The Buddha's Path of Peace

The Buddha's Path of Peace
A Step-by-Step Guide

Geoffrey Hunt

SHEFFIELD UK   BRISTOL CT

Published by Equinox Publishing Ltd

UK: Office 415, The Workstation, 15 Paternoster Row, Sheffield, South Yorkshire S1 2BX
USA: ISD, 70 Enterprise Drive, Bristol, CT 06010

www.equinoxpub.com

First published 2020

British Library Cataloguing-in-Publication Data

A catalogue record for this book is available from the British Library.
ISBN-13   978 1 78179 962 8   (hardback)
              978 1 78179 963 5   (paperback)
              978 1 78179 964 2   (ePDF)

Library of Congress Cataloging-in-Publication Data
Names: Hunt, Geoffrey, 1947- author.
Title: The Buddha's path of peace : a step-by-step guide / Geoffrey Hunt.
Description: Sheffield, South Yorkshire ; Bristol, CT : Equinox Publishing
    Ltd, 2020. | Includes bibliographical references. | Summary: "In this
    book the core of the Buddha's teaching is comprehensively cast in modern
    models of thought--borrowed from science and philosophy--and informed by
    contemporary concerns. It sets out the basic instructions for the
    life-changing way of the Buddha (the so-called 'Noble Eightfold Path')
    wholly in the context of contemporary and everyday life, personal
    experience, human relationships, work, environmental concern and the
    human wish for peace. The reader, who may be completely new to Buddhism,
    is accompanied along the Path with practical exercises that are fully
    explained. The Path begins with an introductory overview and then
    proceeds through Right Speech, Right Acting, Right Livelihood, Right
    Effort, Right Concentration, Right Mindfulness, Right Understanding and
    Right Resolve, and concludes with a short chapter on the relevance of
    the Path to the current global crisis. The reader is mentored throughout
    by practical meditational and contemplative exercises, with tables,
    diagrams, analogies and stories. Gradually the reader who has followed
    this handbook with commitment will feel the benefits of growing
    peacefulness, wisdom and compassion"-- Provided by publisher.
Identifiers: LCCN 2019033502 (print) | LCCN 2019033503 (ebook) | ISBN
    9781781799628 (hardback) | ISBN 9781781799635 (paperback) | ISBN
    9781781799642 (ebook)
Subjects: LCSH: Eightfold Path. | Religious life--Buddhism. | Spiritual
    life--Buddhism. | Buddhism--Doctrines.
Classification: LCC BQ4320 .H86 2020 (print) | LCC BQ4320 (ebook) | DDC
    294.3/444--dc23
LC record available at https://lccn.loc.gov/2019033502
LC ebook record available at https://lccn.loc.gov/2019033503

Typeset by S.J.I. Services, New Delhi, India

Contents

List of Figures, Tables, Exercises, Metaphors and Parables   vii

Acknowledgements   ix

Foreword   xi

Preface   xiii

Introduction   1

PART ONE: Ethics

1 Right Speech: What I Say   15

2 Right Acting: What I Do   25

3 Right Livelihood: How I Live and Work   33

PART TWO: Meditation

4 Right Effort: Directing the Mind   43

5 Right Concentration: Breathing   61

6 Right Concentration: Objects   69

7 Right Mindfulness: Refining Attention   75

8 Right Mindfulness: Anchor and Buoy Model   85

9 Right Mindfulness: Full Awareness   100

10 Right Mindfulness: Insight   108

PART THREE: Wisdom

11 Right Understanding: Ignorance and *Nibbāna*   123

12 Right Understanding: The Horizons Model   133

13 Right Understanding: The Mirror Model   145

14 Right Understanding: The Reflections Model   155

15 Right Understanding: Self and the Waveform Model   170

16 Right Understanding: The Emergence Model   179

17 Right Understanding: Self-Evaluation   196

18 Right Resolve: A Change of Heart   204

19 Right Resolve: Silence   213

Conclusion: A Global Awakening?   221

Appendix 1: Posture   225
Appendix 2: Glossary of Neologisms   234
References and Notes   236
Bibliography   242
Index   244

List of Figures, Tables, Exercises, Metaphors and Parables

Figures

Figure 1: Breathing   65
Figure 2: Anchor and Buoy   94
Figure 3: Walking Meditation   110
Figure 4: Asymptote   135
Figure 5: Möbius Strip   148
Figure 6: Waveform   173
Figure 7: Slipping Knot   174
Figure 8: Newton's Cradle   200
Figure 9: Chair Posture   228
Figure 10: Stool Posture   229
Figure 11: Cushion Posture   230

Tables

Table 1: Some Aspects of Speaking and Listening   17
Table 2: Levels of Concentration   66
Table 3: Vipassī's Loop   186
Table 4: Right Resolve   206
Table 5: Eight Worldly Intentions   222

Exercises

Exercise 1: Mindful Dialogue   23
Exercise 2: Mindful Action   32
Exercise 3: Random Stopping   32
Exercise 4: Mindful Livelihood   37
Exercise 5: The Supra-advert   52
Exercise 6: Tactics for the Obstacle Course   56
Exercise 7: Cultivating Loving-Kindness   58
Exercise 8: Noticing your Breathing   63
Exercise 9: Sensation of Breath   65
Exercise 10: Watching the Abdomen   66

Exercise 11: Drying Leaf   70
Exercise 12: Refining Nostril Sensations   71
Exercise 13: Refining Abdomen Sensations   71
Exercise 14: Satellite Dish   82
Exercise 15: Watchful Walking   85
Exercise 16: The Clocking Tick   92
Exercise 17: The Body Scan   93
Exercise 18: Stand Up and Sit Down   103
Exercise 19: Walking Meditation   110
Exercise 20: Standing Meditation   111
Exercise 21: Mindfulness of Pleasure and Pain   112
Exercise 22: States of Mind Diary   115
Exercise 23: Anonymized Shared Reflection   117
Exercise 24: Mirror of Not-One, Not-Two   151
Exercise 25: Am I My Body?   160
Exercise 26: Wave Motion   173
Exercise 27: Slipping Knot   174
Exercise 28: Ice in Water   175
Exercise 29: Transformation   182

Metaphors

Metaphor 1: How the Buddha Ploughs   37
Metaphor 2: The Cherry Tree   58
Metaphor 3: Torch Beam   77
Metaphor 4: Flypaper Mind   79
Metaphor 5: The Light Switch   103
Metaphor 6: Raymond the Raindrop   142

Parables

Parable 1: The Taste of Broccoli   5
Parable 2: Refusing Anger   31
Parable 3: The Floating Man   46
Parable 4: The Sleepless Woman   51
Parable 5: Buddhist John   89
Parable 6: What's Really on Your TV?   164
Parable 7: Strange Shopping   193

Acknowledgements

I wish to acknowledge the support and kindness of New Buddha Way participants and all friends in the Dhamma.

I must straight away make a special mention of Bhikkhu Bodhi's magnificent English translations of the Pali Canon and the indispensable notes that enhance and clarify those translations. My knowledge of Pali can only be described as rudimentary, which is to say that without Bhikkhu Bodhi's indefatigable translations this book would not have been possible. He is neither responsible for, nor should he be assumed to be in agreement with, my idiosyncratic model-making and interpretations.

I wholeheartedly wish to thank Ajahn Amaro, abbot of Amaravati Buddhist Monastery, UK for reading a complete draft and making valuable recommendations.

I am also grateful to Yamamoto-sensei for looking after me at Jissouji Rinzai temple, Takamatsu, Japan for three months in 2001 and in shorter visits over the years.

More recently I have had opportunities to visit Cittaviveka (Theravada) Buddhist Monastery, Hampshire, UK fairly regularly, and give some talks on the Noble Eightfold Path to the Lay Forum. Tony Halter helpfully chaired the Forum sessions. I am indebted to Ven. Seelawimala Thera, head of London Buddhist Vihara, London for his invitations to present talks on meditation. Thanks to Dr Patrick Baird for some thought-provoking conversations on science and Buddhism.

Given the conceptual innovations in this book I have provided a glossary of neologisms at the end. I bear sole responsibility for any misinterpretations and errors in this book. May I be forgiven for any point on which I have non-intentionally misled readers.

In my quotations of the English translations of passages of the two millennia-old Pali language of the Buddha's teachings we find that the male gender is used preferentially. I wish to state here that we must now understand all such passages in terms of absolute gender equality.

An earlier prototype of this book was independently published in three small volumes in 2008, 2009 and 2010 respectively, and intended primarily for the use of participants in New Buddha Way meditation sessions and contemplative discussions. This edition is so completely revised and expanded that it should be considered as a different book.

I look forward to receiving comments and corrections.

Author contact
g.hunt@surrey.ac.uk | info@newbuddhaway.org |
Website: www.newbuddhaway.org

Foreword

This humble volume is an excellent addition to current materials available on Buddhist practice, particularly those using the language and structures of the Southern Buddhist tradition.

The author has done well indeed in being both imaginative and accurate in the analogies he conjures up, as well as in the models for the many reflective and meditative practices he describes. In particular, such areas as skilful speech and wholesome attitudes in interpersonal dynamics are described in a thorough, practical and helpful way.

This book does not, and could not, cover every aspect of the Buddha's teaching, as represented in the Pali Canon. Rather it aims to dwell on a few specific areas that the author considers, through his extensive experience of practising and teaching Dhamma in the West, to be most pertinent to an English-speaking readership. Thus there is a deliberate laying aside of the cosmological and metaphysical side of the teachings, in order to dwell on the more tangible and accessible aspects of the Buddha's words.

The author intends for this book to be meaningful and useful to as wide an audience as possible; this being actualized through using such language and focusing on areas of the Buddha's teachings that pertain to the universal human experience. This is a noble intention. In describing his objective in following this approach he wrote: '[W]hen I consider how precious and life-changing the Dhamma could be for the "Western" world in this dark age I suppose there's a chance my small contribution might help'.

I sincerely hope it will.

Ven. Amaro Bhikkhu
Abbot, Amaravati Monastery, UK
August 2019

Preface

What's Different about this Book?

I am not a Buddhology scholar. Neither am I a Buddhist monk. My academic training and background are in Philosophy, but my interest in the Buddha's teaching is not just academic, nor is it just devotional. The Buddha himself realized that an answer to the profound question of human peace was not just a scientific or 'rational' one. He saw that he had to find a way between sterile 'objectivity' and dogmatic religiosity. Commitment had to come into it, but in a way that was part and parcel of his peace project, a kind of 'middle way'. Neither science nor religion, in themselves, could resolve the matter at hand.

In several ways, some of them critical, the analogical modelling of the Dhamma ('*Dharma*' in Sanskrit) in this book may be regarded as deviating from the usual presentation of mainstream Buddhism, whether Theravāda or Mahāyāna. However, that was not my intention. The intention behind this book took shape from the difficulties that lay people in the 'West', including myself, have in understanding and engaging with the Buddha Dhamma. We are often faced with the dilemma of a decontextualized 'mindfulness' torn from its conceptual and practical setting, or teachers whether monastic or lay who generally fall back on canonical or orthodox doctrines in presenting Dhamma practice in a somewhat uncritical manner. After 18 years of being a lay teacher I gradually felt cornered into garnering novel approaches. The aim was to get the canonical teaching of Buddhism and mindfulness across to 'Western' lay people, especially younger people, in terms of conceptual models they are more familiar with and therefore more likely to help them comprehend the Dhamma.

I intend this to be an attempt at a fresh and 'contemporary' presentation of the (probable) core teachings of the Buddha and his disciples. This does not imply that I regard the Buddha's teaching as deficient in some way, and therefore needing some improvement or 'updating'. In fact I think the Canon is complete, despite some rather haphazard shuffling, inconsistencies and irrelevancies. Everything you need to know, all the instructions that you should follow, are present and correct. It is just very hard work for a young intelligent person to follow them in the original texts of the Canon. That is a fact, and one that I attempt to address.

Models

This book deploys models to assist the understanding of the lay person seriously engaged with the Buddha Dhamma. But what is meant by 'model'?

By 'model' I mean a conceptual representation of something that cannot be seen or understood directly or easily. In science all kinds of models abound, for they have the explicit purpose of causal explanation and prediction and theoretical construction. The reader may remember school days and the simple model of billiard or pool balls bumping into each other to explain the gas laws and relationship of volume, temperature and pressure. I fully understand that the Buddha was not a scientist in the usual modern sense. However, he was trying to give an account of human life which is, and was even in his time, an account inherently difficult to understand. Maybe contemporary models will help us. Models are akin to analogies, metaphors, parables, allegories and similes. The last of these are particularly abundant in the Buddha's method of teaching.

Of course, no model replicates reality. They are crutches for the mind. They may be refined, extended and replaced—but they are always limited. In deploying any model the author hopes for an 'Aha!' moment when the reader or listener jumps beyond shallow attention to the model to the *point* of the model.[1]

A model might, for example, take some aspect of contemporary common sense or science and use it 'laterally' to clarify something unfamiliar or difficult. However, what is regarded as common sense is not static; it is historically transient, shifting with changes in social structure and culture. It is perhaps surprising that 'new' models may help us to understand the teaching of a man embedded in a late Iron Age society of 2,500 years ago. Still, ultimately, the Buddha's teachings are about *human* life, the core of our own human experience of birth, learning, growing, declining and dying. It may help us to look at something from a new angle, but it is still ultimately the same thing. This same thing is, in Buddhism, called 'The Dhamma' (Dharma).

The obvious limitation of modelling, it may be said by those familiar with meditation, is that it places the Dhamma in the domain of *conceiving* (thinking) rather than practising. It could be seen as an attempt to reach the benefit of Dhamma by conceiving it rather than practising it through meditation techniques. Some might conclude that modelling is therefore futile. I understand the value of what is being said there, but the boundary between conceiving and 'practising' is not so sharp. In fact the relationship is 'nondual', and one has to take a 'middle way' (see later).

Some Innovations

Those with some acquaintance with the Noble Eightfold Path of the Buddha may wish to know immediately what aspects of the Dhamma I have adapted or applied the models to. The Noble Eightfold Path is usually presented as: (1) Right View (Understanding), (2) Right Intention (Resolve), (3) Right Speech, (4) Right Action, (5) Right Livelihood, (6) Right Effort, (7) Right Mindfulness and (8) Right Concentration. Here is a summary of my changes. (Readers new to Buddhism can skip this section and may wish to return to it later.)

In the first chapter I begin with 'Right Speech', whereas it is traditional and 'logical' to begin with 'Right Understanding'. Right Speech gives a common sense accessibility to the path, and for lay people new to Buddhism it is a better place to begin, and finally to return to.

Another point concerning the order of the eight factors is that I put 'Right Concentration' before 'Right Mindfulness', whereas traditionally it is the other way around. This is because I believe that concentration practices are best understood as a precursor training for mindfulness and insight.

The first model appears with a meditational technique I call 'Anchor and Buoy' (Figure 2 in Chapter 8), which is my graphic illustration of a teaching implicit in the Buddha Dhamma, bringing together concentration and mindfulness in a preliminary fashion. Walking meditation, in my account, has been refined in terms of mindfulness of sensations in one foot. For walking meditation one does not need two feet.

Ultimately, with deeper understanding, we see that there is in truth no 'right' sequence for the 'Path'.

There are several other departures from the orthodoxy. To start with, and needless to say, I do not think (except poetically) in terms of *devas* (gods), *yakkhas* (spirits) and *Mara* (the devil). Vital concepts such as *kamma* and *nibbāna* (*karma* and *nirvana* in Sanskrit) are presented in terms of modern models of thought.

A model of mirror reflection is used to clarify the Buddha's 'middle way' (*Majjhimāpaṭipadā*) and a model of the waveform to clarify 'emptiness' (*suññatā*). I interpret 'co-dependent arising' (*paṭiccasamuppāda*) in terms of an adaptation of the modern scientific model of 'complex emergence'.

'The Four Foundations of Mindfulness' are laid out as four levels of self-evaluation along the Path.

I give consideration to a representation of *nibbāna* as a 'horizon' ('vanishing point', 'asymptote') rather than a point of arrival. I have found that this way of talking about it has an immediate appeal. Everyone, with few exceptions, can move towards that point. It is certainly not restricted to a spiritual elite.

The Structure of this Book

The book is laid out in the traditional eight distinct but integrated factors (aspects) of the Buddha's instructions, which together encapsulate the practices necessary for cultivating a new way of life. These 'right' factors were probably set out by the Buddha's followers rather than the fluid mind of the Buddha himself. One should note at the outset that in the Buddha's way of thinking, 'right' is not a moral imposition; the term signifies what is conducive (skilful, helpful) to awakening (enlightenment; see later) and the peace, wisdom and compassion that go with it. The eight may broadly be divided (in my choice of order) into three segments, as follows:

1. **Ethics:** (1) Right Speech, (2) Right Action (Acting) and (3) Right Livelihood. This is about what we need to accept about ourselves as humans living and working together, and our potential to move towards truly cooperative and non-harmful living and working.
2. **Meditation:** (4) Right (mental) Effort, (5) Right Concentration (focus) and (6) Right Mindfulness (inward awareness). This segment is about how to practise meditation and contemplation.
3. **Wisdom:** (7) Right Understanding and (8) Right Intention (Resolve). This is about a general reorientation in understanding; and a motivational transformation of the divided 'me/world' delusion, thereby enjoying wisdom, compassion and non-harmfulness.

In the West there is a widespread misconception that 'meditation' (or just 'mindfulness') can work alone as yet another useful technique for our already weighty and untidy toolbox of therapeutic commodities. Whatever meditation can or cannot do alone, it cannot change your life in the way that a reality-challenging awakening can. For that to happen all eight factors must be integrated and lived out.

Using this Book

This is not a dip-in recipe book or reference work. It should be read in an orderly and reflective fashion over an extended period of time with repeated practice of the 29 exercises. Besides seeking clarity of explanation, this is also in part a *work* manual, a lay instruction handbook to be used for *seeing* things differently and *doing* things differently.

I recommend that, for example, the reader read the chapter on Right Speech, practise the relevant exercises, then read that chapter again, and gradually cultivate and *establish* the practices as natural aspects of attitude and behaviour. That could take some weeks or longer, before proceeding to the chapter on Right Acting. Working through the whole book productively should take a year or more of diligent attention. At the same time, one should try to find a decent meditation teacher and group to practise with on a regular basis. After that, one continues on the Path for life.

Not wishing to labour the point: this is not the kind of book that one reads through at once, concluding with the thought 'that was very interesting', before placing it on the bookshelf and moving on to the next interesting thing. The presence of personal exercises and advice is an indication of the *engagement* of this manual with real life. It seeks a shift in one's perception of human reality. What the serious follower of this way will find is that while an earlier chapter prepares one for the next, the next one throws light on the previous, until the last one lights up the first and second, and so on.

I try my best to avoid all non-English words. A few of the very important words in this book are given in the Pali language as well as in English. Pali is unique to Buddhism and is the language of most of the oldest recorded Buddhist teachings. In this book a Pali term is sometimes followed by the corresponding Sanskrit in brackets. This is because much of Buddhist classical literature is cast in Sanskrit too. For example, 'action' is usually given here as *kamma (karma)*.

A final word of counsel: although I hope this book is scholarly enough for its purpose, scholarship is not in itself its aim. It is rather a 'curved ball' attempt at *advocacy* for a Buddhism that can have a greater appeal to non-monastic people in the modern world—free of the impediments that stilted academic scholarship can place in the way of commitment and creativity.

Note on Permissions

The author is grateful to Wisdom Publications for kind permission to reproduce excerpts of the translations from Pali in its series, 'Teachings of the Buddha'.

Introduction

The Buddha

What are the origins of humankind's apparent inability to live in peace? If we humans could find and stay aware of these origins with honesty and rigour would it then become possible to live in peace, or at least in greater peace?

Once upon a time a 30-year-old hungry man spent another whole night under a tree searching within himself for answers to these questions. Then, after strenuous efforts, he saw that his craving and rejecting were extinguished for a timeless moment. But he had not died or become invisible! He was still just an odd, half-naked man sitting under a tree in the dawn light, in need of sleep, warmth, food, drink, a wash and somewhere to squat in private.

As that man got up from his meditation, and returned to the sensations of this world, everything had changed for him. His understanding was transformed. His reality had re-created itself.

From then on how he spoke, acted, worked and endeavoured could not be the same. The man looked upon his prior ignorance. He did not feel shame, embarrassment and remorse over his previous life. He now understood that he had until then been enthralled and misled by a delusory view of reality, a view so credibly patched together by the demands of material survival. Since it was his own beloved but paltry previous self he was now looking upon with fresh eyes, he felt compassion for himself and all humanity. This was a compassion that comes with the understanding that one need not suffer but has always suffered needlessly.

That man was Siddhartha Gautama, the Buddha—the *Tathāgata*, the *Arahant*, the Rightly Self-awakened One, the one who turned the world the right way up.

The Discovery of the Noble Eightfold Path

Having left his family, property and princely comforts, the Buddha went in search of the cause of suffering and how to end it. He practised meditation in different ways and with great determination. In his first public talk following his awakening the Buddha delivered what is now known as 'Setting the Wheel of Dhamma (Dharma) in Motion' (*Dhammacakkappavattana Sutta*),[1] a summary of what he had discovered. It came to be structured in terms of 'The Four Noble Truths' and 'The Noble Eightfold Path'. The Path he recommended took 'the middle way' of neither rejecting 'the world' nor blindly indulging in it. He had tried self-mortification and it nearly killed him. What he discovered was not just a common-sense case of 'moderation in all things' but a radical transformation of the perception and understanding of the roots of human life. He was awakened in the sense of realizing, or knowing directly the underlying reality of delusory human life. His awakening was a revelation of the self-harming and self-replicating fantasy of the human story and where the fundamental possibilities of peace and compassion lay.

In the detailed account of this radical transformation, delivered to anyone who would listen over a period of 45 years, he sometimes had to use novel or re-shaped concepts such as 'emptiness' (*suññatā*), 'not-self' (*anattā*) and 'co-dependent origination' (*paṭiccasamuppāda*). He knew that his new view of our reality was so unfamiliar, so at variance with what was apparently 'obvious' to his contemporaries, that he hesitated to try and teach it to anyone. He was, after all, attempting a Copernican revolution of the human mind. Fortunately, he decided to try his best, and at the end of his first discourse he was relieved to find that one person in his small audience, named *Koṇḍañña*, immediately understood. Koṇḍañña, a brahmin already versed in the old Vedic teachings, awakened and thus became the first member of the Buddhist *sangha* (ordained community). Delighted, the Buddha declared: 'Koṇḍañña has indeed understood! Koṇḍañña has indeed understood!' The nickname 'Aññā Koṇḍañña' (meaning 'Koṇḍañña's Got It') was irresistible. Here is a snippet of what the Buddha is recorded as saying to the *bhikkhus* (monks):

> *Bhikkhus, these two extremes should not be followed by one who has gone forth into homelessness. What two? The pursuit of sensual happiness in sensual pleasures, which is low, vulgar, the way of worldlings, ignoble, unbeneficial; and the pursuit of self-mortification, which is painful, ignoble, unbeneficial. Without veering towards either of these extremes, the Tathāgata [Buddha] has awakened to the middle way,*

which gives rise to vision, which gives rise to knowledge, which leads to peace, to direct knowledge, to enlightenment, to Nibbāna.

And what, bhikkhus, is that middle way awakened to by the Tathāgata which gives rise to vision ... which leads to Nibbāna. It is this Noble Eightfold Path; that is, right view [understanding], right intention [resolve], right speech, right action, right livelihood, right effort, right mindfulness, right concentration.[2]

Civilization ... What 'Civilization'?

The Buddha felt in his heart and bones that something was very wrong with human life as ordinarily understood. Today, and increasingly, very many people also feel that something is fundamentally wrong, but so far only a few are exploring the very roots of our self-destructiveness. Anxiety is growing, and with it grows fear, blame and hatred. This is the time, of all times, to reflect on our very notion of reality, of human existence, of what it is 'to be here'. The crisis that our world now faces on every front—cultural and philosophical, economic and environmental, political and social, moral and ethical—will no doubt have the effect of deepening religious fundamentalism, institutionalism, populism and authoritarianism. At the same time the countervailing opportunity arises for people to move in the opposite direction, into a re-evaluation of the possibilities of open-hearted and compassionate peace.

When we face such crises it is a sure sign that our old ways of thinking have become dislocated from the realities of our lives. Nothing seems to make much sense, and no obvious way forward can be envisioned. We may fall back into denial, cynicism or, much worse, become fearful and angry and seek scapegoats. In this situation it is vital to examine and challenge our way of thinking at its roots.

An individualistic, pleasure-seeking and consumerist ideology has now spread across the world, setting fires in every corner, from California to China, from the Antarctic to Amazonia. And we are ill-equipped; none of the viewpoints we have depended on for so long now seem to help us. There is surely something very inadequate in our broad views on the most important things: our moral and ethical values, the limits to the role of science and technology, our religions, cultural leadership, our family life and friendships, and our daily way of life. Many of us know that something is very amiss and very unstable. We may feel disoriented, but have no clear idea of how to make any headway. There is a strong temptation to fall back on what helped us in the 'Great' past, without thinking that this may make things worse, not better.

Back to Square One

Maybe what we have to do is go back to square one. Put everything aside and start again. Is it possible to do this? Indeed, is it possible *not* to do this, if our blindly engineered climate catastrophe tears up the book of human history? Where would we begin? Would it be a matter of finding a completely new beginning in understanding our human nature? Or, would it rather be a matter of relocating beginnings that had already been made and partially accumulated in human history and then misunderstood or lost? Have we really understood those who have delved deeply into human nature, tried to tell us what we are and how to rise above it, and warned us of the consequences of remaining in ignorance?

All the great spiritual teachers over the millennia have told us, in one way or another, in different languages and with different imagery, that we are strongly inclined to be self-centred, blinkered, clinging and craving creatures, and that (as useful to short-term biological survival as that may once have been) this inclination is ultimately self-destructive and does not do justice to our potential. They have told us at the same time that there are ways to mellow and soften this inclination. The strange thing is that while on the whole the human race has accepted that this is true it has done one of two things. It has shrugged its shoulders and gone on as before, or it has gradually turned the recognition of this truth into yet another form of self-centred clinging, particularly institutional religion and aimless technology.

Perhaps our best hope is in a return to the core truth of these teachers in a radical spirit. By that, I mean making our best effort to understand the core truths about humanity, while cutting away from our minds all the subsequent encrustations of excuses, compromises, embellishments, hypocrisy, misunderstandings and inconsistencies. It might be like cutting back a tired and tangled garden, only to find that the following spring, pure white snowdrops appear that one did not even know were there all along. Is an alternative way of life possible?

Monastic and Lay

This book is intended as an introduction to an alternative way of life for ordinary individuals, and thus is also intended for contemporary society at large. However, the distinction between *lay* people (ordinary people with families, property, jobs, etc.) and *monastic* people (monks and nuns) is still of importance. In an ideal world, proper monastic people brook no compromise in following the Noble Eightfold Path of awakening. They have left family and property behind, and depend for their sustenance on lay people. In a paradigm of this social structure lay people are embedded in the ordinary struggles of work, family, acquisition and achievement—and depend for existential guidance and support (wisdom and compassion) on monastic people. Thus the two social dimensions combine doctrine and practice. It is perhaps time to review this Jungian archetypal view in terms of the harsh realities of modern life.

This book covers the whole ambit of the path and is primarily intended to make the path intelligible and helpful to *lay* people, people who (like the author) have chosen not to follow the full-on monastic living-out of the path. To become a Buddhist monk or nun is a serious decision and resolution that some people make.

The author is convinced that a true 'Buddha Dhamma of the people' is not just a possibility but is of immense real value. It is time for the monastic living-out of the Dhamma and the lay living-out of the Dhamma to come much closer together than ever before, in an embrace that is not-one, not-two.

The Taste of Broccoli

To understand the Buddha's Dhamma (teachings) is not like grasping knowledge of arithmetic or plumbing or astronomy. The teachings really become learnings only when they are in the process of being recognized and accepted into someone's life. So 'Dhamma' stands for all three at once: the teaching, the accepting, and the realization.

This might seem peculiar at first, but it is very ordinary. We can more easily grasp it perhaps with a parable (below). The point I am coming to is this: it is because the Dhamma is this way that teaching and learning the Dhamma *has to be participatory*, a shared practice of and between people. It is not a piece of knowledge held by one person, a kind of super-human, to be handed over to others who receive it passively.

Parable 1. The Taste of Broccoli

> Janet likes the taste of broccoli. She tells her friend Fiona about it. Fiona has never tasted broccoli, so how does Janet describe or explain it? Firstly, she tries to compare the taste of broccoli to something else that Fiona is familiar with: cabbage and cauliflower. 'Broccoli is rather like cauliflower, but stronger, a bit like cabbage and ...'. Fiona is now a little nearer to the taste of broccoli, but what she has is the thought or image of broccoli not the taste of broccoli.

> Fiona persists with her questions about broccoli. Later, Janet gets hold of some broccoli, cooks it, invites Fiona over to dinner and serves it to her. Fiona tastes it; now she's got it. 'And how does it taste?' asks Janet. 'Well ... I can't describe it, but it's good!'

Fiona had never tasted broccoli, so how could Janet describe it to her? In fact, she cannot do so fully or directly. She can do one of two things. One is to compare the taste of broccoli to something else that Fiona is familiar with, like cauliflower. The second way is to *do* something: to go and get some broccoli and invite Fiona to taste it. This requires effort on the part of the giver and the taker, the teacher and the learner. Very often we are not prepared to make any effort, partly because it takes us outside our 'comfort zone'. 'I'm happy with cabbage', says Fiona. 'Why should I try this foreign-sounding broccoli-thing of yours?'

There are key metaphors or models at work in this book. The unavoidable difficulty with this way of teaching is that the listeners have to see through the analogy (model, metaphor, simile, allegory, symbol, parable, ritual) to what it 'stands for' or indicates. And they have to do so by themselves. But what it points to is precisely what they have not seen before, so they might or might not be able to do that. It is a wonder that metaphors and parables ever work, but they very often do, of course. Spirituality, art and poetry depend on them. So there is the danger of misunderstanding: the listener might take it literally. It depends on whether they are able to discern the difference as well as the similarity between metaphor and the 'thing indicated'. Literalism (connected with 'fundamentalism') causes a lot of difficulty and disagreement between us. People and groups have even killed each other because of it, sometimes on a large scale, and sometimes even within the same religion. Unsurprisingly, this tendency re-defines 'religion' and turns many people away from it.

The Four Noble Truths

The Noble Eightfold Path is an element in a wider framework: the Four Noble Truths. In fact the Path is the last of the four 'truths'. The four truths of human life are as follows:

1. **Anxiety** (suffering, fear, dissatisfaction, insatiability). (*Dukkha*)
2. The **origin** (basis, cause, source) of that suffering, which lies in craving and rejecting. (*Samudaya* = literally the coming together of conditions.)

3. The **cessation** (ending or softening, attenuation) of that suffering. (*Nirodha*)
4. The **path** (way, method) to end or soften suffering, which is the Noble Eightfold Path set out in eight factors or aspects. (*Ariyo aṭṭhaṅgiko maggo*)

In a sentence: human life involves mental, emotional and physical suffering, which is basically brought into being by wanting more or not wanting what one has, but it is possible to attenuate (weaken, lessen) or even eliminate that suffering by following a mental discipline which largely involves the generation of a kind of de-centred inward-awareness that is at once an understanding of the divisive delusion of 'me and world'.

In the light of what we have already noted about the lay and the monastic life, it is no surprise that the Four Noble Truths may be understood on a worldly, everyday, mundane level and on a 'spiritual' (existential, supramundane, metaphysical, transcendent) level. This book attempts to set out both, but with an eye primarily on *lay* understanding, since monastic people should have an environment supportive of daily actual practice as well as direct Dhamma guidance from their seniors and elders.

The Noble Eightfold Path for You Now

In Part One of this book I shall embark on the transformative path of right speech, acting and livelihood. In Part Two the meditational factors of effort, concentration and mindfulness are set out. Then in Part Three the wisdom factors of understanding and intention (resolve) are presented. But first it may be important to say something about how this is a way for you now in your twenty-first century life. It is not only a way for monks and nuns, not only for people in distant lands, not only for an elite of cushion-sitting intellectuals, and not only for people who have customs that are strange to some of us, whoever we are.

The Path is for the person with family responsibilities, the one who has a job and the one who does not, the bus driver, the office manager, the person who delivers parcels, the lawyer, the social worker, the farmer, the taxi driver, the head of a corporate human resources department, the person who has just started her own business, the mother, father, grandfather, grandmother, the teenager; in short, for all of us as we are now. In this way we may envision the laity-become-sangha and the sangha-become-laity; there is no sharp boundary, but only a fuzzy transition.

The Path in Context

The Noble Eightfold Path is the fourth Noble Truth in detail, so working with it means accepting the context of the three other Noble Truths: suffering, cause of suffering, and end of suffering (peace). The teachings of the Buddha—which we call the Dhamma (*Dharma*)—forms a single coherent approach to life in which everything has a place co-created by the meditator. Of course, it is not a system of beliefs which is to be imposed on people. Quite the opposite. It teaches us to let go of imposition and let life speak for itself. But we have to listen very carefully and persistently. The Buddha sometimes said that the teaching of liberation is unified in the way that the ocean has but one taste, the taste of salt. In the case of the Dhamma the one taste is that of tenderizing our judgements and freeing ourselves from unhelpful opinions, routine assumptions and dissatisfaction.

Suffering (the first Noble Truth) takes many forms on different levels. On quite an obvious level we all sooner or later suffer anxiety, pain, frustration, illness, grief, loss, disappointment or mental confusion—to mention a few! But it will certainly not escape our notice that we may, especially if we are 'lucky' and 'talented', enjoy pleasures, success, good health, wealth, and long life. The pleasant experiences might just outweigh the nasty experiences in the lottery of life. Maybe most of us think this way. It is to think of a life as a kind of cosmic casino, with candy and sex as a reward, and cancer and divorce as a penalty. If we get the former we are happy, and if we get the latter we are miserable.

This is one way of looking at dissatisfaction. As something that comes and goes. But are we looking at ourselves hard enough and with complete honesty? Is there an underlying and abiding anxiety or dissatisfaction? Take death. That is a bit awkward, isn't it? We cannot wager, play games or negotiate with that. Maybe that is like being thrown out of the casino. Not for a month or year, but forever.

One way of dealing with that is not to think about it at all. If I do contemplate my own death, thereby making myself uncomfortable, I have (eventually) to put up with another fact: I am not the only one who is going to die. Everyone I love is going to die, and some of them before I do. Furthermore, I almost certainly do not know *when* they will die or when I will die.

As if that isn't enough, it might occur to me that *everyone* that is alive right now (2019)—about 7,700,000,000 people like me—will be dead in just 120 years (assuming there is not a global annihilation before then). Most will be dead within 80 years. Billions of other people will have been born, of course. But they will die too. It is all a bit scary; far better not to think about such things! On the other hand, maybe there is something vital to be learned there? Something that in the long term would make life easier for us all.

Acceptance

Most of us will agree, perhaps reluctantly, that it is far better to accept whatever has the unfortunate qualities of being both thoroughly unpleasant and inevitable. For example, what a difference it might make to me to grasp fully how precious every single moment of my life is! But I am jumping ahead. First we have to clamber over a rugged stone wall before we can enjoy the peaceful pasture on the other side. So, returning to the liberating ugliness of death for just another unbearable paragraph.

Before one dies there is the prospect of becoming unattractive, sick, or at least weak and fragile, and seeing loved ones in such a state. Before these things happen we also have to suffer the fear and anxiety of their happening or the uncertainty of when they will happen. And speaking of fear and anxiety, it may occasionally dawn on us that everything else that is most dear to us could be lost at any moment: homes, furniture, gardens, money, job, hair, teeth, eyesight, memories and photo albums ... you name it.

During certain periods in our lives many of us, wherever we are, will pose some disturbing and unanswerable questions: What am I really? Why am I me rather than anyone else? Where do I come from and where am I going? Is there an after-life? Is there any meaning in life? Is time an illusion? Is there something all-powerful behind it all? The questions are hard to pose in any meaningful way, and there is not even a way of determining whether they *are* meaningful. Supporting such questions may be feelings of unease, bewilderment, fear, emptiness and even desolation.

I am not making this up just for a shock effect. If anything is shocking here, it is that I am *talking* about it. We are now thinking about a largely taboo area. You may be already concluding that this book is hardly likely to be a best seller!

The point has been made. The Buddha's starting point, the first Noble Truth, is that there is an *abiding* malaise, an anxiety, discontent, dissatisfaction, even an insatiability, in human life, and that if we do not face it, understand it, and overcome or transcend it, or at least soften it, then it will push us into all kinds of disappointing, destructive and self-destructive fantasies. As we look at the incredible follies and man-made catastrophes of just the last one hundred years, and those yet to come, we may begin to see that the Buddha was onto something big. Is it perhaps too big for us to accept?

Craving, Clinging, Rejecting

While meditating, and contemplating (reflecting) on what meditation had revealed to him, the Buddha came upon the second Noble Truth: the fact of craving, clinging and rejecting, that is, wanting, holding on and not wanting. 'Craving' may not be a word we are very familiar with. Perhaps we cannot really identify with it. Isn't that what 'addicts' feel? Yes, it is what addicts feel, in a self-destructively intense manner about *one* thing: alcohol, cocaine, heroin, sex, tobacco, gambling and the like. But these are only special cases of physical addiction. In a broad sense we are all addicts, feeling a deep lack or emptiness that we seek to fill with material gain, fashionable clothes and possessions; with pleasure, sex and entertainment; and with fame, recognition, status and popularity. While there is nothing intrinsically 'evil' about any of these any more than there is about alcohol or cocaine in certain contexts (where they may be medicinal or have other benefits), there is something deeply harmful in giving them an all-consuming prominence in one's life.

Putting aside the extreme case of substance addiction, there must be in most things in a given context a middle way between destructive indulgence and destructive self-denial. Usually a balance can be achieved with some awareness and effort. One needs to learn where the tipping point is. Applying this middle way to all things in life is known as 'wisdom'. It is not entirely what the Buddha intended, but is pointing in the same direction. Attaining deeper wisdom is a slow and sometimes painful process, and is part of learning that the Path is ultimately the better way, perhaps the truly human way.

It should be possible to look into our cravings, our wants and see their nature. If we can do that it should be possible to eliminate, lessen or soften them (third Noble Truth). But for that to be possible there would have to be a definite and practical way of doing so, a way we can understand and apply (fourth Noble Truth). This means gradually moving along a virtual 'path' from ignorance of the source of deep dissatisfaction, to greater freedom from ignorance and the peace that goes with that freedom. So let us begin.

Know for Yourself

The Buddha counsels us to 'know for yourselves'.

> *... do not go by oral tradition, by lineage of teaching, by hearsay, by a collection of scriptures, by logical reasoning, by inferential reasoning, by reasoned cogitation, by the acceptance of a view after pondering it, by the seeming competence [of a speaker], or because you think: 'The ascetic is our guru'. But when you know for yourselves, 'These things are wholesome, these things are blameless; these things are praised by the wise; these things, if accepted and undertaken, lead to welfare and happiness', then you should live in accordance with them.[3]*

So the best we can do is to actually *practise* the Buddha's teachings, and in the light of that practice study his words with discernment, and observe possible limitations, until the consistent core of meaning emerges and *lives* in us.

What is that core of meaning? The Buddha had a profound and very fluid way of thinking as well as a great determination and deep concern for humanity in our endless unhappiness. He would teach according to the capacity, assumptions and character of the individual, and generally as a response to a particular question he had been asked in a particular situation. His answer could be given from different angles according to whether the hearer understood his first response. This means that it would have been difficult to repeat, let alone write down, in any systematic way what he was teaching even when he was alive and speaking. It is unlikely that he taught in terms of doctrines, frameworks and tables. His teaching, as we now read it, sometimes has a hidden context that we can never retrieve.

However, those who followed him were in a quite different situation from the Buddha himself. Not everyone shared his genius, so they not only had the tough job of understanding and remembering what he had taught (at a time when writing was absent or a rarity) but also of passing it on to others in a way that made some immediate sense in a changed context. Then, those copyists and transcribers who wrote it down over the centuries had (usually unwittingly) their own thoughts, values, interpretations and views. The transmission of the Buddha's Dhamma (Buddhadhamma) was subject to semantic impermanence (*anicca*), and still is.

PART ONE

ETHICS

Chapter 1

Right Speech: What I Say

> **Right Speech**
> *sammā-vācā*
>
> Speaking, and communicating generally, in a skilful manner, i.e., without lying, divisiveness, abuse, harshness and gossip. Expressed positively, it is speaking truthfully, promoting concord, kindly, gently and when appropriate conducive to the liberating transformation offered in the Dhamma. It also includes listening to the speech of others in an attentive, open-minded, honest and compassionate manner.

1.1 The Ethics of 'Self'

Many people think that the Buddha was only really interested in sitting under a tree meditating; meditation is what he was all about. Speaking and listening rightly might seem like optional extras, or perhaps pacifiers for lay Buddhists or mundane advice for non-Buddhists. This is not correct, however. Everything he was about has the 'taste of salt', that is, all his teaching and his life are about liberation from abiding dissatisfaction and suffering. This liberation is about the *whole* of your life, and the whole of our lives together. We do not understand what we are, so we do not behave or speak in accordance with what we are, so we do not practise a way that would help us to understand what we are, so we do not understand what we are, so ... It's a vicious circle. The whole of human life is caught up in this fantasy-land vicious circle. It would be immediately appealing to many if meditation were another quick fix, but it does not really work unless it is part of a wider re-orientation.

Our ignorance, our lack of compassion for ourselves and each other, and our unawareness and uncontrolled minds and speech are all unhappily entangled. What binds this process of entanglement is my sense of self, 'me', which attaches, craves and clings. It takes hold, holds on tightly and craves for more. This is not about being 'selfish', for even those who are not 'selfish' in the usual judgemental sense will cling to the sense of self. This is not a 'bad' thing; but just how things are. The deeply entrenched root of this entanglement is my sense of being a separate, independent 'self' that wants, wants to be more, wants to be secure, wants to live, wants more of everything. Thus our moving towards understanding, towards ethical living, towards awareness and measured minds is a process of disentanglement, of cutting out the root 'I-me-mine' (as we shall see later).

My point is that the Dhamma is as much about the ethics of speech, action and livelihood as it is about meditation, and as much about spiritual understanding as it is about ethics. The sense of being 'myself', that needs to be protected and built up, manifests itself in my constantly attaching to the things that can apparently serve those two purposes: *clinging* to them when I 'have' them, and craving for them when I do not have them or do not have enough of them. At the same time I am constantly excluding or *rejecting* anything that apparently hinders or threatens or undermines those things that I am clinging to.

Pride (ego) is my clinging to my sense of 'I' and 'me' and all those things that 'make me' what I am in my own eyes: my name, my gender, class, race, achievements, role in society, loveable-ness or unworthiness, and so on. Supporting this sense is all that I have or possess: 'my' and 'mine'. My body, my clothes, my home, my personal belongings, my partner, my family, my friends, my reputation, my money, my qualifications and so on. When the sense of 'I', 'me', 'mine' is threatened or apparently threatened there will be a reaction such as indignation, humiliation or anger. This sense is expressed in all that we think, say, do and relate to—in short, to all that we take ourselves to be.

1.2 Mindful Speaking and Listening

What more obvious place to start on the path of awakening and peace, on unravelling the ordinary way of entanglement, than considering the ethics of the way we speak and listen. We cannot really extract speaking in isolation from the rest of our understanding, attitudes and activities, but we have to start somewhere in a clear and specific way. Speaking seems a simple enough matter—but is it?

We are speaking with each other (and even inwardly to ourselves) from morning to night, but generally pay little here-and-now attention to the assumptions and intentions underlying this speech. The Buddha taught about this, and he distinguished between skilful speech and unskilful speech. That is, between the ignorant speaking that springs in one way or another from our craving, clinging and our rejecting and the wise speaking that springs from letting go of that triumvirate.[1]

The Buddha's aim is not divisively to judge personally some speech as 'bad' or 'wrong' and other speech as 'good' or 'right'. It is to generate awareness and insight into ourselves. If he considers much of ordinary speech to be 'ignorant' he does not mean 'stupid', but simply 'without knowledge', *unaware* of the cloying forces and habitual channels underlying our communication. Also, his teaching on speaking is not meant to be used as a means of divisively judging *others*, for that would be to turn his intention into its very opposite. I also emphasize that he does not mean to stipulate a standard of perfection, setting us up for failure, but is simply providing a guide to gradually developing one aspect of self-awareness and peace. Speech is nuanced, shifting and often fuzzy. I think the Buddha knows that, but he suggests that we might begin to develop a liberating mindfulness of speaking by paying attention to a number of provisional aspects (Table 1).

Table 1: Some Aspects of Speaking and Listening

	NEGATIVE	POSITIVE
DHAMMA-related	Entangling, gossip, etc.	Liberating, edifying, etc.
ATTITUDE	With ill-will, hatred	Good-will, love
INTENTION	Discord, divisiveness	Concord, unity
TRUTH	Lies, deception	Truth, integrity
MANNER (tone etc.)	Harsh, rude	Gentle, pleasant
TIMELINESS	Untimely, unhelpful	Timely, helpful

1.3 Subtleties

It will occur to the discerning reader that in actual circumstances there always has to be room for subtleties, indeterminacy, irony, hints, dilemmas and misunderstandings in conversation and discussion. One cannot reduce speech to some perfect robot-like rules of communication. The Buddha is simply pointing us in a direction conducive to peace and away from obstacles, and where there is deep listening and good-will that direction will prevail despite, or because of, the subtleties. And there is always room for apology and forgiveness. This observation applies to Right Acting and Right Livelihood too, as we shall see.

At this stage on the path the question may also arise of how ethical concerns, which are by definition person-based, are at all consistent with a view that apparently asserts that in truth there are no persons, namely, the 'no-self' (*anattā*) concept. This is a serious misunderstanding and is addressed directly when we have gone much further down the path.

1.4 Attitude

Speech is intimately involved with the matter of peace and understanding, and conflict and hostility. Speaking is not always what it appears to be on the surface. It may be harmlessly trivial or idle chatter. But it will often reflect a person's beliefs, past experiences, needs, wants and defences. Speaking, or any part of it, may flow from a negative orientation such as cynicism or mistrust, or from particular feelings such as resentment or anger, which may often be concealed. Such an attitude will be *revealed*, sooner or later, even if the speaker is not aware of it. The listener too may not be aware of it, or only dimly in feelings of uneasiness. The listener may even join in the negativity, and the whole dialogue becomes a feedback cry of unhappiness expressed as negative opinions. They may depart from each other none the wiser, and at worst have reinforced in each other a rejecting outlook, convinced it is 'realistic'.

A negative orientation of reactions is often revealed in speech that begins with 'People do or don't do X', and is something negative. For example, 'People don't really care', 'People drive badly', and 'People are chasing money'. There are three important things to note about this way of speaking. Firstly, nothing good is being said about 'people' (such as 'People are kind', 'People drive well', or 'People are not chasing money'). Secondly, it is a generalization. There may well be truth in saying '*Some* (or many) people don't care' just as there is some truth in saying '*Some* (or many) people do care', and so on. Thirdly, the speaker is curiously *absent*, even though they are speaking. That is, when the speaker says 'People don't care', are they including or excluding themselves? If they are including themselves then they are making a confession at the same time that they are tarring everyone with the same brush. If they are excluding themselves then they infer that they are the uniquely caring person on the planet. Neither of these alternatives is very convincing.

We are led to the conclusion that statements like '*People* don't do X' are empty of information and are simply direct expressions of a negative outlook (like making a rude gesture), which is unhelpful both to the speaker and to the listener. The negative outlook will have its causes in the person's life and character, and the point is not to condemn or reject this but understand the underlying unhappiness. That is, not to *condemn* oneself for speaking in this way, nor not to condemn others for doing so, but to acknowledge, recognize, understand. With self-awareness may also come the question: 'Is this attitude me; is it mine?' With that question we embark on the path of insight, liberation and peace.

Speaking, or any part of it, may also flow from a positive orientation such as helpfulness or equanimity, or from particular feelings such as gratitude, generosity or joy over someone else's happiness. These too may be concealed, for example, where there is fear of seeming vulnerable, naïve or sentimental.

An attitude or orientation is also behind our listening. I can always examine myself and ask: 'Am I listening with a negative attitude of irritability, a positive one of kindness or a neutral attitude?' The attitude will make a great deal of difference to what I hear, and being aware of my attitude will also make a difference. Naturally, speaking and listening feed off each other in a cycle of reactions. The attitude shaping what I say to you will affect the attitude shaping what you say to me, which in turn will affect the attitude shaping what I say to you, which ... Awareness is a way of breaking out of this cycle of reactions.

Not speaking is always an option. What pressures us to speak, even when silence is the best option? The path of not-speaking can sometimes say more than the ordinary choice of saying something.

1.5 Intention

On reflection we can often discern an intention behind what we say or omit to say. An intention will often be a manifestation of a wider attitude. The intention may be obvious ('How do I get to the train station?' implies that I have an intention of getting to that particular place), or it may be indirect or oblique. When it is the latter the intention may be kindly or exploratory, for example, or it may be indirectly comparative ('Is yours as good as mine?') or to 'size up' the listener ('Are you as great as I am?') or tacitly to get something from the listener ('Are you influential?', 'Can you do something for me?'). It may even be demeaning, or an expression of prejudice and rejection.

Speaking and listening rest on a network of tacit assumptions, of which the participants may be unaware. In speaking with mindfulness (enhanced awareness), many of those assumptions will come to the surface and one may choose to speak more wisely, more helpfully and less harmfully.

The important point is simply for me to develop some awareness, especially at critical moments, of what I am intending (if anything) to bring about by what I am saying: is it helpful or unhelpful to others and to myself as a person seeking wisdom and peace?

The Buddha does not mean to make us neurotic about every conversation. We cannot always be clear about what our intentions are in saying something, or even if we *have* an intention. Strangely, the 'intention' may appear *after* what one has said. Furthermore, we may not be clear what someone else's intentions are when we are listening. But we can give them the benefit of the doubt. Misunderstandings may arise, and our attitude and intentions will be crucial at those moments. What, then, does it mean to be 'generous' in interpreting what another person is saying? We all tend to 'infect' the words of others with our own intentions, preconceptions, expectations and desires.

When someone else's speech is unskilful, how do we 'deal with it' skilfully? Do we sometimes avoid responsibility for our attitudes and intentions in our speech, for example, shifting responsibility with: 'You *made* me angry!'?

1.6 Truth

Truth would appear to be a simple matter. Either a statement is true or it is not. On the whole, one should say what is true rather than what is false. However, a lot of what we say does not consist of 'pure' statements, but of questions, suggestions, expressions of emotion and preference, commands, explorations, thanks, hints and so on. And everything depends on the context of the conversation and the setting. When we are making a statement it is not always as clear cut as 'It is raining', and even that is sometimes debatable. Is a light and fleeting drizzle really 'rain'? Am I *really* just making an excuse for not walking down to the shop for the loaf of bread that is needed?

Our attitudes and intentions will make a world of difference to the truth or falsity of what we are saying. If my attitude is one of ill-will then even a true statement may aim to hurt. If my attitude is one of conceit or arrogance then my true statement may aim to boost my ego rather than throw any light on the situation under discussion.

Even a true statement may mislead, if it is said in a context in which other significant matters are deliberately omitted. In other words, one can lie by telling a falsehood or more subtly one can lie by telling a truth. When there are strong interests or emotions behind what we are saying then it may be very hard to admit that one is not being truthful. In many ways the most harmful kind of lie is the one that one tells to *oneself*. This is closely connected with the 'ignorance' that the Buddha claimed lies behind so much of our human conflicts and unhappiness. For the Buddha, 'ignorance' was not only about not knowing the truth, but not *wanting* to know the truth, that is, not admitting it.

One might say that the entire teaching of the Buddha is this: the human race is deceiving itself about life, but there is also a human potential to stop doing that.

When we look into ourselves honestly, observe our reactions, and note the arising of envy, spite, impatience and resentment can we *acknowledge* their existence without passing destructive judgement on ourselves? When we note the arising of kindness, generosity, patience and gratitude, can we acknowledge them without smugly patting ourselves on the head? Do we find it easier to be truthful about others than about ourselves? In fact, *can* we be truthful about others if we cannot be truthful about ourselves?

1.7 Manner

Imagine that you are participating in a meeting in which some matter has been hotly debated and you have not yet said anything. You suspect that a significant truth, the 'elephant in the room', has been avoided by everyone so far, maybe because it is difficult to raise without conflict breaking out and someone getting blamed. It seems to you that those present are afraid to mention it, and as a result the situation is becoming increasingly dishonest. 'I am going to speak up', you say to yourself, but how do you do it? It seems timely, you feel that you have good-will towards everyone; your intention is to break the deadlock so that a good decision can be made, and you will clearly state the truth.

Unfortunately, you feel rather nervous, and when you speak you do so in a rather direct way, with a loud and emphatic voice, which is taken by some present to be a supercilious manner. Someone snaps, 'We know that! Do you think we're stupid?' You might be tempted to snap back. From then on nearly everyone's manner of speaking seems to rapidly deteriorate in a cascade of rudeness, interruptions and sarcasm. Perhaps everyone joins in the fray, some feel offended and before you know it the good decision you had hoped for is even further away than it was before.

Entanglement reigns. What has gone wrong here, and could it have been prevented?

The manner of speaking can also take the shape of cynicism, sarcasm, exaggeration, hurtful jokes, sneering, being triumphant, demeaning words, cursing, giving the wrong impression, flattering, patronising, manipulation and 'spin', speaking behind someone's back, and so on. It can also take the shape of the opposite of these—which is a choice one is free to make, but one needs to be *aware* that there is a choice.

The manner of speaking is always significant, but even more so in situations like this, in which an evaded truth needs to be brought into the open. This is a real test, and it is not easy to get it right. Since everything else is in place—attitude, intention, truth and timeliness—the ingredient that could have promoted awakening here is a gentle, humble and reassuring tone. Admittedly, this is hardly the dominant style these days, but one can understand why someone in the position of Kofi Annan (at one time, Secretary-General of the United Nations) found it essential. And did you notice Nelson Mandela's *manner* of speaking? We can all take a leaf out of their books perhaps.

Gentleness of manner is not an optional extra, and not to be affected, but cultivated in the context of the whole Dhamma it promotes. It comes with a subduing of the sense of 'I, me, mine', which is the main source of all our human woes. It is not about mere politeness, which sometimes papers over an underlying ill-will, but something deeper, connected with letting go of clinging/rejecting words, and indeed letting go of talking too much.

The manner of listening is sometimes what directs a conversation. However well-intentioned and gentle you may say something to a certain person, it may touch a nerve and that person will feel hurt. They may respond by accusing you of being hurtful.

Even in Buddhist circles I have sometimes heard a person use 'Right Speech' as a weapon of revenge: 'You are not using Right Speech in speaking to me!' But the points being made here are for *self*-analysis, not as more weaponry to throw at other people.

1.8 Timeliness

Timeliness was mentioned in the example above. It is also crucial, and like the manner of speaking it can be the one missing ingredient which underlies everything else. Take the truth, for example. Is it a good thing to tell the truth *just* because it is the truth, regardless of whether this is or is not the best time to do so? To take a rather crass example, is it *always* right, no matter the circumstances, to give immediately to a person one cares about some news that will distress them? Should one not, in *some* circumstances, wait a while perhaps? There is also the possibility of mentioning some matter too late (or not at all), perhaps because I did not care enough to remember it, or because it is not in my 'interest', or because I am afraid of the anxiety or embarrassment that might follow.

As in the example of the meeting (given in the previous section) it may be beneficial for individuals to be allowed the space to work towards the truth themselves, rather than be told 'the truth' by you. Waiting to see what emerges may be an awakening for all in a way in which having it handed to one 'on a plate' would not be. However, a moment might come when it seems right and proper to say what needs to be said. That might require courage. In some circumstances the moment may pass, and saying it later would not be as beneficial. What often gets in the way of this discernment is the usual human baggage of personal attachments and rejections. If only I could drop the baggage then the right moment will often appear of its own accord.

You can begin now. It is not enough to understand intellectually what I have said here—one has to start *doing* something with oneself. Here's an exercise.

Exercise 1: Mindful Dialogue

> Next time you are in a group of people (for example, at work or at a social or family gathering) which is speaking negatively of an absent individual, for whatever reason, try to heighten your awareness of what *you* are saying, what you are tempted to say and what you do not say. Note that it is your awareness of what *you* are saying that will help you, not what others are saying. Observe your mood, what it is you are saying, why you are saying it here and now, your intention or motivation in saying it, the manner in which you are saying it, and why you are saying it to *this* person or persons. Also observe how you are listening, and what you are bringing to your interpretations of what is being said.

Of course, in the above example you may not be able to 'observe' what you are saying at a certain moment *simultaneously* with actually saying it. But you could have some success in observing what you are about to say or what you have just said.

There is more to communicating with awareness than speaking and listening. There are body language, facial movements and eye-contact, tone, volume, inflection, and there are writing and recording, phoning, emailing, tweeting, texting and blogging. There is the matter of cultural norms. There are choices about to whom you speak and when and why, and considerations of why you may speak differently to one person compared with another. Should the position or status of the person to whom you are speaking make a difference, and if so, what kind of difference?

Some readers may be wondering what this chapter on 'Right Speech' has to do with the Buddha's path of peace, and what it has to do with 'meditation'. The short answer is that speaking is a manifestation of the ontology (the innermost structure) of 'I-me-mine'—which is exactly where the trouble lies. We have started the path of *uncovering* the self.

We are now moving into the area of the ethics of Right Acting. Speech is, after all, a form of action in and upon the world. The Buddha has a great deal to teach us about action, so that comes next.

Chapter 2

Right Acting: What I Do

Right Acting
sammā-kammanta

Usually translated as 'Right Action', but perhaps more dynamic is 'Right Acting'. Also translated as Right Conduct, Right Doing, Right Behaviour or even Right Working.

Generally to be understood as *intentional* acting which is skilfull or unskilful in the light of the Dhamma.

2.1 Kamma (Karma)

When the Buddha teaches about what we do in everyday life, in his own language, he sometimes uses the term *kamma* (*karma*). It is just an ordinary word in his language, often used in ordinary contexts. Before the Buddha it was also used in the special sense of a ritual action in a Vedic brahminical setting.

It seems to me that originally the Buddha emphasized *kamma* as act*ing* (participle) rather than action (a substantive or nominal). If correct, this has some importance, because in popular Buddhism *kamma* has come to be conceived and treated as a 'thing'—albeit an ethereal thing—that can be accumulated, transferred or diminished rather like coins in a piggy-bank. This has come to support the belief of many lay people, or ordinary people who see themselves as Buddhist, that what is paramount in life is the accumulation of this coinage in order to win a better 'rebirth', example as a *deva*, or at least avoid a worse rebirth, for example in hell. I think this popular metaphysics, despite giving solace or anxiety to many, will increasingly become a hindrance to the flourishing of the Buddha Dhamma.

Anyway, by taking '*kamma*' out of its Vedic ritualistic context and reforming it as any person's acting intentionally (volitionally)[1] in body, word or thought, the Buddha was a cultural revolutionary. He taught that moral nobility rests in one's intentions or responses (*cetanā*) and their consequences. It did not rest on obedience to the rituals and secret protocols of the brahminical (priestly) Vedic hierarchy. Anyone could be 'noble' by cultivating goodness and wisdom. His 'Eightfold Path' was the true path of nobility.

However, vestiges of the brahminical view continue in Hinduism to this day and also persist in swathes of popular Buddhism. In this way contemporary Buddhism for ordinary people, particularly in Asia, is often largely about individuals donating (*dāna*) to the monastic order in order to accumulate enough of the *kamma*-substance, supposedly, to attain a more peaceful and pleasant after-life.[2] Paradoxically, despite the Buddha's teaching on craving, it has in some quarters become an institution founded on the personal craving for heaven and fear of hell, calling to mind the medieval indulgences of the Christian church just before the Reformation. Of course, it is important, even crucial, that lay followers cultivate generosity and materially support the monastic life; but they should be guided to do so without threat, inducement or illusions.

2.2 Action-reaction

It is not, then, a matter of 'becoming a Buddhist' by attaching to a religious belief in *kamma*. In some quarters one finds complex metaphysical theories of the working of *kamma*. Yet the Buddha was not interested in valueless theories and belief systems and was a critic of dogmatic attachment. He said so many times, and also said that he had no secret (esoteric) teaching.[3] As far as he was concerned, what he had to teach could be discovered by people for themselves, if only they would look hard enough into themselves, sincerely enough and in the right way. So I will not show off some mysterious doctrine of *kamma* but simply speak of intentional action and reaction, doing and not doing, acting and reacting, and the like.

However, one thing does need to be said about our individual action, which should be obvious, but which we have forgotten in our contemporary culture, and which the currently confused notion of *kamma* does dimly reflect. While it would be helpful to let go of any clinging to the metaphysical view of *kamma* as some kind of personal return after death (see my discussion of 're-becoming' and 'transformation' later), there is something vital we need to understand. That is, my every action on something or someone is intrinsically and *at once an action on myself*. If *kamma* has any meaning at all, then it is that and only that.

In the Dhamma, *kamma* means every act is at once action-reaction. That is, my every intentional action on something or someone is intrinsically and *at once* an action on *myself*. We can all see this if we wish, but usually pay no attention to it. There is a vivid saying in the Dhamma teachings that getting angry with a person is like picking up a burning coal with one's bare hand to throw at that person.[4] When I am *directing* anger towards you I am *suffering* anger. It has become '*my* feeling'. If I had a choice would I take ownership of such a thing? In fact I have taken hold of anger like I might take hold of a hot coal. Not very wise! The intended destruction, which may or may not result, is at once and necessarily a suffering, in the sense that it is supportive of the delusory self. This is especially clear if my anger has no impact on the other. I am left feeling the discomfort, even the pain, of the anger. I may feel foolish, regretful or even angrier. 'I' has arisen in this feeling which is here and now entangling life. This is not a *consequence* of the anger, it *is* the anger. I repeat: It is the anger itself.

Every single action is in its very nature an inner 'boomerang'. You might say, in religious language, that the 'Day of Judgement' is built into every nook and cranny of our lives. Every action is its own light or darkness to the actor, and does not await consequences. In this existential sense, those who set out to hurt others never 'get away with it'.

We need to keep this in mind throughout the following consideration of action.

2.3 Reaction or Choice?

It may be asked why I should pay particular attention to what I do in my everyday relations with other individuals. I may already have a good idea of 'who I am' and what sort of person I am. 'I am quite a good person really'. But the idea or self-image may not actually fit the manifestations of who I am in my day-by-day, hour-by-hour, behaviour and activity. I need to cultivate self-awareness. I can train myself to stand a little apart from my actions. Actions and non-actions show who and what I am.

The teachings on personal action are, like all the Buddha's teachings, ultimately based on the fact of the abiding dissatisfaction that results from deep-seated craving, clinging and rejecting, and what is necessary to free oneself from those and thus from the dissatisfaction. Actually, our attaching, clinging, craving, as well as our rejections, appear most vividly in how we 'act out' as individuals, in our relationships with others such as family, friends, acquaintances, strangers, groups and humanity at large.

The Buddha's teaching suggests that most of what we do—and the when, where, how and why of it—is a matter of ingrained attitude and reaction, not a matter of conscious choice. Each of us is formed by a long, patterned series of causes and conditions of all kinds. Mostly, we do not really choose what sort of person we are. Modern scientific research bears this out.[5] Although we can change, it is difficult and sometimes appears impossible. But the Buddha had enormous confidence in the capacity of human beings to liberate themselves from themselves, if they go about it in a certain way. After all, *he* liberated himself, but only with the aid of previous teachings; and with his own independence of mind, courage and effort. Everyone has some degree of these virtues, with very few exceptions. We know this because we see them at work every day in the notable things that people achieve. The Buddha suggests that we tap into that energy and courage and at least channel some of it, some of the time, into nurturing the roots of wisdom and peace.

If we can put enormous and sustained effort into learning to play a musical instrument, or a sport or how to be physically fit, or learning a foreign language, then how much more important it must be to channel effort into self-understanding and wisdom. Just consider how much time we spend standing before a mirror, attending to our faces and bodies, our hair and teeth, our clothes and shoes, and then compare that with how much time is spent reflecting on how one acts out one's life, on seeing into the nature of one's short lifetime, and on developing a wiser and happier outlook.

As we shall see, while the key thing for a 100 metre athlete may be their muscle tone, the key thing for a 'wisdom athlete' is self-awareness. If we have little awareness of ourselves then change in the direction of wisdom and peacefulness is almost impossible. Meditation, as we shall see, provides us with certain exercise equipment for developing self-awareness. But, just as we have to start learning a sport or how to play a musical instrument with some very basic movements and by addressing certain hindering habits, so in following the Buddha's Dhamma we need to do the same.

2.4 Precepts

It is true that for those men and women leading a monastic life in a *sangha* (monastic community) there are over 200 rules to be followed. These rules are, or should be, about *training* in the Dhamma rather than setting up a disciplinarian structure. For lay people, we find that nearly all Buddhist schools put some emphasis on at least five rules ('precepts' or 'abstentions'). These are to refrain from:

1. Killing; physical harm
2. Stealing; taking what is not given
3. Sexual misconduct
4. Lying; deceiving
5. Intoxicants; drug abuse

Negligent and cruel destruction of life is generally based on clinging, craving and rejection, and is endarkening. There is no fixed rule here absolutely prohibiting the taking of life under *any* circumstances. Arguing from extremes is not helpful. An *attitude* of respect for life is what the Path points to. It is on this basis that, for one example, we may consider vegetarianism. Respect for all life-forms is de-centring; it challenges the I-me-mine delusion.

The same considerations apply to the other four precepts. What they warn against is the priority given to the grasping and pleasure-seeking of I-me-mine. By implication, what they promote is life-nurturing, sharing, sexual respect, truth-telling and a balanced mind.

2.5 Attachment to Rules

There is a caveat about rule-following. One may ask, what part do rules play in the Buddha's conception of intentionally acting? If we understand the heart of his teaching about craving, clinging and the way to subdue them on the path of a more awakened life, then there will be little need for attachment to rules. In fact, a strong attachment to rules is quite likely to give rise to poor judgement, and insensitivity to the actual situation. The Buddha's ethics is not *based* on rules, although rules may have their provisional utility. We touched on this matter in the previous chapter (Right Speech).

While for some people this is just common sense, others yield to the temptation to build a whole theory on these rules, and endless refined arguments may follow.

If one understands the heart of the Buddha's ethical teaching, which resides in letting go of clinging and its harms, then it will be obvious what these five precepts amount to and that *attaching* to them is not necessary or helpful. Dogmatically following a rule cannot be awakening. While the Buddha warns against dogmatic attachment to rites, rituals and rules, still, in lay life, laws, rules and regulations certainly have their social function and importance; but even they have their exceptions, mitigating circumstances and interpretations.

2.6 Collectivizing Ethics

The Buddha lived in the late Iron Age. It was a period of rapid urbanization and commercialization, but he did not live in a society anything like our profit-based globalized world. His ethics now requires extension to be wholly relevant in modern times. For example, a contemporary extension of the first precept, beyond anything the Buddha could have imagined, concerns the wholesale destruction of other species as a consequence of collective human action—action that the cossetted and comfortable individual may (understandably) be blind to. Consider that never again shall we see the colourful and harmless Tahitian red-billed rail—human activity exterminated it. There are hundreds of such cases, probably thousands if we include invertebrates such as insects. Somewhere on the growing list could be *Homo sapiens* itself.

The same goes for taking what is not given, or does not belong to you. On an individual basis that is clear enough. However, a contemporary example, beyond the individual level that the Buddha generally speaks of, is the daily humanly organized appropriation on a massive collective scale of a decent standard of living for millions of fellow humans by means of economic and financial structures and values that mask the ethical truth. Oxfam recently reported:

> Last year saw the biggest increase in billionaires in history, one more every two days. Billionaires saw their wealth increase by $762bn in just 12 months (March 2016–March 2017). This huge increase could have ended global extreme poverty seven times over. 82% of the new wealth created has gone to the top 1%, while 0% has gone to the world's poorest 50%.[6]

Obviously, it is time to connect basic Buddhist precepts with the collective outcomes of action and non-action, as we shall see later.

2.7 Catching Oneself

The nature of action, as outlined above, clarifies the importance of my general attitude to other people and living things along an axis of hostility at one end and kindness at the other. At one end of the axis I may catch myself acting with anger, frustration, irritation, resentment, sneering, impatience and the like. And it has been already emphasized in this book that if your ill-will aims to harm or hinder someone else in some way then it is hindering *you* completely. At the other end I may catch myself acting with genuine kindness, love, encouragement, support, patience and the like.

It does not matter what I *believe* I am like—I can *find out* for myself what I am like through meditation techniques, and the guidance of a suitable teacher. Nor does it matter so much what others believe I am like, when I am fully equipped to find out for myself. At the same time I do need to listen to others who speak to me honestly about myself. As I watch myself I will have to be fair on myself and note the kindliness as well as the hostility. Again, this is not about judgement and guilt or smugness. But, no cheating; as the tally mounts I get to know myself. At first, I do not have to do anything, just note. After a while, I may notice that I am beginning to catch myself out *just as* or even before the negative or positive action. Later we shall develop this much further with certain techniques. I may begin to get a feel for where I am on the axis, and I may begin to question whether I *have* to be at a particular location along it.

It is true that particular 'unavoidable' circumstances will have an impact on which pole I appear to be gravitating towards, but I may be drawn towards using that as an excuse. What we shall find is that I do not *have* to react, for example, with hostile action, even under provocation. Here is a story from the Buddha's teachings to make this point graphically.

Parable 2: Refusing Anger

> Once the Buddha was abused by a brahmin (member of the priestly caste) who was angry that his relative had left home to become the Buddha's follower:
>
> *When he had finished speaking, the Buddha said to him: 'What do you think, brahmin? Do your friends and colleagues, kinsmen and relatives, as well as guests come to visit you?'*
> *'Sometimes they come to visit, Master Gotama [Buddha].'*
> *'Do you then offer them some food or a meal or a snack?'*
> *'Sometimes I do, Master Gotama.'*
> *'But if they do not accept it from you, then to whom does the food belong?'*
> *'If they do not accept it from me, then the food still belongs to us.'*
> *'So too, brahmin, we—who do not abuse anyone, who do not scold anyone, who do not rail against anyone—refuse to accept from you the abuse and scolding and tirade you let loose at us. It still belongs to you, brahmin!'[7]*

Anger is one of a family of ill-feelings: pique, resentment, fury, grudge, vengefulness, irritation, frustration, grievance, bitterness, contempt, exasperation, hatred, lasting disappointment and so on. The Angry Family are in pain, and they apportion their pain everywhere. Then there is the Kindly Family: kindness, peacefulness, equanimity, joy in someone else's happiness, love, appreciation, respect, cordiality, amiability, acceptance, forgiveness, patience and so on. The two families may live in the same house.

The Angry Family are holding feelings against others, and not noticing that they thereby hold them against themselves. Meanwhile, the Kindly Family first learned not to hold feelings against others, and then had to go deeper and learn not to hold them against themselves. Living as they do, in the same house, the Angry Family cannot really hurt the Kindly Family, because the latter does not accept the abuse, but remains peaceable and kind. The Angry Family gradually learns that it is only hurting itself and expressing its own pain, and finds that the Kindly Family, being what it is, is more than happy to help. This might be a story of the human race.

Exercise 2: Mindful Action

I sit down alone and review the last week. I think of my encounters, tasks and demands one at a time. I try my best to think of *my* role in these, not the role of others. I ask myself how much in the last week I have taken from others, and how much have I given. Before starting I have to reassure myself that this is not about praise and blame, defending myself or congratulating myself. It is about honestly understanding myself, with no praise or blame attached. Giving includes a smile, encouragement, assistance, time and effort, and use of one's belongings, joining an NGO for human welfare. Taking includes snubbing someone, demeaning someone or their efforts, avoiding the giving of assistance, time and effort. Once I have made the 'tally' I do not have to do anything with it, or feel anything about it, just acknowledge it.

Exercise 3: Random Stopping

Here is a simple exercise in non-action. By stopping non-mindful action, one can for a moment restore mindfulness of action.

Now and then, in random but careful fashion, stop what you are doing. You could be climbing up steps, writing an email, about to check your mobile phone, typing a sentence, combing your hair, putting on a hat, putting garbage in the bin—in fact, anything that is relatively 'meaningless' or trivial. Stop, freeze, and *be aware* in the mid-flight of the action itself. After a few seconds continue the action, with greater self-awareness, firstly of the continuation of the action itself and then of the repercussions of the action.

In the next chapter we proceed to actions as purposeful daily activity. It is the third factor in the ethics segment of the Noble Eightfold Path, namely Right Livelihood.

Chapter 3

Right Livelihood: How I Live and Work

Right Livelihood

sammā-ājīva

This aspect is about everyday living and working skilfully, in the light of the Dhamma. A mode or style of living, or subsistence, which does not cause unnecessary harm to people or animals nor rest on exploitation. Instead, it is one that promotes caring, honest, fair and accountable relations in all encounters with people and other living things.

3.1 Progress?

Everything that we have so far considered about speaking and acting is just as true in the workplace as it is in generally leading our daily domestic lives. Turning our attention to the work I do 'for a living' is to bring the social dimension of my identity into focus.

It may come as a surprise to discover that the Buddha's teachings embrace the question of livelihood or work. Of course, he lived in a society very different from our own. It was very rural with a majority of people involved in subsistence agriculture. However, his society was beginning to urbanize into towns, although there was nothing like the cities, industries, railway stations, airports, banks and corporations of today. He probably could not have even imagined the kinds of work many of us do today, and the sheer complexity of it would have baffled him. However, given the replicative and cumulative course of entanglement (*saṃsāra*) it may not have surprised him.

Still, the Buddha was an 'existential' teacher, not an economist or sociologist, and what he has to say about the fundamental human condition is as ethically relevant today as in his time. So maybe he *could* have imagined the general trend, if not the details. The trend to self-destruction was clear to him. It follows from the logic of the grasping and craving human condition. He would recognize the humanity of the contemporary condition, even if he would not know what a 'double hamburger and French fries' is, what an ATM is for, or how it is possible to speak to someone in another country by holding to one's ear a small shiny object bearing numbers 0 to 9. Clinging, rejecting and ignorance would, if anything, be even more 'in his face' today. Hundreds of years of fuel would have been added to the fire. Progress would just be more of the same, but much bigger. Could he conceive the intensity of hatred behind the Holocaust, or that of the greed behind Wall Street, or that of the ignorance behind the nuclear arms race and the impending climate catastrophe?

If he were here with us now and we were to ask whether he thinks that the human race is on the whole more awakened, what do you think he would say? Cleverer certainly, but wiser? Smart technological wonders abound, but ignorantly we take technology to be the *purpose* of our civilization rather than one *means* among others for attaining civilization.

One thing that might intrigue the Buddha is that human beings *choose* to earn their living working in Wall Street, to work at making nuclear weapons, and to work at persuading people to eat more processed flesh of cows, sheep and pigs. As he notes that J. Robert Oppenheimer became a celebrity for designing a weapon for the mass destruction of innocents, that Milton Friedman earned a world prize for celebrating Wall Street and the *non*-altruism of corporations, and Saatchi & Saatchi was acclaimed for its ability to persuade millions to act in favour of their cravings and fantasies (before it collapsed of its own greed), he might just give a knowing nod and mutter, 'Well, I told you so'. And we might ask him, 'And what should we do, then?'—to hear the reply, 'Let's start again, yet again, shall we?'

3.2 Loss of Balance

What would strike him more than anything perhaps, is not the concentration and collectivization of human harms in social catastrophe so much as how the humdrum work of millions of human beings has become separated both from its source and sustenance and from its consequences. We are all sleepwalking in increasingly fragile and unstable organizational complexity. Balance has been lost, and it cannot go on.

We find some clue to the Buddha's thoughts on the matter, but they are incommensurate with our contemporary predicament. It appears that he mentioned a number of kinds of livelihood which bring harm at once to the workers and to the recipients of the work: dealing in weapons, dealing in humans (slavery), and dealing in meat, intoxicants and poisons.[1] We certainly still recognize these in contemporary forms, greatly intensified: global arms trade, human trafficking, mass underpaid 'casual labour' and child labour, factory farms, alcohol, cigarettes, cocaine, sleeping pills, and so on. He also mentions several dishonest means of gaining wealth: practising deceit, treachery, soothsaying (quackery), trickery, and usury (lending at an interest). Telling lies and doing harm by means of one's work are at the kernel of his concern.

There are many in our society today who see nothing to concern ourselves with in any of these. Indeed, all of these are perhaps the mainstay of our 'national interest', 'economic development' and 'economic growth'. At the same time, we have to remember that the Buddha's practice does not entail moralizing or condemnation. Like Socrates (who was a Greek contemporary of his), the Buddha maintains that all those activities that some of us call 'sin', 'evil' or 'wickedness' are all plain ignorance. The 'worse' they appear to be, the deeper the ignorance they flow from, and the greater the compassion we may increasingly feel for ourselves. Condemnation and retribution have not worked, but insight and compassion are worth a try.

3.3 Work on Three Levels

In what way is the work many of us do in the modern world based on 'ignorance'? Surely it is not ignorance to take the opportunities provided by our society to purchase food and shelter, accumulate some wealth and belongings, make ourselves more secure, and have some fun? Isn't the Buddha the one who is being unrealistic about life and work?

We could think of work as resting on three possible levels: the naïve, the manipulative and the insightful.

At the first level there is the naïve ignorance of taking the world of work for granted, accepting uncritically that there is a range of jobs 'out there' and I should choose one. Choose 'the best one for me' and 'success' will follow.

At the second level, comes the realization 'with experience' that work is suffused with conflicts, unfairness and disappointments. Whereas before I was naïve, now apparently I am worldly-wise. I am learning to manipulate the situation to my own advantage, to 'survive'. While I look back, and think I am now less ignorant than before, in fact I have reacted against my previous state by adopting a stance *against* the world: a stance which floats somewhere in a brew of caution, disappointment, manipulation, pessimism, fear, cynicism, hardness and defensiveness. I take this to be knowledge or even 'wisdom', that is, worldly-wisdom. This arises purely by a reactive contrast with what I now regard as the naïveté of childhood and youth. I could stay in this condition the rest of my life, and many do, and some gather more and more negativity as they look forward to 'retirement' and go into old age. But they need not. However, to go beyond this attitude to life I need to *see* it as a pattern of life-reactions. I need to rise above it. How do I do that?

At the third level, I deeply question the conception of what is 'best for me'. It might gradually dawn on me that if it is true that I, like all humans, have a strong inclination to clinging and rejecting then why should that inclination stop simply because I am at work? The same applies to everyone else at work. What happens to us all when all that clinging and rejecting is added up and collectivized in an 'organization'?

Maybe the way out is in learning to let go both of trying to counteract every clinging with a rejection and every rejection with a new clinging; instead, standing aside and watching my reactions and attitude, at least now and then. From this viewpoint, what previously looked like knowledge is now revealed as a deeper form of ignorance than the one I was immersed in as a child or youth. I may even congratulate myself with the thought 'As a child I was happy in my innocence, but now I know what the world is *really* like...' That is, I take myself to be knowledgeable but unhappy. But that's impossible. From the third level viewpoint, true happiness and real knowledge turn out to be the same thing.

The second-level ignorance which permeates work these days is multiplied a thousand-fold by complex organization. Whereas once upon a time in my dullness of mind I could destroy *myself*, and perhaps a few others around me, now we can heap up all our ignorance in wondrously complicated and sophisticated ways and destroy the entire human race without realizing it. This is called progress. It is a progress we neither intended nor created, but stumbled into by not paying attention. It is in truth an existential and ethical regression.

3.4 Questioning the Meaning of Work

So, to update the Buddha's list of harmful and inauthentic ways of going about a living, perhaps we should all ask ourselves: What do I do for a living? Why do I do it? What is its purpose? What is the point of my employing organization? What impact does it have on society, on other creatures, on the environment, on future generations? How is it connected with what others do? Are those connections harmful?

Is harm only to be found in the direct actions of the arms trader and drug trafficker or also in the considered decisions of the suit-and-tie executive in his or her immaculate office who follows precisely the procedures, the law and the code of conduct of the profession?

The ethical issue of livelihood in this epoch is generally not about going out and doing a bad thing to make money, but not having any ethical idea at all about what my work is for, what it is doing to me as a human being and its wider consequences for my fellow creatures. This is a precarious position for a global civilization to be in. Our problem is not the economy, it is not 'peak oil', it is not climate change, it is not technology—*we* are the problem.

Increasingly we work in order to consume, and we consume in order to ... well ... in order to consume. Can we escape the powerful attraction of this black hole of our own making?

Exercise 4: Mindful Livelihood

> Next time you go to work try out some of these questions on yourself. Why do I personally do the work that I do—what are my intentions and purposes? Am I, through the very nature of my work, manipulating others to my own ends? Am I being manipulated to ends I do not agree with or am unaware of? Am I being carried away with this just because everyone else is doing it, or am I reflecting on it? What is the ultimate purpose of the organization I work for? Does it do harm to people, to their health, to their understanding, to other creatures and the environment? Is there something else I could do for a living that is less harmful in its indirect consequences?
>
> Am I stressed out by my work, and what is the rationale for that—is it worthwhile? Is it making me a calmer, a more insightful and compassionate human being? Is it contributing to peace for me, for the organization, for society—and are these the same thing? If not, which is or ought to be the most important? Who takes responsibility for the consequences of my organization's activity? Do I, at least in part? What will my work mean to my grandchildren and great-grandchildren, and all future generations?

The Buddha himself was an itinerant monk of sorts, and it will be said that he did not have a livelihood, so can hardly be an expert on the meaning of work. Did he work?

Metaphor 1: How the Buddha Ploughs

> During his wanderings the Buddha once joined a workers' food-distribution line in order to receive a monk's alms. The brahmin responsible took issue with him. Here's the story:

> [Brahmin:] *'Recluse, I plough and sow, and when I have ploughed and sown I eat. You too, ascetic, ought to plough and sow; then, when you have ploughed and sown, you will eat.'*
> [The Buddha replied:] *'I too, Brahmin, plough and sow, and when I have ploughed and sown I eat.'*
> [Brahmin:] *'You claim to be a man who works the plough, but I do not see your ploughing. If you're a ploughman, answer me: How should we understand your ploughing?' ...*
> [The Buddha replied:] *'Faith is the seed, austerity the rain, wisdom is my yoke and plough; shame is the pole, mind the yoke-tie, mindfulness my ploughshare and goad ... Energy is my beast of burden, carrying me to security from bondage. It goes ahead without stopping to where, having gone, one does not sorrow* [nibbāna].'[2]

3.5 *Mindfulness as a Consumer Commodity*

Considering right livelihood, how about making 'mindfulness' one's livelihood? The very idea of 'mindfulness as a commodity' is, from the Dhamma point of view, a contradiction in terms. Certainly, we see that 'mindfulness' has caught on big time in the West. Human resource managers, counsellors and consultants offer courses. Money is being made, celebrities are arising. It would be quite wrong to deny that as a medical therapy it has benefited many people for specific maladies, especially depression. This is very important. But it is a sad thing if that blinds us to the 'whole of life' benefits of mindfulness in its Dhamma context, freezes us on one step of its whole journey. For some reason we do not yet see the same level of interest in the Buddha's teachings on, say, Right Speech or Right Livelihood, even though they are integral to a more peaceful life and spiritual awakening.

Some managers are now becoming concerned that mindfulness training is undermining 'motivation'. How soon will the more basic question arise: 'motivation to do *what*?' Exploit people, living things, trees, water, mineral resources, human labour, and the human hope for happiness? Or build a sustainable world without war? Suspicions may arise among dealers in mindfulness that it does not promote 'motivation' and 'ambition'. How long will it be before the mindfulness-commodity is drained of its last drop of utility and the cynical reaction to mindfulness and Buddhism emerges from the wreckage? Nearly every good thing to come from the human heart is now grist to the merciless mill of pleasure, praise, fame and gain. Putting mindfulness in context is one aim of this book. A heart taken out of the living human body does not beat. One should remember that the Buddha speaks of '*right* mindfulness', as that mindfulness which is conducive to enlightenment, as opposed to endarkenment. This is the mindfulness that has the power to reveal to us the three marks of existence: insubstantiality (especially that of the self), flux or impermanence, and suffering or dissatisfaction.

We are all ensnared by our utility-obsessed, management-pushed, consumption-pulled society and always on the look-out for an innovation or fad. Must wisdom, peace, honesty, compassion and love be put up for sale? Can they be? Except for short-term fantasy or dupery?

3.6 Integrating Right Speech, Action and Livelihood

To have existential understanding is to drop all divisions and boundaries and in so doing lose one's small grasping self, have compassion for all things, live in peace and lose one's dissatisfaction and fear of death. This is not a theory but a kind of holistic experience and outlook which a person can work towards. The work involved has been experienced and clarified by many existential teachers and taught by them in diverse manners. One such teacher, who gives us a great lead, is the man now known as the Buddha, namely, 'the awakened one'.

The Buddha's approach in helping others follow this life-work programme may be set out in three dimensions: ethical, meditational and compassionate understanding or wisdom (*pañña*). In the first Part of this manual we clarified the ethical dimension. This involves paying *deep attention* to what we say, how we act, what we do for a living, and how we deal with inner obstacles to existential understanding and, instead, develop its catalysts.

In paying this attention we learn how so much of our abiding dissatisfaction has its roots in ourselves, not outside. In particular, we are attaching, craving and clinging creatures in a reality that cannot be attached to, cannot be craved for and cannot be clung to.

We learn that an infinitely greater security and satisfaction lies not in holding on to the world, but living and working with it. In order to reach this deeply human outlook we have to work, not on the world 'out there', but on ourselves. Only when we have learned about ourselves can work on the world 'out there' take a shape which truly fits our fundamental needs and our potential for love, because only then will it be based on the recognition of our inexplicably *human* limitedness.

3.7 Not Just an Intellectual Exercise

The matters we have covered in Right Speech, Acting and Livelihood are indispensable to the journey of awakening yourself and finding peace. You cannot do without them if you choose to embark on that journey, but it is far from being enough. There is little point in thinking 'Well, I have read about the first three of the eightfold path, got the picture, now on to more exciting stuff'. You should have spent some time, at least some weeks or months, going through it and doing the exercises for significant periods of time.

Besides having some intellectual grasp, which can be lost in even a few days (as anyone cramming for an exam knows), the lessons have to sink into one's heart and muscle. If one reaches a point at which one can honestly say, 'Yes, I look at life rather differently now', then that may be the time to move on to the meditational segment of the Noble Eightfold Path: factors 4, 5 and 6, namely, Right Effort, Right Concentration and Right Mindfulness.

3.8 The (Apparently) Toxic Environment

The workplace can be a particularly stressful environment, having to work sometimes with people who seem incompetent, unduly criticize you, disagree with your approach to tasks, sabotage your work, take credit for what you have achieved, make unethical demands, betray you and tell you or others lies. Add this environment to what appears to you to be a similar family environment and there will be times you may 'explode' with frustration and anger and a feeling of despair and even guilt and shame.

Following the Buddha's path may often help you 'cope' with such an environment—or *perceived* environment. Sometimes, however, things do get out of control and you lash out. This generally makes matters appear even worse. Also you may be left feeling that you have failed. You may get a snide remark from someone such as '...and I thought you were supposed to be a peaceful Buddhist!' At these times it is best, if possible, to take time out, confide in a friend, avoid alcohol, double your practice of mindfulness of breathing, be patient and, above all, understand that the Buddha's path is not all smooth and lined with roses. It has rocks, thorns, stumbles and challenges. Just keep following it and get up when you fall. Remember that this situation too will pass, as all things do.

PART TWO

MEDITATION

Chapter 4

Right Effort: Directing the Mind

> **Right Effort**
> *sammā-vāyāma*
>
> Endeavouring, striving or making an effort to deal with arisen (actual) and unarisen (potential) unwholesome or hindering thoughts and emotions such as desire and doubt. But also to accept, nurture and support arisen and unarisen wholesome ones such as good-will and generosity.

4.1 Mindful Living

Some readers may think that all I have said so far is not 'meditation'. Some may go so far as to think, 'I don't need all that moralizing stuff, just tell me how to meditate and become enlightened'. Well, ask yourself this question: is any meditation technique likely to work in a sustained way if returning from the meditation group I am sarcastic to my partner, grumble about the rain, kick the pet dog and curse having to go to work tomorrow? And there is another angle on the importance of the ethics segment of the Noble Eightfold Path. When we come to the mindfulness factor of the path we shall see that speaking and listening, intentional acting and not-acting, and everyday livelihood provide us with an every-day substrate or 'food' for practising that mindfulness. In fact, actual everyday living is the very foundation of meditation, and once we learn the specific features and techniques of meditation we shall start to see Right Speech, Acting and Livelihood as 'mindful living'. Hence we can and should practise mindfulness of speaking, acting, working, and so on. The Buddha's meditation is a 'whole of life' endeavour.

There again, sometimes we may come across the word 'meditation' used very generally to mean a kind of relaxing calming of the mind. Thus listening to music, peacefully looking at flowers in the garden or reflecting on pleasant moments in one's life are sometimes referred to as 'meditation'. Calming the mind is a good thing, but in itself it need not bring about insight or wisdom. It may even work in the opposite direction if it unleashes unacknowledged tensions and cravings that one does not know how to control.

The word 'meditation' is also used to refer to a *focused* way of calming the mind, such as deep breathing. We find this in the context of stress therapy, anger management or prenatal clinics, for example. This is also a good thing and should be encouraged, but it does not have the whole-of-life context and discipline of the Buddha's Dhamma meditation.

The abuse of substances to bring about altered states of mind is never meditation in any sense.

A small but helpful step towards Dhamma meditation is the more focused meditation we find in the recitation of a mantra (repetition of an inner word or sound), that is derived from certain wider practices now called 'Hindu'. It is not to be found in the recorded teachings of the Buddha. Meditation may also be treated as a kind of devotional (worshipping) practice. Again, this is not what we find in the Buddha's recorded teachings. Dhamma meditation is certainly not any kind of worship of the Buddha himself—he very clearly put aside that idea.

Finally, it may be worth pointing out that the Buddha was not simply a 'yoga' teacher as popularly understood in the West. The Buddha quickly mastered certain yogic concentration practices of his time and lifted them to a higher level by reshaping them with a novel dimension of awareness, self-scrutiny, ethical understanding and a holistic view of human life and 'the world'.

To summarize: the Buddha puts all the emphasis on a whole-of-life individual reorientation aimed at diminishing mental/physical anxiety or suffering. In this reorientation process, meditation is a fit-for-purpose, integrated set of reflective mental techniques. This reorientation begins in the individual and ends in community and society at large.

4.2 Effort and Non-Effort

To awaken from unaware engrossment in the world is also *work*. It is work on myself, and work for and with others. The usual way of work may often, on deeper reflection, be a kind of anti-work, a counter-productive effort, and energy spent on digging a hole that serves no purpose and is not filled up, until one falls into it.

'Energy is my beast of burden', says the Buddha. We all know that energy is our beast of burden, but is our beast carrying the burden even vaguely in the same direction as the Buddha's? Peace, insight and compassion are not possible without effort, and that is why the Buddha emphasized it as an essential part of the Path. A 'meditation' which is an occasional relaxation from stress, so that I can return refreshed to the very causes of the stress until the next break (or breakdown), is not what the Buddha was talking about. The Buddha was not teaching us how to take a rest on the merry-go-round but how to stand back from it. Deeper than that, he was showing us that there is no merry-go-round, except for the one we create by our constant craving.

It is not necessarily a matter of giving up my bread-winning work to become a monk or a nun. Rather it is a matter of reappraising the meaning of the work I do as I continue to practise the Buddha's way. Whether as a result of this practice I do my work in a different spirit, or change it in some practical way, or even give it up entirely, is not for an 'enlightened person' to *tell* me to do. There is no value in that. The value is in discovering for myself, even if I need a hand.

It is the same with effort generally. The effort that may be expended in doing what someone tells me is 'right', or even in doing what I tell myself is 'right', is not always going to be any less harmful than the same effort expended on doing what is 'wrong'. It may even sometimes be more harmful. History is littered with the damaging self-righteousness of accusations, correcting others, evangelism, just wars, inquisitions, bombing the innocent, crusades and guilt-ridden self-flagellation. Great harm may (as mentioned earlier) be secreted in the collective outcomes of the innocent efforts of the individuals playing their innocent part in large organizations. The global tragicomedy of human beings expending over the centuries just about enough energy to steam the Earth in its own atmosphere now perhaps gives us a vantage point to pose two questions: energy for what? And, what kind of energy is really worth expending? The latter follows from the former.

Thus, we have already seen that often the effort required of self-liberating speech, action and livelihood is not so much the effort of doing but of *not-doing*. That is, the effort of letting go. This is not a 'Don't do this or that!', but a case of the 'this' and 'that' simply not arising in the first place. It is not so much a matter of having to hold my tongue in speaking ill of someone, but of it just not occurring to me to speak ill. The former is an attempt to counteract doing by rejecting the doing. The latter is neither a doing nor a rejecting of doing.

It is also the same with meditation. The effort required is not that of the attaching, grasping, clinging, craving and rejecting that goes with building up, protecting and reassuring myself.

Once we question the effort of getting more and more, because of the bigger and bigger black hole it eventually threatens us with, we then have to question what *kind* of energy is appropriate to civilized life. It cannot be the energy of grasping. Nor can it be the energy of rejecting. It must be quite different: it is surely the effort of not-grasping.

If you think that it requires no effort to learn to let grasping lie where it is, think again. Here is a parable.

Parable 3: The Floating Man

> Ade is teaching Wu to swim. Wu is very nervous, and fears drowning. Any time his face goes under water he panics and grasps at anything he can hold on to. Ade provides a kickboard and Wu holds on tightly to that. After some weeks, Wu does know that if he is going to swim then he has to let go of the kickboard. When he tries this, however, he panics and grabs hold of Ade's hair instead, holding her under water. Ade recovers and jokes that Wu really should not try to drown his teacher. 'Sorry, but I was scared! Oh, I'll never swim!' says Wu. 'That's the only problem you really have: fear', says Ade. 'Do you realise you can already swim, you just need to let go'.
>
> Ade explains that Wu is trying too hard, grasping at the water, grasping at doing the right leg and arm motions, grasping at the bottom or side of the pool, grasping at Ade's hair, as well as rejecting his own clumsiness and failure. She suggests that Wu lie back in the water with his head back, his body in a relaxed horizontal position, and very gently move his arms and legs together in one motion like a sleepy frog. Ade shows him.
>
> This action of (almost) not-doing anything seems to work. This also requires an effort, but it is not the effort of 'overcoming' the water in order to make progress from A to B. It is instead, for Wu, the effort of trusting that the water will hold him, because he and the water are made that way. After all, they grew up together, you might say.

I need not cling to the water to force it to work for me. That is futile. I need not reject the water as stuff that threatens me with death by drowning. I need not even reject my futile grasping, for which I might instead feel compassion. What would benefit me is learning to let go of clinging *and* rejecting, so that this 'water v. me' problem does not arise at all. I can already float; what 'problem'! This letting go requires an effort, and it is the kind of effort involved in meditation.

It would be really useful if we could devise a way of looking into effort, watching how it is from one moment to the next being harnessed for this, but not for that. That will take us deeper into the nature of meditation, attention and non-attention. But first we need to take our making of effort to a deeper, more fundamental level.

4.3 *Ethical Detox*

Classical texts of the Buddha-Dhamma often speak of 'purification' (*visuddhi*), a kind of ethical 'detox', often as a prelude to meditation and other practices.[1] Admittedly, in the West (broadly understood) our culture is not in a mood to give this much serious consideration. Western culture is now fundamentally hedonistic, that is, it seems obvious to the vast majority that the main aim of life is fun. So obvious is this that any alternative does not appear realistic.

For many it makes perfectly good sense to make truly heroic efforts in 'physical fitness', but it is patently silly to spend any effort at all on moral fitness. While there is nothing wrong with fun now and then it is hardly sustainable as the moral foundation of a person's life, let alone a civilization. The 'West', and its sphere of influence, is probably the first society in the history of the world dedicatedly to attempt this feat for the last half-century or longer.

So, effort is *apparently* well understood—it is what is involved, for example, in packing one's belongings into a confined space and hauling them across the planet at 500 miles per hour and back for something called 'a holiday', which is often so exhausting that one needs a peaceful rest before returning to work.

Now, we just have to imagine taking, say, 10 per cent of that energy, and using it to undertake some internal travel—a journey into oneself. Of course, just as that holiday far away often turns up unpleasant things like cockroaches, malaria, sunburn, diarrhoea, a noisy hotel and theft, so too the internal travel has its unexpected discomforts. The difference is that the 'holiday' is often motivated by the fantasy of advertising brochures (and perhaps a dose of rivalry with one's neighbours and colleagues: 'Oh, you went to Blackpool … mmmh … we went to Bali'). Discomforts are definitely not in the brochure, and must be stamped out with complaints or defended against with insurance policies. The internal travel, however, is motivated by a call to get to grips with what this life really is. Surely, it can't be holidays all the way down?

To re-orientate oneself in life it is not sufficient to pay attention only to one's efforts 'out there in the world', such as the effort involved in studying for an exam, in a sport or in furthering one's career. One has to go deeper. The reason for this is that the outer efforts are working in concert with very powerful inner energies, of which we may be unaware. Patterns of inner energy, which continue year after year, become so much a part of us that we may not see that *that* is where a lot of our total effort is going.

In a way, who we are is defined by these patterns, so it is really important to become aware of them and choose to re-direct them or let go of them, if we can only begin to see that this is necessary for peace and wisdom.

4.4 Habitual Energy

Some of this habitual energy may be unhelpful or even self-destructive, and sometimes without your knowing it, or knowing it only dimly. Some of it may be helpful. The unhelpful and the helpful efforts may be at war with each other within yourself, and this is the basis of much dissatisfaction, frustration and anger directed at others. If under certain social circumstances this inner-conflict anger is collectivized and seized upon by narcissistic power-hungry politicians it can be channelled and aimed at a scapegoat social group, perceived as different in some way. Here is the kernel of misery on a large scale.

Nothing, then, could be more important than coming to see for oneself what pattern of habitual energies is at work within oneself. Without this inner 'clearing out', meditation will be difficult and may not work at all. It is a widespread misconception that one can start on a rather 'heady' kind of meditation or 'mindfulness practice' *without* first looking into one's deep-seated pattern of reactions in order to re-orientate oneself.

A person who functions, in their attitude towards others, on a perpetual bias of distrust and ill-will over hope and good-will will not awaken by practising meditation, even in one hundred years of doing so. A person who shifts that bias to the positive side will have benefited enormously, even if they never meditate.[2]

What can be done about these habitual energies? In order to clarify them, some Dhamma teachers distinguish between 'unwholesome' and 'wholesome' states. These words might have for some people a rather 'Mary Poppins' quaintness about them. It seems our values-impoverished society feels almost embarrassed by many such terms, including 'honour', 'noble-mindedness', 'tenderness', 'commitment', 'diligence', 'self-discipline' and the like. So that I do not ring the wrong bells, I choose another pair of words: unfruitful and fruitful.

Some mental states do not give fruit to peacefulness, wisdom, compassion and existential understanding. Others do give fruit to these.

One can look at the flowers on an apple or plum tree and hope that fruit will one day appear there. The potential is there, but the fruit is not ... not yet. One of three things can happen. A fine fruit will grow; no fruit will grow at all; a deformed or diseased fruit will partially grow before withering and possibly infecting the other fruit. What happens will depend on a number of interrelated conditions including, most importantly, how I take care of the fruit tree.

First we consider unfruitful states.

4.5 *Unfruitful States*

If we think about the fruit tree about to bear fruit, there is another distinction which cuts across whether it is unfruitful or fruitful. Has the unfruitfulness or fruitfulness arisen, or not emerged yet? Is it just a potential, hidden from view in the bud or flower, or is it actual? Plums do not grow on apple trees, and apples do not grow on plum trees. If we have a plum tree in flower, we assume that plums will emerge when the tree begins to fruit.

It is often the same with good fruit and bad fruit. A particular tree may always produce small untasty fruit, whatever one does. When the tree has not yet borne fruit, that smallness and un-tastiness are not apparent; they have not arisen. We might say the smallness and un-tastiness are 'unarisen' or non-emergent at this point in time.

With unarisen states of fruit, good or bad, one can apply remedies such as more light, water or fertilizer. This is how it is with us too, from the point of view of personal character. In a sense, our 'goodness' is arisen or unarisen, and our 'harmfulness' is arisen or unarisen. The Buddha teaches us to examine all four and indicates how we should apply the appropriate remedy or support. He said:

> *And what, friends, is right effort? Here a bhikkhu* [monk/nun] *awakens zeal for the non-arising of unarisen harmful unwholesome states, and he makes effort, arouses energy, exerts his mind, and strives. He awakens zeal for the abandoning of arisen evil unwholesome states, and he makes effort, arouses energy, exerts his mind, and strives.*[3]

To make things easier to grasp the Buddha mentioned five very general unwholesome or unfruitful states in particular (often called 'The Five Hindrances'), which are always obstacles to meditation—both concentration and mindfulness—and indeed to existential liberation. They are:

(1) Sensual desire.
(2) Ill-will or resentment.
(3) Lethargy or apathy.
(4) Restlessness or worry.
(5) Doubt or distrust.[4]

Of course, there may be combinations of these and other more subtle hindrances, such as fantasy, obsession and ambition. This is not that complicated, if we recall his simple teaching that craving is at the bottom of it all. What the five amount to perhaps is this: we want more stuff, we get frustrated and angry when we don't get more (or can't get rid of what we don't want), we get tired chasing around after what we want (or rejecting what we don't want), we worry about whether we can or will get what we want or about losing what we have, and finally we doubt that there is any other way of going about life.

4.6 Unarisen Unfruitful States

So this is how it works: Every hindrance begins (for our purposes here) with a mere 'sign', a flicker of the senses—a sight, sound, touch, taste, smell, a sense-memory. We might think of these flickers as little fly-papers to which mind-contents, such as memories, attach like flies and gnats, and in attaching thereby shut off the mind's natural openness.

When that which is a sign of one of the hindrances to meditation first appears then, with training, *before* the harmful state of mind arises the person sees the risk *in* the sign, and immediately lets it go, not letting it develop into associated ideas and feelings. Entanglement is discouraged. In other words, the senses are guarded, but not in a tense or hostile manner.

A sign which could lead to trouble is nipped in the bud, so it gets no chance to give rise to desire, greed, lust, anger, jealousy, apathy, anxiety, and so on. After all, even with a kindly disposition, one does not let just *anything* through one's front door—a rabid dog, a stranger with a knife, or for that matter a smiling salesman.

If it is too late, and the grasping state has *already* arisen in one's mind, then more effort is required to dispel the associations which are growing around the original sign. There are a number of ways of doing that. As with an infected fruit on a tree, the longer one leaves it, the more it develops, the more it infects other fruit, and the more the effort required to get rid of it. To make this clearer we need some examples. Here is an example of the hindrance of restlessness or worry.

Parable 4: The Sleepless Woman

> When under stress or unhappy, Joe occasionally finds himself becoming fix-
> ated on something very trivial but irritating. This most often happens when
> he has gone to bed and is about to sleep. On one occasion he remembered
> something that a senior colleague, Jan, had said at work earlier that day.
> He was not sure whether the colleague meant to blame him for an untow-
> ard event at work or not. He re-played it in his mind, trying to remember
> whether the tone was sarcastic, what precise words were used, what the
> context was, what had previously been said by others, whether other col-
> leagues generally thought he was negligent at work, and so on. Restlessness
> ruled the cranial roost.
>
> He began to feel insecure and wondered what would be said about him
> at the annual review. He began developing a feeling of dislike towards Jan.
> 'Why can't Jan be clear? Is Jan saying other things behind my back?' In this
> agitated state Joe did not sleep for several hours.

This may seem like a silly story about a silly man. Unfortunately, millions
of people suffer torment from such fixations. Far more than that, this
story even does service as an iconic history of the human race.

It is an illustration of a much more general point about the human
inclination to attach, to stick, in ways that become obstructive to existential understanding. What can helpfully be said about Joe's state of mind
in this context is not intended to be primarily psychotherapeutic, that is,
in the professional sense, but rather how all human beings can remove
or mollify the conditions of attachment, craving and clinging. Clearly, it
raises issues about the inner environment of anxiety in which clinging
arises, and whether one can let go of clinging the moment it shows some
sign of arising, as well as whether anything can be done once it has arisen.

Things might be quite different, or at least easier, if Joe acknowledges
this tendency to latch on in this way. Let's consider the unarisen state.
He's lying in bed, lights off, and there is some low-level 'wandering of
the mind' going on, but Joe has learned about the stickiness of certain
thoughts. He knows that when he is anxious or upset he may be laying
the ground for a 'latching on' to a recent memory. So, he notes whether
he feels that way, and 'observes' it if it is there. Observing the anxiety
itself, but not the thing he is anxious about, it subsides. If the anxiety subsides then those troublesome 'signs' are less likely to arise. Then, if even
for a millisecond there is a 'sign' of a sticky thought, he lets it go, perhaps
by practising a simple meditation exercise or by putting his mind onto a
completely unrelated object, whether a play of light in the window or a
pleasant memory.

4.7 Advertising

One only has to look at advertising to see how well the desires and fears of human beings have been understood by those who, far from wishing to allay them, wish to inflame them to their own ends of gain and power.[5] It is designed, in the first instance, to make *unarisen* states of mind arise. Then, it is designed to intensify arisen states. Hardly any advertising is designed merely to inform. As we all know, most of it is designed to multiply and deepen our desire (wants) and do so by playing into a quite small set of habitual energies: sexual desire, desire for food and drink, desire for security—in short, pleasure, praise, fame and gain and avoidance of pain, blame, ill-repute and loss (see Table 5 in the Conclusion).

Our next exercise turns the tables on the advertisers. We can look at their advertisements and deploy them to understand ourselves and transcend the manner in which advertisements entangle us. Thus the advertisement becomes a supra-advert, to coin a word.

This is a use of the advertisement that is 'above' or 'beyond' the advertisement itself, and a means by which we re-empower ourselves. Thus any advertisement can become a means of liberation rather than imprisonment, and to be welcomed as a free teacher, a supra-advert.

Exercise 5: The Supra-advert

Next time you are walking down a railway platform, look at the poster advertisements and instead of simply reacting to the half-naked body-beautiful or noting the particular product being advertised, do two quite different things:

(1) Note what the initial 'sign' is (flesh cleavage, gleaming car, silky chocolate, whatever) and note your own reaction to it. You can ask yourself: 'What was the very first thing that I noticed?', 'Did I linger on it?', 'Did I have to linger on it?', and 'What feelings and thoughts did it evoke in me?'

(2) Ask yourself whether the poster fits into one of these eight categories in regard to what it is evoking (or trying to evoke) in you: pleasure-fulfilment, pain-avoidance; praise-fulfilment, blame-avoidance; fame (popularity)-fulfilment, bad reputation-avoidance; gain-fulfilment, loss-avoidance.

For example, an insurance advert might carry a powerful image of loss-avoidance and/or pain-avoidance. An alcohol advert might carry one of pleasure-fulfilment and/or obscurity-avoidance. Note out of 10 or 20 posters which categories are most common. Maybe you will notice some that do not fit into any of these categories, so you can create in your mind your own liberating supra-advert.

When you find you can do this, and it has thrown light on the way your own mind works, the next stage is to 'nip it in the bud', which means dropping the 'sign' the very moment it appears. You have to be quick. This is the effort of non-effort; so quick there is no real effort involved. Quicker than catching a ball thrown to you.

Let's consider a scenario. You walk through the tunnel onto the underground system in the city, your mind on the appointment you have to keep, and suddenly there is in your face a 3-metre high poster of a young, half-naked woman (or man) with a seductive look and lying on a beach with a bottle of alcohol between her (his) legs. If this does nothing for (to) you, good, but think of an advert that does arouse your interest, in order to learn about yourself.

By now, with a little training, you have got used to this, if you weren't already. Instead of gaping or embarrassedly turning away, you did not even get as far as 'Wow! Look at that!' Instead, in the time it takes to blink you have registered the initiating 'sign' of 'pleasure' and let it go. Not only your eyes, but your mind is elsewhere in a flash.

Sounds impossible? Well, just think that you already do it every day without noticing it, but not for the 'enticing' things but for the neutral or 'nasty' things. The senses dart quickly over all sorts of things and simply do not register them but immediately drop them because of the complete *absence* of any inclination of the mind to stick to them. Thus, it is hardly likely that walking down Oxford Street your vision would linger on a splatter of last night's vomit in the gutter and even less on a small, discarded piece of paper of no significance. While the vomit might be momentarily noticed and let go of, the piece of paper would almost certainly not be noticed at all.

So, just try it and keep trying it. You already know how to let go in milliseconds, it is your native effort of non-effort; you just need to extend your application of this liberating technique. After all, what are advertisements but 'desire-me' psycho-tricks? Do we *have* to fall for them? And, it is not just about advertisements of course, but all of our daily experience. When you get to the chapters on meditation you will see how important this control over attention is.

Some readers may object that this kind of exercise could make me quite neurotic, having the opposite effect to the one proposed, because I may become obsessed with trying to 'catch myself'. This is an understandable objection. However, one does not have to try and do this every waking moment of the day, unless one chooses a monastic lifestyle, but only sufficiently for the lesson to be learned. If I once had to make an effort to learn the 'times tables', and repeat '...6 × 7 = 42, 7 × 7 = 49, 8 × 7 = 56...' apparently without end, these days I hardly ever repeat any part of it, but nevertheless I do know my times tables for they have become part of my background knowledge and I have no neurosis about it.

4.8 Putting out of Reach

It should be obvious that there is another simple (if not always convenient) method of not allowing unarisen unfruitful states to arise. It entails not putting oneself in a position where they will arise. Since we live in a consumerist society in which advertisers are continually giving us strong 'signs', this is not always easy. But we may become so immured in consumerist signals that it never occurs to us that there are lots of opportunities to shut them out or simply be where they are not.

A recovering alcoholic or cigarette-smoker knows that it is better not to be present where there is an abundance of the signs of these things, or to deliberately avoid them, or to shut them out. For example, we can mute the TV when the advertisements come on. On the other hand, we might look forward to the opportunity to practise the supra-advert technique! We can avoid people and situations which 'drag us down', at least until we have the Dhamma maturity to benefit from the lessons there might be in them.

There is a danger of being misunderstood here and in a number of ways.

Firstly, this is not just about advertising, but about all those signs and signals that we allow to give rise to thoughts and feelings which block our deeper understanding.

Secondly, I do know that many of us have become 'hardened' to advertising, and most people understand what advertisers are up to. However, research shows that advertising *does* on the whole have the effects that manufacturers and distributors want, and that is why they are willing to pay high prices for advertising campaigns. Ask yourself how it is able to work, and whether it *must* work on you.

Thirdly, this is not at all about some kind of Victorian prudishness. You might say, 'What's wrong with being offered a bit of free sexual titillation on the underground platform?', 'What's wrong with some advice on insuring against a real risk such as a shark attack while on holiday in Australia?' Well, nothing is wrong with it, except that when they all add up (especially for a child or young person) day after day and year after year, without awareness and challenge, one may find it harder and harder to tap into inner resources for some lasting meaningfulness in life.

The point of developing awareness of these unarisen and arisen states is that we would really like to be free, peaceful and wise; and all the money, food, sex, holidays, cars, insurance policies and cosmetic surgery in the world cannot achieve that except for the briefest of interludes.

4.9 Arisen Unfruitful States

What if it is too late, and the associated thoughts and feelings have already started to arise? There are fine lines between the unarisen, the just arising and the arisen. If you are already caught by the reaction 'Wow! Look at that!', then you are hooked. There are five techniques we can use for the unfruitful states which have emerged:

(1) Divert attention.
(2) Use the opposite feeling to dispel the harmful feeling.
(3) 'Stare it down'.
(4) Marshal the forces of revulsion and dread.
(5) As a last resort suppress it, or release it elsewhere non-harmfully.[6]

All of these require effort on an ascending scale. The 'nip it in the bud' effort is tiny (or no-effort) by comparison. And all of them require that you first acknowledge that the state has arisen and may grow. Some states, untreated and fuelled by other factors, may grow to horrendous proportions in which horrendous things are done, but let us consider the more ordinary situations. The ability to acknowledge comes earlier and earlier with practice, until one day one acquires the 'nip it in the bud' ability. The meditation practices considered in this part of the book will enable you to develop your abilities of controlling attention, and this will help enormously with the growth of acknowledgement of your inner experience.

Diverting attention involves moving it as soon as possible on to something unrelated. It could mean moving it to something completely and utterly banal and paying close attention to it. You may find yourself investigating the delicate motions of a tiny and insignificant scrap of paper as a train approaches, or last night's vomit which has formed a fascinating stalactite on the edge of the platform. The latter is really an example of the fourth tactic, of marshalling forces of revulsion.

Have you ever thought that one way to put yourself off sexual thoughts when not-so-appropriately attracted to someone is to think of the 8-metre tube of foul-smelling matter just an inch or so under their clothes? Yes, there really is a very long smelly tube in there—unless this person is some kind of space alien. Still, one would not wish to dwell on this. It is just a passing supra-advert tactic. Or is it? For a fun-loving society the very idea of deliberately marshalling forces of revulsion is itself revolting, and enough to put one off Buddhism for life. This tells us a lot about how *real* we have succeeded in making our fantasy lives.[7]

Using the opposite feeling to dispel the harmful feeling is worth a try with irritation, anger, envy, jealousy and the like. Staring it down is not advisable with desire, but may work with other members of the hindering family of five, such as apathy and doubt (see section 4.5, 'Unfruitful States').

As a last resort, especially if thoughts of revenge and violence are getting a grip on you, suppress them and let the energy out harmlessly. However, hammering nails into an effigy in your backyard is only a stopgap, and anyway you should be able to find other things to do with your time that are more conducive to awakening.

Making such recommendations for dealing with arisen unfruitful states of mind does perhaps present life as a kind of obstacle course. However, if you allow it, life will be an obstacle course anyway, and the point is to find out and put into practice a way of not allowing it. Your life need not be all obstacle course, and so far as it is one you can just *watch your experience* of the obstructing (rather than the obstacles) and ask yourself whether it might be you that is allowing the obstacles to arise.

Exercise 6: Tactics for the Obstacle Course

Try the above five techniques in the following situations.

(a) Getting out of bed when you really do not want to: try the 'ignoring of sign' or 'nipping in the bud', that is, just get up before a thought or feeling arises. You have to be quick. The moment that the thought arises, 'Oh no! I have to get up!', is the moment that the suffering starts.

(b) Seeing/smelling food which you really do not need: try engendering the opposite feeling, such as an image of your giving it away to someone starving.

(c) Despising or looking down on someone: try feeling the opposite, some kindliness and compassion, which is best done by *doing* something considerate for that person.

4.10 Fruitful States

Having dealt with some habit-energies which hinder meditation, we now turn to those habit-energies which are conducive to meditation and to the preparation for it. The Buddha put it in a nutshell:

> And what, friends, is right effort? ... He awakens enthusiasm for the arising of unarisen wholesome states, and he makes effort, arouses energy, exerts his mind, and strives. He awakens zeal for the continuance, non-disappearance, strengthening, increase, and fulfilment by development of arisen wholesome states, and he makes effort, arouses energy, exerts his mind, and strives. This is called right effort.[8]

First we shall consider the conducive states which have not arisen in us. In view of what we have just learned, it should be plain that one reason that they do not arise, or not as often as we might expect, is that they are drowned out by the arising unfruitful states. So we have to harness these 'Four Endeavours' (to use the classical term for channelling unarisen/arisen unfruitful/fruitful states) in a unified effort. If we can make even a little headway with this we shall find that our 'formal' meditation, when we get to it, is so much more beneficial.

4.11 Unarisen Fruitful States

To arouse unarisen fruitful states, we have to make room for them and invite them in. It is like planting seeds in a seed box on the window sill. We can sit there and watch and watch, and we know the seeds are there. But how do we get them to show themselves? After all, it is not the seeds we want, but the flowers and the delicious fruit that emerge from the flowers as they wither away. Wishful thinking is not going to do it.

In the case of seeds, certain factors have to be present, such as fertile soil, water, light and warmth, and removal of competing shoots. And we have to go on nurturing and caring for the seedlings: transferring them to a garden, caring for the growing tree, the flowers and the fruit through the whole cycle of life. In the case of the seeds from which fruitful states of mind arise, we need certain so-called 'factors of enlightenment'.

The Buddha suggests that the most important of these factors are seven in number: mindfulness, the investigation of phenomena (mental analysis), energy, joyfulness, tranquillity, concentration and equanimity (balance, poise). This may sound like a tall order, but then ask yourself whether growing a cherry tree is a tall order. Yes, and no, depending on how committed you are and how you go about it. Anyway, the classical 'seven factors' express matters in rather an abstract way. Let's simplify them by taking further the seed box image.

Metaphor 2: The Cherry Tree

> Imagine the whole life of a cherry tree. The bright flowers are those states of mind which give rise to the sweet fruit of existential understanding. The flowers are the mindfulness and concentration which precede such understanding. Joyfulness is the radiant colour of the flowers.
>
> Tranquillity is the peaceful refuge the tree provides for tired and hungry creatures. Equanimity is the balanced proportions of the whole flowering tree. 'Investigation' is the close attention the gardener has to pay (and indeed, you might say, that the tree itself has to pay) to the soil, buds, leaves and so on to ensure healthy growth. Energy is the power the tree has to grow and bear fruit—activated and nourished by light, water and nutrients.

We can now appreciate perhaps that nurturing unarisen fruitful states of mind is a large part of the Buddha's instruction. We must assume that human beings everywhere at all times have the sort of latency to produce fruit rather like wild cherry trees do. While farmers know in an abstract way that not every seed they wish to plant will grow, they can never know which ones for sure. So their actual practice is the generous and hopeful one that all are given that chance, for it is not in the farmer's gift to cause growth itself but only assist its conditions.

Unarisen fruitful states are assisted by letting go of the dominating role that desires have in life, letting go of ill-will and resentment, of apathy, anxiety and (gradually perhaps) letting go of the doubt that there is a 'path of peace' at all.

As in all the Buddha's teachings there is a 'roll-up your sleeves and do it' suggestion for sparking off unarisen fruitful states. It has been used world-wide by hundreds of generations of followers of his way, and is essentially no different from the exhortation by Jesus to love your neighbour as yourself. We may call it the practice of 'the cultivation of loving-kindness'. Here it is, significantly adapted, in the form of an exercise, which has several steps.

Exercise 7: Cultivating Loving-Kindness[9]

> Sit by yourself, or in a community of meditators, and close your eyes.
>
> **(1) Self:** Imagine you are looking at yourself, encapsulating your whole life. Then take a deep breath in and let it out slowly, like a sigh. After some minutes, sincerely express good-will to yourself inwardly in these words:

'May I *now* be peaceful, may I be happy, may I be free'. When you say it, mean it, and emphasize the word 'now'. Hold this for a few minutes.

(2) **Loved one:** Imagine you are looking at someone you love or care about deeply. Then take a deep breath in and let it out slowly, like a sigh. Then sincerely say these words inwardly to that person: 'May you *now* be peaceful, may you be happy, may you be free'. When you say it, mean it, and emphasize the word 'now'.

(3) **Neutral:** Imagine you are looking at someone you know only in passing, but perhaps see quite often, and that you have no liking/disliking feelings about (the postman, perhaps). Then take a deep breath in and let it out slowly, like a sigh. Then sincerely say inwardly these words to that person: 'May you *now* be peaceful, may you be happy, may you be free'. When you say it, mean it, and emphasize the word 'now'.

(4) **Disliked:** Imagine you are looking at someone you do not (did not) get on with very well or not at all. Some feelings of discomfort or hurt may be involved. Then take a deep breath in and let it out slowly, like a sigh. Then sincerely say these words inwardly to that person: 'May you *now* be peaceful, may you be happy, may you be free'. When you say it, mean it, and emphasize the word 'now'.

(5) **Local view:** Imagine you are in the air looking down on your local neighbourhood or town. Then take a deep breath in and let it out slowly, like a sigh. Then sincerely and inwardly say these inner words to that neighbourhood: 'May you *now* be peaceful, may you be happy, may you be free'. When you say it, mean it, and emphasize the word 'now'.

(6) **Global view:** Imagine you are on the moon looking at the whole planet earth, as in the famous photos taken by astronauts. The whole human race is there: some in darkness, some in light, some being born and some dying. Then take a deep breath in and let it out slowly, like a sigh. Then sincerely say these words inwardly to all the billions of human beings and creatures: 'May you *now* be peaceful, may *we* all be peaceful, may we be happy, may we be free'. When you say it, mean it.

It will not always seem appropriate to do such an exercise. Still, if you feel some persistent antipathy to this exercise, it might be worth asking yourself: 'Am I in an arisen unfruitful state?'

You may have to run through the description of this exercise a few times before you can do it without looking at the words as you carry out the exercise. The precise words do not matter that much, of course. What is essential is that you are making a genuine effort to expand feelings of good-will outward from yourself to the whole human race, step by step. It is probably best done in a group of meditators with a facilitator taking everyone through the stages. It is important not to hurry, so that the whole exercise takes about 20 to 30 minutes.

4.12 Arisen Fruitful States

Once fruitful states of mind have arisen in you, such as a higher degree of kindliness, equanimity and so on (and correspondingly less distractedness, irritability, anxiety, etc.) then they should be sustained by continuing practice. That is, not just maintainable for a while, but *sustainable*. I quite like the way the Buddha expressed it:

> ... suppose a cloth were defiled and stained, and a dyer dipped it in some dye or other, whether blue or yellow or red or pink; it would look poorly dyed and impure in colour. Why is that? Because of the impurity of the cloth. So too, when the mind is defiled, an unhappy destination may be expected ... [but] ... suppose a cloth were pure and bright, and a dyer dipped it in some dye or other, whether blue or yellow or red or pink; it would look well-dyed and pure in colour. Why is that? Because of the purity of the cloth. So too, when the mind is undefiled, a happy destination may be expected.[10]

So, one has to put the fruitful states on such a footing that they are not easily lost, dissolved or obliterated. Persistent but gentle effort (largely non-effort, letting go) can strengthen them, link them, bind them into a whole change of outlook, which is further reinforced by meditation and further existential practices and understanding. Sustainability will depend on regularity of practice, practising with a community of like-minded people, and using what one has learned to facilitate the learning of the way by others, and dealing productively with setbacks in life. If one feels a waning of fruitful states, perhaps due to some stumbling-block in life, then *that* in fact is the time to learn from the inner dimension of the outer turmoil, and make a special effort. After all, almost anyone would make a special effort if their own child were in danger of being lost.

Fruitful states can and should also be helped to arise and be sustained on the level of friendships, family, the workplace, civil groups, voluntary groups, artistic creativity, one's neighbourhood and the whole human race and environmental life. Things do not have to get busier and busier, greedier and greedier, more and more stressful.

We can eat slowly and together, slow down our cities, slow down our travel, get to know our neighbours and neighbourhood, and volunteer to assist those who are in the desperate condition that we might be in ourselves later.

Chapter 5

Right Concentration: Breathing

> **Right Concentration**
> *sammā samādhi*
>
> Focusing the attention and quietening the mind; centring the object of meditation (such as the motion of the breath) in such a way as to raise the mind to one-pointedness, eventually unifying other mental factors in pure awareness.

5.1 Concentration's Place in the Path

Right Concentration is usually placed *after* Right Mindfulness; but there are good reasons for putting it before Right Mindfulness, as we shall see.

Building on the clearing of the ethical ground, the effort now has to be turned to the practices of meditation. Right Effort was about consciously controlling what is arising and falling away in the mind, so that some non-coercive control is gradually being attained over mental activity. This light-touch control encourages what is helpful for deeper meditation and peace and discourages what is intrusive and disturbing. The attention required in Right Effort is now to be deployed like the single beam of a torch. This focus means that other mental activities are dropping away and one is aware of the inner quiet and tranquillity. The more one attains concentrative tranquillity the more one is creating a kind of space for higher-level liberating activity, especially mindfulness and its fruits.

Right Concentration is about taking an object of meditation, such as the motion of the breathing, and focusing on it persistently enough as to unify the mind and take it to a single-pointed awareness. With this awareness one is nearing a vantage point of seeing into the delusory nature of 'I-me-mine' and 'external world', and the suffering consequences of that delusion. When 'I-me-mine' is dissolved, so is suffering.

5.2 Attending to Attention

The effort made to 'manipulate' arisen fruitful and unfruitful states required inwardly directed attention. Attention is all-important. Now, you would not be able to move the mind from shifting kaleidoscopic fragmentation to a more unified state if you were unable to *attend* closely and continuously to an outer or inner object. In fact, inner attention (*manasikāra*) in its various forms is the bedrock of Dhamma meditation taught by the Buddha. Where there is little or no attention, there can be no meditation. The development of the ability to direct and pay attention is therefore paramount in the cultivation of meditation and the benefits it brings. In the present factor of the Noble Eightfold Path we learn how to pay attention inwardly in a sustained and concentrating way. It is vital to attaining the benefits of meditation. No attention, no meditation.

5.3 The Agitated Mind

If we can learn to focus the mind on one thing, then it will have to let go of the other things randomly arising in the mind, and in letting go it will become calm, tranquil and peaceful. A space opens up in which we can learn about our own minds—the source of unhappiness and the source of contentment. The agitated mind is the enemy of peace, and the enemy of understanding oneself and others. It is the enemy of right speech, action, livelihood and effort; and the ability to concentrate is their friend and supporter.

In ordinary life we sometimes notice that if we try to focus on one thing the mind will keep wandering off. Familiar examples are keeping the mind on the page of a book one is reading, or having to listen to some talk that does not hold our interest, or trying to calculate mentally or even just trying to follow a complicated plot in a movie. This wandering off may have a specific cause, such as tiredness or alcohol, external distractions (e.g., traffic noise) or just lack of interest. The mind is nearly always in some random state of agitation, even if we do not usually notice that. When we choose to give it an object such as the motion of breathing then initially the state of agitation becomes more obvious. This is primarily for two reasons. Breathing holds no interest as an object (unless one has an asthma attack or pneumonia), and the agitating thoughts just seem to be more important. There is a craving to return to such thoughts when practising concentration with focus on breathing. Secondly, and more significantly, one is unaccustomed to fixing the attention *inwardly*.

Attention seems to be designed to 'look outwards' at people, food, furniture, trees, cars and opportunities to gain something. Later, we shall begin to see that such distinctions between 'inner' and 'outer' are part and parcel of our delusory confusion. For the time being they serve an explanatory purpose.

If we try to keep the mind resting in the ongoing experience of the breathing, or the ticking of a clock, or a coloured disc, and nothing else, we shall at first find that we can hardly go a couple of seconds without a 'distraction'. This could be a thought, hearing something, a desire to sneeze, a pain in the back, a memory, or curiosity about what my fellow meditator is doing or what the time is. You may notice that there is something of an irony in the fact that the mind is generally all too sticky, like flypaper, but when we want it to stick to one thing it is very reluctant to do so. Who is in charge here!

Being able to fix the mind on one object of meditation is fundamental to the Dhamma practice, but we cannot take it for granted. We need to develop this skill before we go on in meditation and Right Understanding. Inward focus requires training.

5.4 Breathing for Meditation[1]

The character of your breathing is always important in meditation. You take your first breath at birth and your last breath at death, and yet you may spend your whole life and have little awareness of the breaths that come in between. People who are unfortunate in suffering from asthma and other respiratory conditions will probably be much more aware of breathing and the total dependence on it.

In normal conditions the state of your breathing is both a reflection of and a modulator of your state of mind. Have you ever noticed what happens to your breathing when you become angry, upset or even just impatient? One's breathing will speed up, and when very angry or upset you may even feel you are choking.

This chapter has some exercises in breathing and it is important to *do* them as you read about them. The first exercise is simply to draw your attention to your breathing and its character.

Exercise 8: Noticing your Breathing

Consciously adopt one of the postures described in Appendix 1 (at the end of this book) and close your eyes. No slouching—it will constrict and alter your breathing. There are two stages. The first stage is to breathe in as deeply as you can, noticing what is happening in your chest. Then, breathe out as far as you can, again taking notice. When you have recovered to normal relaxed breathing you go to the second stage.

This time do not change anything about your natural breathing; just let it continue as it was but pay close attention to it. As you breathe normally try to follow the whole subtle motion from the intake of air through the nostrils and/or mouth, like this: sensation of air around and through the nose, expansion of chest, shoulders moving up, expansion of abdomen, a release of tension, abdomen falling in slightly, chest falling, air passing out through nose and/or mouth. Repeat this about twenty times, paying close attention to the cyclical motion in a relaxed, easy-going way. But neither thinking about it nor imagining it—just be aware of the ongoing experience.

Now look at Figure 1, below, which is a simplified diagram of the chest and abdomen regions. You will see that there is a sheet of muscle, almost dividing the inner body into two 'halves'. This muscle is the diaphragm and it is like a flexible wall between the lung and the abdomen areas. It is this sheet of muscle that largely controls the inflation of the lungs, although you will not be aware of it but only of its effects. Other muscles are involved in breathing: the small muscles between the ribs and the abdomen region as a whole.

The contraction of the diaphragm pulls the ribcage down and draws the air in, pushing down on the abdomen. There is a brief moment of tension and then the diaphragm lets go so that the ribcage moves up to its previous position while pushing out the air. Then there is another pause, when the lungs are inactive, but the need for air starts the cycle again, and this is repeated roughly about six hundred million times in a lifetime of 70 years.

This is a big bodily activity, but we do not generally notice it much. When one reflects on the whole body you may realize that there are countless millions of interconnected cycles at different scales, down to the molecular, going on at any one time in the living human body. But you generally do not or cannot pay attention to them. Then you may wonder whether we have a vastly inflated view of the importance to life on Earth of consciousness or mind. Look at the birds of the air and the flowers of the field: they are born, live and die, like us, but they have no thoughts and no worries.

There are (at least) two other ways of doing breathing meditation, and you should try both and find out which works best for you.

Figure 1: Breathing

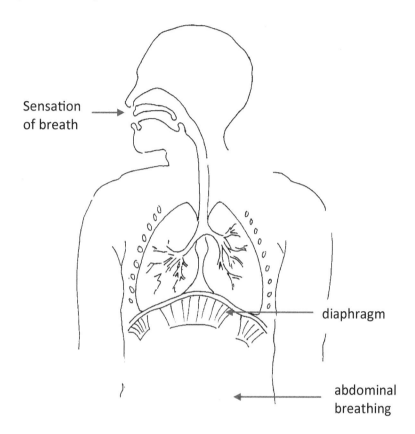

Sensation of breath

diaphragm

abdominal breathing

Exercise 9: Sensation of Breath

This time, focus on one small aspect of breathing: the sensation of breath around the nose. Again, adopt a meditation posture, close the eyes, and breathe normally (assuming you do not have a cold or hay fever). Now identify and then follow the 'touch' of the air at the nostrils or just inside them. You may need deliberately to puff in and out a couple of times to locate this sensation, since you will not be used to attending to it. Now spend about five minutes watching this sensation of breath. Count each out-breath, counting from one to four, and then repeating. If, after a while, you do not feel the need to count in order to maintain focus on the breath, then let it go. This will soon form the basis of a deeper meditation technique.

Exercise 10: Watching the Abdomen

> Once again in your meditation posture with eyes closed, pay attention to the rise and fall of your abdomen. At first you may not notice that the abdomen is rising and falling slightly when breathing. To develop your awareness of this motion, place your hand on your abdomen just under the ribcage, and deliberately breathe in and out quite deeply. Once you have acknowledged the abdomen-motion, return your hand to the position recommended, and continue to breathe normally, spending about five minutes being aware of your abdomen rising and falling. Count each pulling-in of the abdomen as breath goes out, counting from one to four, and then repeating. You should find that exhaling takes longer than inhaling. If, after a while, you do not feel the need to count in order to maintain focus on the abdomen, then let it go.

5.5 Strengthening Concentration Levels

An analysis into three stages of concentration is to be found in Table 2 below. You may stay in the initial stage for quite a long time, before you begin to see that the 'bouncing' is slowing down, the gaps between 'distractions' are widening and that you are experiencing some degree of tranquillity. The gaps keep on expanding, and the tranquillity goes on growing, depending on factors such as state of mind, your background level of agitation, your posture, your degree of effort, the time you are prepared to stick with it, and the letting go of any feelings of frustration or failure. Remember that trying to achieve a *perfect* state is counterproductive; you should keep your mind on the motion of breathing and not on any imagined or desired state or achievement. You are not *thinking* about breathing, but *just* breathing and staying *aware* that you are.

Table 2: Levels of Concentration

STAGE	DESCRIPTION	MIND
Initial stage: *Bouncing*	Training	Keep bringing the mind back to the object or image.
Middle stage: *Fixing*	Meditation	Single-pointed, resting in object or image.
End stage: *Opening*	Fully concentrated	Erosion of, and ultimately loss of, distinction between 'me inside' and 'world outside'.

The table shows us how concentration develops (roughly) through three stages. This process must be preceded by, and continue to work alongside, the ethical practices and the right kind of effort already discussed. All the methods or techniques of meditation are mind trainings, and that is why it is a misconception to think that one is 'failing' when the mind wanders off its object. Of course it wanders off its object! That is why we are practising meditation! And, as we shall see later, we can learn a lot from the nature of the wanderings.

It is rather like the persistence needed to train a dog to sit at the kerb instead of running into the road where it may harm itself and others. At first, resistance is strong and the dog just does not seem to understand what is required. There would be no point in feeling frustrated, getting angry or feeling that one is failing with the dog. The dog is only as smart as its teacher. And the attention is only as smart as the directing mind. In the case of the dog we know that it requires not only patience and persistence but also some affection for the dog. Gradually, those scattered mind-waves will die down and the mind will start moving to the middle stage.

The middle stage is 'meditation' in its very strict sense. It is the single-pointed (non-scattered) settling of the mind in an internal object. The rise and fall of thoughts, feelings and sensations give way to a steady crystalline sense of awareness. You still feel some sense of separation from what you are attending to, but this is getting weaker. You are becoming absorbed in the object (or the object is becoming absorbed in you).

In the end stage, attainable after long and determined practice, description may fail us. It is no longer necessary to focus on an internal image. There is no thought or awareness of 'I am meditating', for it is a so-called 'nondual state' in which the subject-object separation of 'I am in here', and 'the world is out there' is dissolved or at least quite faint.

5.6 Breathing Meditation as the Main Practice

It is possible to persist in concentration, making it your sole meditational path. This would require a level of secluded dedication that may be possible only in a monastic setting. Some Buddhist traditions do indeed follow this course and do not emphasize the path of mindfulness and insight meditation. Questions may arise about whether such a path really leads to the existential insight into the *saṃsāra* (suffering) cycle, spoken of by the Buddha, or whether, at best, it limits the practitioner to the benefit of nondual awareness. I will not discuss these meditational niceties here.

Suffice it to say that were you to have the courage to follow exclusively the path of concentration, then with long and hard practice you would pass, it is said, through four phases of refinement as one moves from the middle to the end stage. In the standard accounts these are as follows.

> First, feelings of want and aversion subside and a joyful wonder emerges that this state should be possible at all. One feels happy about this, as opposed to sad.

> Second, thinking starts dissolving to a very low level, and the mind becomes single-pointed, not scattered and wandering. Joy remains.

> Third, thinking ceases and joyful wonder also dissolves, while a general feeling of peaceful happiness remains.

> Fourth, even happiness dissolves, tainted as it is with worldly pleasure and a tension with its opposite, 'sadness'. Nothing now remains but an aware equanimity, in which there is no sense of a self/world division (duality).

It seems to me that such mental states are too subtle and unstable to allow for such a neat stepwise pathway. However, this manual is written by a lay person for lay people, and certainly does not rule out monastic training with its greater sustainability and depth and abundant benefits. Accessibility is my key concern here, and I suggest that, if with practice in concentration, you find that you are able to stay with sufficient stability in a place of joyful vicinity to single-pointedness, with your thinking at a very low level, this is when you should gently switch to greater effort in insight meditation, as described below.

Chapter 6

Right Concentration: Objects

6.1 Age of Blindness

In our shallow and unstable global society, concentration is best developed by ordinary (lay) people *as a preliminary* to insight meditation. This is because in contemporary 'globalized' culture we mostly 'live outside ourselves' in unparalleled blindness and conceit. Looking at whole populations, the Buddha's core teaching is at a low ebb in the East and struggling to be heard in the West. Our times are not congenial to the intense inwardness required by higher levels of concentration.

However, at the same time our society is generally at a much higher order of general awareness than in the past, albeit the kind of awareness that stands in need of reversal from outer to inner. Still, this awareness may play a part in facilitating insight meditation, and even the fleeting fragmentariness of our contemporary experience may dispose us to what insight meditation can teach, as we shall see in later chapters. The absurd narcissism of a society in which one may be famous merely for being famous perhaps holds out the hope of a liberating flash of self-awareness, since the next stage of being famous for being famous for being famous is hardly tenable. In other words, insight meditation is meditation for all of us in the Age of Blindness.

Some teachers suggest that we could forget about concentration meditation and beginners should go straight to insight meditation. I am not sure what is meant by this suggestion. It surely cannot mean that beginners should not bother to develop some level of concentration first, even if they intend to leave that track and switch to insight meditation at an appropriate point. I see concentration and insight working together in complementary fashion. We can adopt a three-stage approach of teaching and learning meditation. That is, concentration to a level necessary for beneficial insight meditation; followed by 'anchor and buoy' (preliminary insight meditation, anchored in an object of concentration); followed by direct and anytime insight meditation for adept meditators.

6.2 *Other Objects of Concentration Meditation*

The Buddha gives many examples of objects of meditation, and these are quite different from one another and may be selected by a teacher for individuals who are at different stages of attainment, are in different circumstances, have different cravings and aversions, and have diverse characters. To give some examples: one could focus on an external object such as a pebble, a leaf, a bowl of water or earth, a candle flame, or a sound; or an internal object such as an afterimage of a candle-flame, or an invented image in the mind such as a figure of the Buddha or a ball of light.

It would be tempting to think that such an object of meditation must be something 'nice and relaxing' such as a flower, a tree, a bird, bird-song, music, the ocean, goldfish, a fountain—but this is not the case. The Buddha does not mention any of these. There is a good reason for that. We choose our object of meditation not for reasons of pleasure, joy or excitement but with no motive except to meditate and learn—in the longer term—about the workings of our own mind. And we do that so that gradually we become more peaceful, wiser, more understanding of others; and ultimately for spiritual (or ontological) reasons. It is best, for our present purposes, to have a *neutral* object of meditation, so that the mind is not encouraged to wander into fantasies, memories and stories. We now have to subdue or attenuate (weaken) the senses and the wanderings of the bobbing buoy of the mind as much as we can, and have to make a concerted but gentle effort and sustain it for quite a long period, say 30 minutes at least.

Exercise 11: *Drying Leaf*

> Here is a simple exercise which requires both simple concentration and simple mindfulness, and should help to lead to contemplative understanding.

> Take a fresh green leaf and place it where you will see it regularly (e.g., your bedroom or kitchen window sill). The best is a tough, deep green leaf such as laurel or rhododendron. Whenever you see it again, focus on it for three minutes. Then start observing its colour, texture, shape etc., without judgement or wordy descriptions or biological explanations, for three minutes. Then contemplate on the changes you see in the leaf from one viewing to the next. Over a few weeks you will see it change slowly in almost every respect. This may lead to a reflection on the birth, growth, flourishing, decline and death of everything around you. Such is the impermanence of

all things. No need to become morbid about it; after all, compost is a condition for renewal in the cycle of flourishing life.

6.3 Deeper Meditation

In the previous chapter you practised two exercises in breathing. This was mainly from a postural point of view. Now we practise them again in an expanded context, that is, a more refined, meditational point of view. When we consider these we shall see how there is no firm line between fixed attention (concentration) and momentary attention (mindfulness), because everything ultimately depends on your mental vantage point, so to speak, in the ongoing moments of awareness.

Exercise 12: Refining Nostril Sensations

Re-read 'Exercise 9: Sensation of Breath', and then follow these additional instructions. After five or ten minutes of attending closely and continuously to the sensation of the airflow through the nostrils, the 'bouncing' will have subsided and you will start to feel calmer. Now you are in a position to pay even closer attention to the sensation. Do not hold onto it or grasp it, but rest in it as though you were floating in a stream. Now, here is the crucial refinement: as you float, watch the airflow sensation *in all its detail*. It fluctuates, deeper, shallower, longer, shorter, slightly different locations, colder, warmer, etc. Patiently go on practising this over a matter of weeks. Practise and practise until one day the joyful sense of single-pointedness arrives of its own accord. At this point the mind may be so calm that, like the surface of a pond on a windless day, it merely reflects, since it has no ripples on its surface.

If you have worked with the sensation of breath as described above for some weeks, you might like to try an alternative: watching the abdomen rise and fall. It is not required to move from sensation of breath to abdomen watching. You could move from one to another, or you could stay with one or the other from the very beginning. Still, I recommend that you try sensation of breath for some weeks, and then move to abdomen watching to find out whether this is more effective. It is often of greater efficacy for those who feel that they 'think and talk too much'.

Exercise 13: Refining Abdomen Sensations

Re-read 'Exercise 10: Watching the Abdomen', and then follow these additional instructions. After five or ten minutes of attending closely and continuously to the rise and fall of the abdomen, the 'bouncing' will have subsided and you will start to feel calmer. Now you are in a position to pay even closer attention to the abdomen-motion. Do not hold onto it or grasp it, but rest in it as though you were floating on a gentle, soothing wave. As you float, watch the abdomen-motion in all its detail: it fluctuates, deeper, shallower, longer, shorter, slightly different locations, 'shapes', etc. Patiently go on practising this over a matter of weeks. Practise and practise until one day the joyful sense of single-pointedness arrives of its own accord.

6.4 Worry and Restlessness

We may recall that the Five Hindrances were mentioned earlier under section 4.5, 'Unfruitful States'. It is worthwhile to re-read this, and recall desire, ill-will, laziness (lethargy), worry and doubt. There can be no doubt that worry (restlessness), for example, can be a major obstacle to settling into fruitful meditation. The Buddha himself regarded worry as being like a bowl of water stirred by wind in which one cannot see one's face; and even likens worry to 'slavery'. He said:

> Bhikkhus [monks/nuns], *I do not see even one other thing on account of which unarisen restlessness [worry] and remorse do not arise and arisen restlessness and remorse are abandoned so much as pacification of the mind. For one with a pacified mind, unarisen restlessness and remorse do not arise and arisen restlessness and remorse are abandoned.*[1]

Ethical living and meditation pacify (bring peace to) the mind. What is more, in developing insight we will come to see the Five Hindrances in a more positive light: as our private tutors! For in observing our states of mind, including the disturbing states and hindrances, we learn what we are and we also learn how to transcend those states. Note that a dumbbell is very heavy yet it is not a hindrance to a weightlifter, but that by which he or she becomes an adept weightlifter.

Look into worry and you may see that it is either about the past or the future. It may be remorse about what you have done or failed to do, or fear of what one might do or fail to do, or what some other person might do to you or fail to do for you. Look deeper and you will see that these concerns have no substance in your mind and no permanence. Look even deeper and you will see that the object of worry exists only in so far as you grasp it, and vaporizes when you let it go by saying inwardly 'It is not me'. In the next chapter we learn more about how to do this 'deep looking into'.

6.5 Concluding Concentration

To summarize this chapter, we should now see that concentration meditation has a number of benefits, which includes the following:

- It strengthens your power of attention, which is a central aspect of controlling the mind generally.
- It eventually brings about tranquillity, clarity and single-pointedness.
- It teaches you more about how the mind works (and how it does not work) and indeed what 'the mind' is or is not.
- It prepares you for insight meditation and Right Understanding.

6.6 Lay Practice: Beginners Start Meditating Right Now

Select or create a Still Point for yourself. This is a place at home where you would have an opportunity to be alone at some time during the day. The best time for many people would be when getting up in the morning, having just finished in the bathroom.

(1) At the Still Point you could, if you wish, place a candle, and/or flower, and/or some peaceful and inspiring image and a small bell. (Such bells are available from meditation goods suppliers.) Unless you wish to stand, place your chair, stool or meditation cushion in front of the Still Point. I believe a Still Point should be simple rather than elaborate—but it is up to you.

(2) Let anyone else around know that you are meditating. Adopt one of the recommended postures (see Appendix 1). Look at your Still Point and give a deep sigh of relief. Now make yourself generally aware of your body in its posture. If you live with others who do not meditate you might like to invite (gently ring) the bell to mark the start of the meditation period, although that is not always necessary.

(3) Next, close your eyes and 'watch' either the sensation of breath around the nostrils or the gentle rise and fall of the abdomen as you breathe normally.

(4) As thoughts, feelings and sensations arise, do not struggle against them, but acknowledge them briefly and gently let them go and return to watching the breath.

(5) Do this for at least 15 minutes (longer as you develop). You might like to invite the bell to close the meditation session.

(6) Some beginners like to use an 'app' or a timer. These might be useful for the real beginner, but are not recommended in the longer run because they generate a 'waiting' mentality and app-dependency.

Once your simple home practice is established, you could consider joining a meditation group or attending a retreat centre. There are Tibetan temples, Theravada monasteries, Zen groups, 'mindfulness therapists', and so on. Some are good, and some not so good. Try different ones and choose carefully. A group is only as good as its teacher.

Chapter 7

Right Mindfulness: Refining Attention

Right Mindfulness
sammā sati

Sati is from the Vedic *smṛti* meaning memory or recognition. In the Theravāda *Pali Canon* it is mindfulness, paying inner attention (*manasikāra*), intentness of mind, wakefulness of mind, alertness, or in some contexts, lucidity of mind, or even self-consciousness. In any case, mindfulness is always associated with awareness or clear comprehension (*sampajañña*).

7.1 Attention in Mindfulness

Attention is at the heart of mindfulness, and mindfulness is at the heart of meditation, and meditation is the principal means for breaking the chain of conditions that emerge as worldly attachment. 'Breaking' the links in that chain liberates a deep peace and compassion for your needless suffering and that of humanity.

Attention has a dual role in meditation. It is both the source of our problems and the escape from them. It is just a matter of control. Attention out of control may stick and grasp, triggering desires, hatred and anger and many harmful arisings. Attention under control promotes peace and understanding. In a sense, meditation is learning to use liberating attention against entangling attention. The switch from one to the other requires awareness, which is covered in Chapter 9.

7.2 Refining Attention

If attention is in general a selecting, focusing and staying with an object or field of objects (external or internal), then the attention deployed in mindfulness is the directed and sustained, non-judgemental and aware (reflexive), observing of what is mentally arising and falling away: thoughts, sensations, emotions, memories, fantasies, and so on. It is not a thought, memory or concern *about* the experience but mere *awareness* of the actual, ongoing, real-time, unfolding experience as it is.

The point of cultivating finely-tuned inwardly directed attention is the benefits that come from being able to look into yourself honestly. It is like having a magnifying mirror to examine the blemishes on your face and the condition and nature of the skin. As the Buddha expressed it:

> And how, friends, is a bhikkhu skilled in the ways of his own mind? It is just as if a woman or a man—young, youthful and fond of ornaments—would look at her or his face in a clean and bright mirror ... If they see any dust or blemish there, they will make all effort to remove it. But if they do not see any dust or blemish there, they will be glad about it ... So too self-examination is very helpful for a bhikkhu [to grow] in wholesome qualities.[1]

Only when I have honestly examined myself am I in a position to understand others, and understand life itself. Paradoxically, I study myself in order ultimately to lose the attachment to the delusion of a *separate* or discrete self.

7.3 A Torch in the Darkness

In ordinary life a lot of our effort and energy already goes into attention from moment to moment. It could hardly be otherwise, but we are barely aware of it.

So what exactly is attention? It is the mind's selection, attaching and staying with (holding) an object or field of objects. An 'object' could be anything at all that is the target of our mental selection, attaching and holding. I could be paying attention to a football match on TV, or a cat crossing my path, or the words being spoken by my friend, or a song on the radio, or an insect bite on my ankle, or a memory, a plan, an image, an ache in my shoulder, or the words on this page. So the object could be, as we say in dualistic terms, either 'outside me' or 'inside me'. Or so it appears.

Attention is often visualized as a kind of reaching out and grasping by the mind. But actually meditative experience shows that it is much more like closing down everything around the object, like a camera diaphragm, so the object comes to stand alone. This closing down is the 'letting go' that brings about the quieting of the mind, and the feeling of tranquillity.

If we first reflect on the nature of attention we shall be taking a step to understanding ourselves. The Buddha's form of meditation initially demands paying attention to attention, that is, being aware of the act of attending. Making a generally life-enhancing effort requires highly focused attention to a lot of things we may not usually notice very much. It also requires attention to the very moment when desiring or rejecting, caring or giving, arises in us.

7.4 Torch Beam

What are you looking at right now? Obviously you are looking at this sentence and dropping from your mind everything else. How wonderful it is that your mind can do this, otherwise it would be overwhelmed with a chaotic torrent of experiences from all directions.

Actually, you are *scanning* at this moment. Instead of staying in one place your attention is directed along a line of words. You are attending not to one word, but to a line. You now take this for granted, but it took you years of training to be able to do this in a sustained way. (Reading is a lot more than focused looking of course, but we do not need to go into that here.)

When reading a line your vision is in some ways like a moving torch beam. It is a narrow beam, with its effort and energy focused but also moving continuously and rapidly. If you can do that for reading, you can also learn to do it for meditation. (Incidentally, I am not suggesting that reading is reducible to paying attention to words.)

Metaphor 3: Torch Beam

> If you go into a very dark room with a narrow-beam torch, you would probably flick the torch around to find your way around. You would be scanning the room. You would have to do this because the torch cannot illuminate the whole room at once.
>
> As you flick the torch around, you would pass quickly over some things and linger on others. In other words, you would be selective. Some things appear to be more 'interesting' or 'important' than others. You would be discriminating, and would also pass immediate positive, negative or neutral judgement on what you come across: 'I like it' or 'I don't like it'. This would not necessarily be a matter of conscious choice, but just the way the mind typically works.

This point about visual attention largely applies to all other objects of attention: attending to a sound, a touch, a pain, a taste, a smell, a memory, a mental image, a calculation, a feeling, and so on.

The basis on which one is making the selection generally remains obscure. You have to attend very closely to the attention itself, and then contemplate for a while, to have some glimmers of insight into what that basis is. We learned to do this previously to some extent, in the context of speech, action and work. If one were very thirsty, no doubt one would linger on the sight of a glass of water. This would be positive; it would attract. A stretch of bare floor would probably hold no interest. It would neither attract nor repel and would be instantly forgotten.

A coiled object in the corner of the room would arouse fear: 'Could it be a snake?' You would linger on it very attentively in order to detect any motion or serpentine characteristics. At that time your entire being would for that moment be poised in a negative state: rejection, revulsion, readiness to fight or flee.

So there is some broad pattern in our flickering and reactive attentiveness: either a pulling towards (attraction), or a pushing away (repulsion, aversion), or neither (neutrality). You could say that this summarizes the whole of the human condition: pulling in, pushing away, or neither. In judgemental language we might be familiar with the first two as wanting/desire and rejecting/aversion. Greed and hatred would be the extremes of these two states.

Let us pursue this model of a torch beam further. I move deeper into the dark room with my torch. Since I am thirsty I am drawn to the glass of water. I am attending to it. My mind is attaching to that thing, and thereby tending to leave any other thing in darkness.

These reactions are the *bedrock* on which countless refinements and complexities accumulate through life's experience. We shall encounter the Eight Worldly Intentions in the Conclusion: they are pleasure and pain, praise and blame, fame and humiliation, gain and loss. Here is the anatomy of attention and non-attention. As we have seen, the Intentions rest on positive and negative attitudes and reactions, namely, on attaching/clinging and rejection, on moving towards and moving away from. Increasingly complex levels arise, all convoluted variations on the bedrock.

This act of attaching is a very powerful force and, while it is not the only mental force at work, the Buddha suggests we would benefit enormously by observing its nature. There is only one clear way of breaking out, and superseding these reactions, and that is through the development of an awareness of the whole process itself. In that awareness there is the basic condition for release, for liberation. This is at the very heart of the Buddha's teaching, and its implications are radical. It is said that with this awareness, the 'wheel of the Dhamma begins to turn'. Consider this analogy:

Metaphor 4: Flypaper Mind

> Before clever electrical devices were devised for executing insects that find their way into the kitchen, there was the flypaper. This is a strip of brown paper that smells good to insects and is adhesive on both sides. It is hung in a corner of the room and insects are attracted to it only to find themselves terminally glued: a kind of fatal attraction. A large aggressive bluebottle might alight and convulse the entire paper, giving false hope of escape to the immobilized midges. This belligerent, too, would eventually be drained of energy and succumb. After some time, the flypaper would be covered in struggling, dying and dead insects of all shapes and sizes and have to be replaced with another.

How far is this a metaphorical description of the involuntary stickiness of my mind, littered with fading memories and emotional traces of matters large and small, which have been given their place in my personal identity for reasons now painful, forgotten or seemingly ridiculous? How many more of my cravings and aversions will fall into the trap, today and tomorrow, merely from lack of proper attention? Right Effort was showing us how actively to make a change.

On the most general level, we human beings wish to be happy and satisfied and will tend to attach to whatever appears to fill that lack, that perceived need, that gap in our lives. Unfortunately, because we are not very aware of the nature of attaching, it tends to happen without our awareness or real understanding. Attaching therefore can often serve short-term gains but also mislead, block out, bring clinging, craving for more, disappointment and pain.

Do not jump to conclusions: the Buddha is not at this point teaching the *elimination* of attachment, but rather the freedom that comes with an awareness and understanding of it. For this, we first need to fine-tune and direct our ability to attend.

If I feel a lack of water, then water will surely satisfy me, and it is no surprise that all my attention tends to fall on the glass of water. I move towards the water. I desire it, and want to make it *mine*. (Note how 'mine' emerges.) In this wilful state of being, a lot of other potentialities are aroused in me, which may or may not be realized. Consider a few of these: I may be neglecting other things in my field of experience, I may become frustrated or even angry if anything obstructs my getting to the water, and I may be disappointed and even angry if the water is foul or insufficient to satisfy me. I may even develop an obsessive taste for water in a glass, and I may come to think that satisfaction always lies in gratifying my lack as soon as possible.

There is a distinction to be made, in some contexts, between what I need and what I want, but our needs are actually very small and our wants are infinite. I may have a tendency to expand the list of perceived needs when describing my wants, and contract the list of perceived needs ('He doesn't really need that') when describing the wants of others.

7.5 Holding and Joining

The water has been drunk. The experience is now 'in the past' and is a memory. Where there was a glass of water there might now be either a short-term satisfaction or an annoying absence. Either it was not enough or I shall feel thirsty again after some time. Sooner or later I may feel some disappointment. Let us suppose all I have is this dark room, and there is no water tap anywhere to be found. Now I am holding tightly onto the image of water, or perhaps the water has frozen over me in the form of a cloying memory. I am craving. 'That experience of gulping water: Oh, how I want it again!' I am holding on to the very idea of the water, and I join it up with other attachments and rejections and it grows in my mind, grows into my very life. I am in danger of becoming nothing but a concentrated grasping.

Things might go this way, but they do not have to. Just as when I scan this sentence I am joining up words in order to make sense, I am joining things up to make sense of my experience all the time. Flicking my torch around I join up all the passing glimpses, all the attachments and rejections and paint myself a picture of the room. It is painted in the primary colours of my attachments and rejections. There may be all kinds of objects in the room, but only the glass of water and a possible snake have any prominence in my view of it. As far as I am concerned, this 'Water Room Possibly Guarded by a Snake' is the room's reality right now. So now I am attached to a view of reality, and this takes hold and grows. Let any fool dare disagree with me, and there will be trouble!

7.6 Exclusion by Torch Beam

Where there is no torch beam, there is darkness. That which is not in the torch beam is excluded from my view. It is the area where attaching has not occurred. Furthermore, also excluded from my view are all those things that are momentarily in the beam but do not survive the filter of my attaching and rejecting. Attention, as I have pointed out, is not just sticking onto something but also the excluding of everything else. Perhaps it would aid our understanding to think of attention mainly in that way. That is, not as a sticking to something but as an excluding of things, so that one thing remains in the field of view. After all, can the mind *really* stick to anything? What is 'the mind' anyway? Perhaps that is how the mind is. It is a function, like the diaphragm of a camera that closes down around the object. That is why, where there is an obsessive compulsion, it often helps to prise open the mental beam by shifting the attention to a wider and unrelated perspective, such as looking through the family album and recalling stories around the pictures.

Attentive-exclusion is a very important dimension of the way the human mind works. First, my ignorance that my mind works in this way leaves me with the view that the world selected by my sense of lack and need is the world as it is 'really' is. To express myself philosophically for a moment: I take the mind-constructed world as *the* world; take the world as it is *for me (and us)* as the world as it is *in and by itself*. In this alienation by duality the suffering arises.

However, if I can take the higher vantage point of observing the whole inclusion–exclusion process, as it were, then I can shift the mind and my view of the world becomes quite different, for then I see the world as a shifting-construct world. Then, in a sense, I cannot take it quite so 'seriously'. My troublesome 'clinging and rejecting' tend to become less fixed, for I see them for what they are.

Second, even if I accept the possibility of this higher vantage point, I might still be 'ignorantly' excluding the expanse of ordinary experiential possibilities that could broaden my mind sufficiently to reach that vantage point. If I am mentally tussling with a memory or an anxiety then I am excluding the birdsong and flitting insects just outside the window. I am not then in any position even to begin to contemplate the fact that the birds and insects have no worries, but are supported by the very environment which they are not just *in* but *of*. Then the question 'Could the same be said of me?' cannot arise for me precisely because I am fully preoccupied, stuck, cramped, attached. Furthermore, on the dark side, my denial or deliberate exclusion of what I do not find acceptable about the world, such as loss, illness and death, also closes off the emancipatory possibility of learning how *it is* with the world, and how I cannot in truth make it stand as I want or stay still as I need.

7.7 *Distraction*

Attention also entails distraction. If my mind can settle on one thing and stay with it according to the degree of attachment or rejection involved, my mind can also do the opposite. That is, it can let go of, be pushed off or pulled away from any one thing. This is because the mind cannot attend efficiently to two different things at the same moment. Of course, we all know we can mentally attend to something such as the news on the radio while *doing* another thing such as driving a car. But even then the two things tend to interfere with one another. We can also attend to one thing and be marginally *aware* of another or others.

What we cannot do is consciously attend *simultaneously* to two or more things, although we can flit rapidly between one thing and another.

Indeed, we must ordinarily be aware of, or somehow receptive to, a field wider than the object of our attention, or we could not so easily be distracted. As we shall see when we discuss the practice of meditation, the bang of a door will generally distract the meditator who is focusing on their breathing. Such a distraction may be regarded as an 'intrusion'. Besides this, there is a general kind of distractedness in which the mind more or less aimlessly attaches to whatever 'catches its attention'. This is fishing without a fisher.

It is only when one tries to direct the attention to something and keep it there that the tendency of the mind to wander willy-nilly becomes clear. This persistent background restlessness can generate a lot of trouble and unhappiness and, says the Buddha, keep the individual in a deep ignorance. It has been said that we may live our entire lives in distractedness. We shall now turn to the possibility of reining in this wandering through fantasy heavens and hellish realms.

Exercise 14: Satellite Dish

Sit comfortably and alertly with your eyes closed and pretend that you are a kind of satellite dish. You cannot transmit anything, but you are very sensitive to any sounds around you. Without discrimination or judgement, note how many different sounds you are picking up. It does not matter whether they appear important or trivial, pleasant or unpleasant, near or far, just note each one carefully and then be receptive to others. You may focus for a while on one particular sound, and note how it is made up of several different sounds or how it is changing. You may also note some other things about how your mind works with these sounds.

After five to ten minutes of this you should take a pen and paper and question yourself about the details of this experience. The questions might include the following. Was it a calming exercise? How many different kinds of sound were there, such as a car passing by, someone coughing, a pigeon cooing, aeroplane passing overhead, rain falling, your tummy rumbling or a chair creaking? Did your attention shift to a sound that was louder or more 'important' or 'interesting' to you than another one? Did your ability to listen and pick out different sounds improve with time? Did you find yourself becoming absorbed or 'losing yourself' in the sounds? Did you notice how the sounds continually shift and flow and are never the same at any point in time? Did you also notice that it was hard to be completely non-judgemental, in the sense that every sound was not *just* a sound but a sound *of something*—that is, you found yourself trying to *identify* the sound so as to weigh it up?

A very important question is how many of these sounds you would have noticed had you not been asked to notice them? You will probably find that only a small fraction, and maybe none at all, would have been noticed. We could repeat this exercise with sights, tastes, smells and touches, and we might then conclude that if we could add up all the things we could potentially notice at any point in time they are far greater than the number of things we do actually notice at that point. If you are worrying deeply about some matter then it may be that, at that point, you notice almost nothing at all, even if you are in a beautiful and interesting environment.

Another important question, then, is: On what basis am I selecting what I pay attention to? That is, how or why did I come to be attending to it? Indeed, am I *selecting* at all or am I, as it were, driven or guided by some forces I do not acknowledge or understand?

7.8 Two Forms of Meditation?

We now return to the question of the relation of concentration and mindfulness. In fact, attention is what unites concentration and mindfulness. It will have become apparent by now that mindfulness, real-time attention to one's inner experience, can be deployed in two ways: by *fixing* it on one experience, or by watching various *momentary* experiences as they arise and fall away. In fact, one might say that mindfulness is a kind of momentary concentration.

These apparent alternatives have been developed into what some teachers regard as two forms of meditation: on the one hand, 'tranquillity meditation' and on the other 'insight meditation'. Confusing the matter, the former is sometimes called 'calm meditation', 'concentration meditation', '*samadhi*' or '*samatha*' (Sanskrit: *śamatha*), and the latter is called 'mindfulness meditation' or *vipassanā* (Sanskrit: *vipaśyanā*).

We have already discussed Right Concentration in depth. There can be little doubt that concentration meditation existed as a method long before the Buddha, and he learned about it from two great teachers that he encountered. It has continued to be practised from the Buddha's day and is also found in religious practices collectively often called 'Hinduism'. It is also obviously akin to what we now call 'Yoga'. It is referred to with approval many times in the Buddha's teachings. It also appears to be true that his own special contribution to meditation was *insight* meditation, and this is what is often taken to be distinctive about the meditation method we now often call 'Buddhist'.

A choice does not *have* to be made between fixed and momentary mindfulness. It does not have to be one or the other. Only misunderstanding or dogmatism, what the Buddha called 'attachment to views', would insist on such a choice. They should be seen and practised as complementary, as mutually supporting, and united by attention, juggling with helpful and unhelpful attachment.

I shall explain more about how to integrate the concentration and insight methods into the Anchor and Buoy Model in the next chapter. It is the first of our models.

Chapter 8

Right Mindfulness: Anchor and Buoy Model

8.1 Watchful Walking

In this chapter the relation of concentration and mindfulness is further clarified and then practically integrated in what I call the 'Anchor and Buoy Model' of meditation. But first there is a preliminary to Dhamma mindfulness: what may be called 'watchfulness'.

You can lead yourself into the technique of Dhamma mindfulness by doing a preliminary exercise in ordinary life. Let's call it Watchful Walking; but one could also use 'thoughtfulness' or 'carefulness', or the older word 'heedfulness' (*appamāda*). Next time you take the dog for a walk or go for a stroll or ramble, try this. First of all you have to slow down and let go of getting somewhere or achieving something. The point is not to *get* to but to *be* as awake as possible.

You have five senses to awaken: seeing, hearing, touching, smelling and tasting. You are going to deploy each of these one at a time during your stroll.

Exercise 15: Watchful Walking

Let's say you are walking down a leafy lane or weedy back alley. For the first two minutes, put your sense of vision into hyper-drive and notice everything and anything around you, e.g., leaves, stones, grasses, wood, insects, and so on. Do not just note them in general, but one at a time, taking note of the particular features of each item. Also note the unpleasant things, in a neutral way if possible at this stage. Do not try to analyse or explain; just observe closely.

Next, turn up your hearing capacity and for the next two minutes attend to all the sounds around you. For example, wind rustling, rain pattering, dog barking, bird tweeting, aeroplane passing overhead, car door closing, and someone shouting in the distance. Again, there will be pleasant and unpleasant things, but take it all in your stride.

Next is touch, and for two minutes touch whatever you can (but not if it carries a sign such as 'Danger of Electrocution!'). Touch the grass, the leaves, the branches, a mouldy stick, a passing black beetle, a puddle, a pebble or sand. There will be some things you would not wish to touch, so just for a moment imagine you are touching them and watch your own reaction.

Next, be like your dog: sniff everything. For example, smell of damp earth, smell of flowers or vegetation, the neighbour's cooking or some indefinable whiffs. You might like to try smelling a leaf, a grass or piece of bark.

Finally, there is taste. What on earth could we do with that while on a stroll? The answer is: a lot. When I was a boy in Wales I discovered that clover petals were sweet at the roots, that a thistle-head had a nutty bit in the middle and that fresh grass was quite tasty. Lots of wild plants are edible, of course. (This is not a health and safety manual, so please be careful about what you put in your mouth.)

Concerning taste: when you get home and have your next meal, slowly and deliberately eat the food, paying close attention to the taste and texture of each morsel.

If you are in a pleasant place then obviously this 'watchful walking' will be a pleasantly awakening experience. You might even feel quite exhilarated and begin to feel you have been missing a lot. The next thought might be that not all the sense-experiences were pleasant, but they were there in your world and many of them may have been put there or left behind by other human beings. You might now feel sad or irritated. However, another state of mind is possible: to detach one's judgement from these experiences and to become simply aware of them. We come to that in depth soon.

Now we need to fine-tune this watchfulness into 'mindfulness', for the purposes of following the Path. We return to the scenario of the torch beam in the dark room.

8.2 Directed Attention

In the example of the dark room your torch-beam attention settled on the glass of water and the unidentifiable coiled object. You did not necessarily *choose* to attend to them—rather, thirst and fear chose for you. There was a reaction or motive behind the attention: my attention was *led*, not directed.

In meditation we make use of this distinction. For the most part during meditation (but not always, as we shall see later), we choose to direct our attention to something, to an 'object of meditation'.

I may choose as my object of meditation anything that is fit for purpose. It could be a physical object such as a coloured disc or a candle. It could be an inner, bodily process such as my own breathing. It could even be a mental image, such as an imaginary coloured disc, 'invisible' to anyone but myself. In fact, we could take anything at all as a meditation object, but we might choose carefully in order to address such factors as our character, our state of mind and our degree of enlightenment or endarkenment. Generally, a teacher would have to point this out to the meditator.

The key points about this directing action is that it now appears that I am leading, rather than being directed by desires, fears, and so on. To put it another way, I am consciously choosing to attend to a specific object in a specific way. A kind of freedom from willy-nilly attachment emerges in my mind.

8.3 Sustained Attention

In the scenario of the dark room my attention to the glass of water and the coil was fairly sustained. That is, I maintained a focus on these two items for some time. Mindfulness usually involves staying with an experience for a defined period. The duration of the period depends on the particular technique. In any case, the attention is, at the very least, sustained enough to note what the experience is, for example hearing, remembering, feeling an emotion, sensing an itch.

The kind of flitting attention that engages much of waking life, lightly touching on and passing by, is not mindfulness. It is certainly essential to carrying on ordinary life, but it generally goes on without mindfulness, or very little of it. This is because fleeting attention generally does not involve any awareness, or no significant depth of awareness, and therefore no discernment or examination (*vicāra, parikkhā*) that can be activated by that awareness. It is as though the touch is too brief, too light to register in the consciousness, although it may well register at some unconscious level.

In many techniques of meditation, as we shall see, we stay determinedly with the object of meditation, or stubbornly return to it should the mind wander. Every beginner to meditation will confess to the difficulty of sustaining attention. Beginners often remark that they hardly seem to go one second before a thought or sound (usually one of these two) will apparently take them away from the meditation object. Indeed, when we endeavour to keep a small child attending to the spelling of new words or arithmetical tables we see mirrored in them our own struggles with sustained attention in meditation.

Many people who try meditation classes give up after only a short while. Perhaps the realization that there is no failure in being unable to sustain attention to your own experience does not occur to them. Actually, this is an important step in the meditation process: now, we see for the first time how capricious or unruly the mind is, how freedom of mind is possible, and how we may have compassion for the unfree state that we are often or usually in. The key to meditation lies not only in sustaining attention but also in the patient, non-frustrated *returning* to the meditation object.

8.4 Non-judgement

In the dark room my attention settled for a while on two items. This happened because the two items, glass of water and coil, were perceived as significant. That is, I instantly discriminated between or 'judged' them. In the simple context provided here there are definite grasping (clinging) and (rejecting) aversive reactions 'driving' this attention: a thirst for water and a fear of snakes. On the conscious level, a judgement also arises with the perception, that is, that water is good and snakes are bad. Water keeps me alive, but snakes can kill me.

From this simple dualism there cascades an infinite variety of two-sided judgements, some strong, some weak, some rigid, some flexible, some fleeting, some obsessive, and so on. The human world, especially as moulded by Western languages, is painted in two strong tones: black and white, with a few shades of grey in between. On the one side are goodness, kindness, justice, beauty and praise, and on the other are evil, sin, injustice, ugliness and blame.

When we consider 'being judgemental' we usually think only of the advisability of avoiding *negative* judgements, especially regarding other people's behaviour. No doubt this is good advice. However, there is a possible misunderstanding here. Meditation does not involve 'being non-judgemental' primarily in that sense, but rather in the sense of observing (not necessarily *eliminating*) the negative *and positive* judgement embedded in all our experience. Beginners in meditation sometimes imagine that sweet bird-song and flitting butterflies are the kind of thing we should be attending to, and buzzing wasps and slamming doors are an annoying distraction which any decent meditation centre should not tolerate. For some reason it stubbornly escapes our notice that what *attracts* us often hurts us a lot more—sooner or later—than the things that repel us. The teachers in our lives can be found both among the things we like and cling to as well as those that 'make' us irritated, angry or afraid (i.e., that we reject).

So strongly embedded is judgement in our language and outlook that it is difficult to see how we could make sense of experience without it. So we do not notice how often it makes nonsense of our experience. Here is some topsy-turvy behaviour:

Parable 5: Buddhist John

> John, a self-proclaimed Buddhist, once did all he could to avoid hurting earthworms when digging the garden. He secretly admired himself for this improvement in his sensibility. One day, a cute but hungry robin alighted on John's spade handle and eyed him. Devoutly remembering 'Buddhist compassion', he at once dug up some worms or pieces of worms and threw them down for his newfound friend, the robin, to eat. John did his best not to hate slugs (for eating his lettuces) until he noted one day that they also ate the weeds, and then the hating mysteriously vaporized of its own accord. The squirrels, which were at first so furry and adorable, infuriated John when they ate all the nuts he had carefully arranged for the birds. Aware of the supposedly un-Buddhist emotions arising here and there, apparently at war with his good intentions, he eventually concluded that Buddhism is 'unrealistic' and joined the golf club instead. (It seems he was not the sort of person to ask advice from a Dhamma teacher!)

John was vacillating between contrary judgements. What he lacked was *equanimity*, or calm balance, a putting aside of preference.

We persist in thinking to ourselves: 'But there *really is* evil in the world; there *really is* beauty.' Well, yes, there really is; and, no, there really is not. It depends on what vantage point you take, what level you are at. If we remind ourselves of the three levels of life and work we may understand that at the level of clinging/rejecting (level 2) the world will be one of good/evil, beauty/ugliness and so on. After all, to see something as 'good' is to attach and cling, and to see something as 'evil' is to reject and dismiss. We do not cling *because* it is good, for the clinging *is* the goodness. We don't reject *because* it is bad, but the rejecting *is* the badness. Not surprisingly, we sometimes change our minds, and what we cling to at one point we later reject when it does not live up to *our expectations*. Has the good that was once 'really' good, now become 'really' bad? Contemplate this point.

Is it possible, then, to observe in a non-judgemental way, to have bare experience? It depends on what one means by 'bare'. I think the answer is 'No' if we expect to arrive at a ground of 'sense-data', namely, theoretical units of sense-experience.[1] However, if we mean by 'bare experience' a shift of my observation from the 'things of this world' to my *experience* of them then indeed that is what is required of mindfulness. In this sense mindfulness is experience *laid* bare.

8.5 Single-pointedness

The awareness that is a dimension of mindfulness is also focused. By this I mean that it is, in its strict form, attention to the finest detail possible in one 'place'. It would be tempting to say that this focus has intensity about it, but this could be misleading because it might suggest a grasping of an object, whereas it is more of a complete resting in or absorption or even blending into an object *together with awareness* of this resting as resting.

The very word 'focus' perhaps suggests a mental action like trying to hit the bull's eye. It is more like knowingly falling into the point to which the mind wholly points. Imagine a golf ball that is initially aimed at the hole but then the ball circles around and plops into the hole because that is the natural lie of the land.

8.6 The Directly Visible Dhamma

Again, it is not mindfulness at all if it is not awareness of my actual real-time *experience*. (The phrase 'here-and-now' has become a very popular way of indicating this aspect.) In teaching meditation I sometimes find that practitioners of the Buddha Dhamma think they know what this means, when in practice they do not.

The Buddha explains to one inquirer what he means by speaking of 'the directly visible Dhamma'.[2] When I feel hunger I know at the time that there is that particular feeling or craving going on, and when I feel gratitude then I know at that time that that is going on. And this does not mean that there is a one-to-one correspondence between a unit of *experience* and a unit of experiential *awareness*. There is no such separation. There is the Dhamma right there. It is the knowing of that flow of feelings, thoughts, sensations, and so on, and of the suffering or release that goes with that knowing. There is nothing mysterious about 'the Dhamma'—it is right in front of you, you might say. This is not *thinking* about greed or gratitude; it is *awareness* of them as they actually arise, linger and fall away like mist or a shadow.

We humans are now so entrenched in *thinking* about x, y and z that we just do not know about *being with* x, y and z, or even about *being of* x, y and z. Recall our earlier parable on 'The Taste of Broccoli'. The actual tasting in the moment of the broccoli is quite a different matter from the thought or image or memory of broccoli. Thinking about broccoli is not at all the same as actually tasting broccoli. In fact the *taste* of broccoli cannot be thought about, like I might think about harvesting broccoli from my garden. I would have to put down this book and pop some broccoli into my mouth and savour the taste. Behold, the taste-awareness of broccoli is a tiny facet of the Dhamma.

8.7 *Think-ism*

Think-ism (to coin a word) is actually an outstanding characteristic of our information-obsessed 'civilization', which works against the very possibility of Dhamma. It is not here-and-now but there-and-then. In fact, even the 'there-ness-and-then-ness' of a memory, for instance, may reveal the Dhamma, if and only if one is aware of the 'there-ness-and-then-ness'.

There will be some people who will read this book in the spirit of receiving even more *information* and think 'Oh, I've got it; very interesting!', before moving on to the next fascinating (rather than suffering-relieving) subject, such as *The Guide to Shopping in Tokyo* or *Rare Insects of Patagonia*. A few may even manage to squeeze a few minutes of meditation in between shopping and planning the Patagonia flight. Unfortunately, they will not wholeheartedly practise Dhamma mindfulness, and therefore will not *actually* have experienced the Dhamma even if they have learned *about* it. (I should add that there's nothing intrinsically wrong with either shopping in Tokyo or having an interest in insects.)

There is little point in being an expert in swimming on the basis of having closely studied swimming manuals, while never having put a foot in water. Such manuals are meant to help *in the water*. When I've 'got it' *in the water*, then I can throw away the manual. So mindfulness is necessarily awareness of one's *living* experience, which right now is the reading of this sentence by you.

If I am meditating near a window and I note 'bird singing', that's quite near to mindfulness, but it still falls short. This is because in meditation we are not bird-watching, and the bird is not our object. Our object is the *hearing experience* bathed in an awareness. So, examining the experience I inwardly note this: 'hearing'. That is all. If I am meditating and inexplicably recall words exchanged with a friend yesterday, then my object becomes not the words or what my friend meant, but this: 'remembering'.

I note 'remembering', and let it go, returning to my primary object of meditation.

What we are mindful of is just the experience and not the experience *of* someone, namely 'me'. I do not note 'I remember' or 'I am remembering', but instead just 'remembering'. The remembering or the hearing are just 'arisings' in much the same way the sun rises, the Earth rotates, the rain rains, worms consume rotting leaves, the song is sung, insects multiply in Patagonia, and Tokyo continues being shopped day and night. Both subject and object are dropped, and even 'experience' itself becomes suspect—I clarify this crucial point later in this book.

Now we shall try an exercise. It will seem a very simple exercise at first: just listening to a clock. However, this is a mindfulness exercise, so it must become directed, sustained, non-judgemental, aware, focused and here-and-now experiential.

Exercise 16: The Clocking Tick

> Put yourself in a very quiet place, where the sound of a clock is clearly audible. Adopt one of the recommended postures and close your eyes. Listen to the ticking of the clock. At first all is familiar: you are noticing the ticking and feeling 'at home' with it. 'I know what that is: it's a clock ticking and I am sitting here listening to it'. But familiarity is the enemy of meditational insight and we have to intensify our focus on the ticking, listening to it very carefully and intensely, as though trying to penetrate the detail of each tick. Stay with this for about 20 minutes, and note what happens. The tick shows itself as unfamiliar.

At first, it will be very hard to stay with the ticking, and the mind will wander. However, if you do this with some determination, the following may happen. If it does not, then try it another day and, if it still does not, then just move on. After ten minutes or so 'The ticking clock I hear' may become unstable. Ticks will seem to be missing. Some will seem to be louder and others quieter. They may seem to speed up or slow down. Then, it becomes the tick that tries to identify itself as a clock, a kind of clocking tick. Then, it becomes just a tick and no clock. Persevere and it becomes a tick that at this instant makes me the 'I' that is nothing more than a tick-listening. It seems: what am I at this moment but this tick? Then it becomes just a tick, and no 'I'. Now, it is a tick that ticks itself, and becomes even more unstable. Is this a tick? What is this 'thing' suspended in here/out there—'tick' is just a word, and this is not a word, it is ... whatever it is. The existential significance of this will gradually become apparent as we move to our later chapters.

Here is another simple and popular exercise:

Exercise 17: *The Body Scan*

> Sit in one of the recommended postures (see Appendix 1) and close your eyes. Imagine a special kind of body scanner is passing slowly through your body from head to toe. Do not miss any part of your body, inside or on the surface, as the scanner passes down through your forehead and brow, nose, tongue, jaw muscles and so on, and eventually down through your knees, calves, ankles, feet and toes. This may take about 3–5 minutes, so you may find yourself scanning too quickly, which will bring no benefit. Try it a few times until you can do it slowly, and paying close attention to what your body is doing at the scanning point and with *clear awareness.* You may detect tension or discomfort in some places, such as brow, jaw, tongue, neck, shoulders, back, abdomen, hips, knees or ankles, which you had not noticed before the scan. When you notice any tension, do not reject it but gently release it and continue with the body scan. Habitual tension may be difficult to detect and release, which is why you must scan slowly and with awareness.

This exercise should further raise your awareness of your body and bodily motions, both for enhancing posture more conducive to meditation and in preparation for certain meditations on the body (mindfulness of body), which we shall come to soon.

As far as is possible this manual builds gradually on a stage-by-stage approach, so putting down the book and *doing* the exercises recommended at any point will make the next stage so much easier to do and to understand. Gradually we proceed to the attaining of Dhamma *insight.* That means that what you will be working towards is, in general terms, a deeper understanding of what this 'living of a life' is and is not, for you and for everyone that has ever lived and will ever live.

8.8 Anchor and Buoy

In order to move seamlessly from 'Right Concentration' to 'Right Mindfulness' it is very helpful to combine the two aspects in what I propose as the 'Anchor and Buoy' model. If we look at Figure 2 we see an anchor attached to a buoy that is bobbing about on the surface of a lake.

We can think of the sea's surface as the surface of the mind. It is either agitated or calm, or somewhere in between. When it is agitated the surface waves pull on the buoy and it lurches about in random directions, just like thoughts, feelings and sensations do. But if the buoy has an anchor

Figure 2: Anchor and Buoy

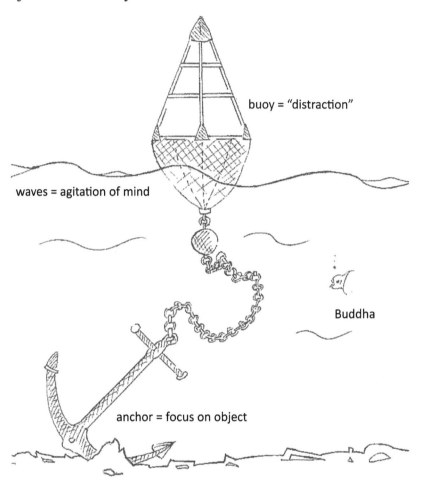

then this lurching about will be tamed. In meditation we could take just one thing, such as the experience of breathing, as our anchor. The buoy of thoughts, feelings and sensations will tend to drift away from the anchor. The further the buoy drifts the more tension there is on the anchor to pull it back. Just imagine if this subduing of the buoy were in turn to help the surface of the lake to calm down. If the anchor were effective then tranquillity might gradually result. (Remember that this is just a model and cannot correspond exactly to the reality it depicts.)

We seem to have two choices here. We could just fix our attention on the anchor, and not pay any real attention to the buoy. That would be tranquillity meditation, resulting in a mind that is 'concentrated'. That would in itself be a great benefit, and indeed some teachers suggest that this is the main thing and some that it is the only thing we need to do.

Alternatively, we could just watch the various momentary bobbing and lurching of the buoy very closely and not pay much (if any) attention to the anchor. That too would in itself be a great benefit, and again some teachers suggest that since this is the main thing, we should go directly to that.

8.9 *Refining the Anchor and Buoy Model*

Assuming you have persevered with concentration meditation long enough to calm, clarify and focus the mind, then you will be ready to return to the Anchor and Buoy method in earnest. Look again at Figure 2. The anchor represents the object of concentration meditation. Its function is to still the mind, just as the anchor stills the buoy. The buoy represents the 'distractions', bobbing off in different directions. The ocean represents the whole potential of the mind: deep or shallow, calm or agitated.

You are now in a position to better practise insight meditation, by taking the so-called distractions as momentary objects of meditation whenever they arise as you rest in your breathing. You might object at this point that if your distractions subside to zero during concentration then the Anchor and Buoy method cannot work, because there is no buoy. Quite right. However, if you get *that* far with concentration then maybe you should go on with it indefinitely, since it obviously suits you very well. For the vast majority of lay people this will not be the case.

You will need to change your attitude to 'distractions'. That is, as dis cussed earlier, you should work on dropping the judgement that these arising things (door slamming, phone ringing, someone coughing, feeling of boredom, etc.) are 'distractions', that is, something negative. They are merely 'arisings', and that is how we shall refer to them from now on. In fact, we could try to take the attitude that these arisings are something positive because they have the potential to teach us what we are. Arisings are teachers.

The Anchor and Buoy method works like this. You rest your attention in, say, the motion of the abdomen, as described in detail above (see Exercises 10 and 13). You will already know that when the mind wanders or 'bounces', following some 'distraction', you immediately return to the abdomen-motion, which is your object of meditation. But now there is a big difference: when the mind wanders you briefly *take note* of 'what it is doing' and then return to the abdomen-motion. This is not to set you up to watch your own failure! Far from it. There is enormous benefit in observing the arisings. How can you reap it?

When the mind wanders, as it will, you label those wanderings as varieties of arising. For beginners, there are three very common arisings:

- Thinking.
- Hearing.
- Sensing (something bodily, such as an itch or pain).

Of course, we could add many more arisings and break them down into dozens or even hundreds, as some Buddhist monks and nuns have done. We shall keep it simple. If you find that nearly all the arisings are thinking then you could take another approach and discriminate between ...

- thinking past
- thinking future
- fantasizing.

In any case, as I said earlier, 'drop the subject and the object'. For example, if I am watching the abdomen-motion and realize that I am thinking about what Juan said to me yesterday, I do not say: 'Oh, I am thinking about what Juan said'. Instead, I let go of the 'I' and of the object of the thought, namely, Juan speaking. I just say to myself: 'Thinking'. Thinking is what has arisen. Not *my* thinking; just thinking. Not thinking *about*; just thinking has arisen.

When this thinking arises here and now, it is like the buoy bobbing off. Then the chain attaching it to the anchor will take up the slack, and the anchor kicks in. The buoy is tethered once again: you are focusing on the abdomen-motion again. After a while, let's say hearing arises: the buoy bobs off in another direction; the anchor takes up the slack; you say to yourself 'hearing' and the abdomen-motion anchors the mind. After a while, sensing arises (for example, an ache in the back): the buoy bobs in another direction; the anchor takes up the slack; you label it 'sensing' and again the abdomen-motion anchors the mind. (In this last case, you might like to attend to proper posture while you are at it!)

When you first try this practice you may find that when the mind wanders you start thinking about what the 'correct' label is. This will happen less as time goes on and you learn to immediately identify the arising. In any case, your default label is 'wandering'. So rather than spend time thinking about the 'correct' label, just stick a 'wandering' label on the arising and return immediately to the abdomen-motion.

As you persist in this practice the bobbing-off will slow down, with fewer and fewer arisings. Furthermore, more subtle arisings will probably emerge. So that little buoys of thoughts, hearings and bodily sensations that you had not previously noticed will tug at the anchor. Persevere with the practice.

If you meditate with a community of those following the Path then you will have the support to take this practice further over months or even years, together with other life changes. You will gradually become calmer, more self-aware, more aware of what is going on in others, more sensitive to other creatures and the environment, and closer to seeing into spiritual questions about birth, growing older, life purposes, sickness, death, suffering and peace.

8.10 Insight Learning

The Anchor and Buoy method stabilizes the mind sufficiently for it to, in a sense, observe its own actions. This skill of watching what the mind is attaching to, rather than (or, as well as) watching the world go by or trying to bend it to your will, is central to the Buddha's teaching. If we are meditating by concentrating on an object such as our sensation of breath or abdomen-motion then of course anything that appears to get in the way appears to us as an obstacle. It is a great leap forward in doing meditation to understand that there are no obstacles except those that you, in a way, 'choose' to identify as such. But to see this you have to detach yourself sufficiently to be able to watch these 'choices' (attachments), which later on you may see are not actions *of* your mind but *are* the mind itself. The mind is an attaching process. There is no 'mind' other than the attaching process.

What this means is that when you watch arisings you engage in a deep form of learning. It is not the learning of books, classrooms, websites and information. It is that learning which the Buddha calls 'insight'. We could call it 'existential' learning, and I am inclined to use that term sometimes. I also use the word 'spiritual', even though it might suggest something to do with spirits or The Spirit, which do not usually belong in core Buddha Dhamma discourse.

If we develop the skill to watch arisings, then we are learning to watch the continuous emergence and dissolution of the mind, like a cloud formation. What is it that is doing the watching? We are hijacking one forceful kind of arising, namely consciousness, and turning it onto itself. This is rather like using the right hand to scratch the right shoulder. Is the right hand of greater importance than the right shoulder, or could it subsist independently of the right shoulder? Of course not. No right shoulder, no right hand. When the right hand makes contact with the flesh of the right shoulder there is the illusion of identifying something separate 'out there'—but it is the arm touching itself.

Earlier I discussed the ethical dimension of attaching, and how we can become aware of what we attach to and do not attach to. We can see now perhaps why the Buddha's ethical teaching is completely at one with his meditational teaching. They are not two teachings, but one.

8.11 Elaborating and Simplifying

When we used the Anchor and Buoy model, we learned to label some arisings as thinking, hearing and touching and all the rest as 'wandering'. Before that we had in fact discussed various other arisings of all kinds, although we had not always called them 'arisings'. It is now time to bring a little order into this, because this will enhance our understanding of the key process of attachment.

In the classical collection of the Buddha's teachings, the *Tipiṭaka*, mindfulness is divided for training purposes into four groups called the 'Four Foundations of Mindfulness', which I shall shortly clarify in detail. These comprise a bodily (physical, material) group, a pleasure and pain group, a quality of mind group and a group of core teachings or 'natural laws' (*dhammas*)[3] to always keep in mind. There is no point in memorizing this classification as an intellectual exercise, but it is useful for keeping our attention on how to learn from our subjective experience. Actual experience is a continuous intertwining flow and does not lend itself to rigid classification. We classify only as a crutch for our struggling understanding as we progress along the Path.

As noted earlier, once the mind has picked up a 'sign' or a sign has just arisen, there will often be a tendency to elaborate this into a story, a kind of recollection or daydreaming, as though you were watching an internal video in which you have the star role (or the victim). In mindfulness exercises we learn to catch this elaboration in its early stages and watch how it begins to unfold. If we do this then the elaboration will usually cease, and we return to a simpler state of mind.

This elaboration is especially vivid and forceful in the case of states of mind or emotions such as indignation, anger, humiliation, infatuation and the like. An emotion is a complex of thoughts, desires, images, bodily sensations that must burst out into action, and not always wise action. Mindfulness in general is the opposite of this emotional elaboration. It is a process of non-attachment, simplification and clarification.

The Buddha emphasized the Four Foundations of Mindfulness as the sure way to 'the purification of beings, for the overcoming of sorrow and distress, for the disappearance of pain and sadness', adding that the meditator:

> ...abides contemplating body as body, ardent, clearly aware and mindful, having put aside hankering and fretting for the world; he abides contemplating feelings as feelings ...; he abides contemplating mind as mind ...; he abides contemplating mind-objects as mind-objects [dhammas as dhammas] ...[4]

Elaboration is a heating up, while mindfulness is a cooling down. Imagine a large metal bucket full of chunks of molten metal: red and yellow and dangerous. We put the bucket down and watch it cool down into a solid gleaming surface of reflecting silver.

Chapter 9

Right Mindfulness: Full Awareness

9.1 Awareness

The next step is critical in understanding the Noble Eightfold Path. We need to become clearer about the awareness dimension of mindfulness (*sati*), a dimension that is usually translated as 'full awareness' or 'clear comprehension' (Pali: *sampajañña*).

While mindfulness in some circumstances may not be fully directed or sustained, and may not be entirely free of judgement, it is not mindfulness at all if it is not *awareness* of direct experience. Full awareness (*sampajañña*) is not easy to define or describe. It has been described by some as 'reflexive', meaning that it is a kind of mirroring, turning one's attention inwards upon oneself. This makes mindfulness a special kind of awareness, namely, self-awareness. But even then there are several kinds of self-awareness. (The question of 'self' and 'not-self' is addressed later.)

The first kind of self-awareness is that by which I am aware of myself as a person (as an *object in the world*). When celebrities or models preen themselves in front of the cameras they may be very aware of how they look *to other people*. This is the self-awareness of appearances. Being concerned with how one looks to others is inauthentic or insincere in the sense that as a model, for example, I am concerned not with *what I am* (and even less with *whether* I am) but with what others want me or expect me to be or not be, at least in appearance. We also recognize the opposite scenario: stage-fright. When one is, for example, giving a speech or playing an instrument, self-awareness of this kind is stultifying and hinders or blocks one's performance. So this, rather obviously, is not the full awareness that is essential to mindfulness. When I am fully preoccupied with how I appear to others I am far removed from mindfulness, for at bottom I have no interest in how things are *with me*, but how they are with others.

The second kind of self-awareness (related to the first) is very powerful and pervasive in modern society: being fictitiously aware of myself *as an object of science* in the world. I regard myself as a biological body, a brain, a species subject to evolution, a survivor or not, a web of psychological relations, a sociological phenomenon, a medical condition, and so on. Absorbed in this supposedly objective self-awareness, 'I' am absent due to being fully absorbed in the 'external world'. This is not the 'emptiness of self' that we find in the Buddha Dhamma. In a way, it is its opposite. This is the dissipation of the 'I' into the object; it is the transformation of 'I' into body or material stuff. It is *total attachment*, and as far from of *nibbāna* as it is possible to get. This curious animal-like state of mind defines our era as 'modern'—that is, blind and ultimately self-destructive.

The third kind of self-awareness is that through which I am aware of in my responses to the things around me. This is not an answer to 'What am I in the eyes of others?' nor is it the popular scientific viewpoint. Expressed (rather awkwardly) it is the demand for an answer to the question 'What is this that recognizes itself as "me"?' It may be summarized in the question 'What am I?', and has a long history among philosophers and theologians in the West, as well as some wandering mystics in the East.

Now, the Buddha acknowledged but leapt beyond this third kind of self-awareness. Ultimately, he dismissed this question as leading us into a 'wilderness of views'.[1] and spiritual suffering. But it is an enormous breakthrough to understand *how* it is misleading. It is confused, you might say, because there is ultimately no separate, independent, discrete 'I' to seek an answer to the question 'What am I?' A deeper understanding comes with seeing into 'co-dependent origination' (see later).

But we are now jumping ahead to the chapters on Right Understanding. Let's slow down and return to the matter of 'full awareness' or the 'clear comprehension' of mindfulness! In Buddhism it first presents itself as a practical matter of the mind knowing, or being conscious of, what it is doing at any point. (Putting aside the question of what is meant by 'mind'.)

9.2 Awareness in Dhamma Meditation

In the Dhamma context *sampajañña* is the *knowing that the mind is doing something now*; it is an alertness to the mental action in the moment, in real time. It is almost as though the mind is doing two things at once: *observing* a sensation (e.g., the motion of the in-breath) and also *knowing* that it is doing so. The importance of this in the Buddha's unique teaching cannot be over-emphasized. Consider what the Buddha says in the *Mahāsatipaṭṭhāna sutta*:

> *Mindfully he [meditator] breathes in, mindfully he breathes out. Breathing in a long breath he knows that he breathes in a long breath, and breathing out a long breath he knows that he breathes out a long breath. Breathing in a short breath, he knows that he breathes in a short breath, and breathing out a short breath, he knows that he breathes out a short breath. He trains himself, thinking: 'I will breathe in, conscious of the whole body'. He trains himself, thinking: 'I will breathe out, conscious of the whole body...'*[2]

The same applies for whole-body movements:

> *Again, a monk, when going forward or back, is clearly aware of what he is doing, in looking forward or back he is clearly aware of what he is doing, in bending and stretching he is clearly aware of what he is doing, in bending and stretching he is clearly aware of what he is doing, in carrying his inner and outer robe and his bowl he is clearly aware of what he is doing, in eating, drinking, chewing and savouring, in passing excrement or urine he is clearly aware of what he is doing, in walking, standing, sitting, falling asleep and waking up, in speaking or in staying silent, he is clearly aware of what he is doing.*[3]

The 'knows that' (is aware of, conscious of), emphasized by the Buddha in a variety of ways and words in the first passage, is that very awareness that we are speaking of here.

9.3 The Awareness Dimension

Many scholars seem to agree that, in the Dhamma context, *sampajañña* and *sati* (mindfulness) go together—they are a couplet (*satisampajañña*): attentive awareness or aware attentiveness.

When I have taught mindfulness to lay people I have sometimes had difficulty getting across that 'mindfulness' is much more than a matter of inner attention. So, what can one do, as a lay teacher like myself, to get across that mindfulness is emphatically a matter of a 'strenuously comprehending attention'?

Certainly, we should avoid investing a concept in just one word. The point being made by a teacher—namely, the *concept*, not the word—may be expressed through a cluster of words that takes its life *from the conceptual context* and that context needs to be relived in meditational and contemplative practice. This is true of all languages but may be especially true in ancient Eastern languages. Anyway, let us not get too 'hung up' on *sampajañña*, which after all is not the only word the Buddha uses to get his point across. The important question is *what was the Buddha getting at* when he used it sometimes, and some other related words other times? Time for another model.

Metaphor 5: The Light Switch

> Consider the Light-Switch Effect. I go up into a very poorly-lit loft in my home. I may dimly see and hesitantly recognize the boxes, old table and chairs, suitcases and paraphernalia. But when the light is switched on for the first time everything changes, although nothing has changed! Same loft, same boxes, old table and chairs, etc. However, in the light I can see unfamiliar objects, colours, well-defined shapes, unacknowledged layers of dust, and a mouse cowering in the corner. And what difference does that make? How does it raise opportunities or potential that weren't there before? Well, the loft may now look unfamiliar in the light but with the light we might bump into things less often and hurt ourselves less often, as we do in life. We might see things we can use or give away to others.

At the deepest level the unfamiliar fleetingness, hollowness and suffering in things can now begin to appear in the field of attention. Awareness draws in things I knew dimly but barely understood before. The Buddha's 'knowing that' or 'clear comprehension' is the light. Here is a simple exercise for getting what is meant by 'full awareness'. It might or might not work for you. The following exercise has to be read to the meditator by an instructor.

Exercise 18: Stand Up and Sit Down

1. Now stand up.
2. Remain standing for 10 seconds or so. Wait.
3. Now I am about to ask you to sit down, *but* the instruction is different. Listen carefully.
4. When I ask you to sit down, I want you to do so very slowly, in *full awareness* of the bending of the neck, the folding of the body, the folding of the knees, the folding of the hips, the pressure in the feet, and the sensation of contact with the chair or cushion.
5. Sit down. Wait.
6. Now I have a question for you: Was the experience of sitting down *different* from the experience of standing up in terms of a *mental* exercise? In terms of what was going on *mentally* were they different?

If you doubt whether the Buddha would have asked anyone to do such an exercise, note that in the *Satipatthāna sutta* he instructs: '...when standing, he understands (*pajānāti*): "I am standing"; when sitting, he is fully aware [*sampajañña*]: "I am sitting"...'.

Note that we do not have to rely on intellectually understanding *sampajañña* to get his point! Do the exercise and see what may or may not happen.

And again he speaks of 'one who acts in full awareness [*sampajañña*] when going forward and returning ... when flexing and extending his limbs ... when walking, standing, sitting, falling asleep...'⁴

I leave it to you to answer the question: was the motion of the body somehow different *mentally* (or experientially) when *you* were fully aware of it? What was the difference or differences? Try it. Remember that getting up you do *not* pay any attention to it—just get up. Sitting down you pay close comprehending attention to the motion of the bodily parts. There seems to be a shift in consciousness.

9.4 The Buddha's Instructions

Let us now go deeper into the Buddha's instructions in the classic text, the *Satipaṭṭhāna Sutta*.⁵ There, we are told that the 'Four Foundations of Mindfulness' are 'a direct path for the purification of beings', 'an ending of suffering', a path to the attainment of *nibbāna*. It is to those ends, that we have these four instructions on mindful awareness of body, feelings, heart/mind (*citta*), phenomena (*dhamma*). Regarding our current societal fascination with mindfulness we should always beware and keep in mind the context and *purpose* of the instruction. Without holding in mind the purpose we are likely to lose or misconstrue its meaning or turn it inside out. Elsewhere the Buddha warns us about the persistent worldly lure of pleasure, praise, fame and gain in which everything is grist to the mill. Can 'mindfulness' really be a commodity?

9.5 The First Foundation (Body)

Let us focus on the sutta's First Foundation as a kind of template for all four (although they are quite different), all four making the point about the critical significance of full awareness. The Buddha is recorded as speaking of: 'contemplating the body as a body, ardent, *fully aware*, and mindful'. But this is not contemplation in the mundane sense of attentiveness to, and awareness of, worldly aspects of body (the body of cosmetic surgery, Botox and beauty products), for he immediately adds: '...having put away covetousness and grief for the world'.

Now, returning to the short quotation from the 'Mindfulness of Body' teaching, what about the rather strange repetition of words found in 'contemplate body as a body' (etc.)? The eminent scholar-monk Bhikkhu Bodhi cites a classical commentary (*Atthakathā*) on this point. It is said to be a means of 'precisely determining' and 'isolating' the object of contemplation.[6] This may be true, but I do not think that quite penetrates the critical—even momentous—feature of awareness that the Buddha is pointing to. There is something here we really cannot afford to miss, and that is the dramatic shift in understanding; a shift that is 'wonderful and marvellous'. This, by the way, is a phrase used sometimes in the Pali Canon to describe the Buddha's Dhamma (see below).

Let me emphasize: When we light up with awareness any actual experience and do so with committed and penetrative investigation, we come across, not the familiar body we take for granted, but the unfamiliar, something or other we have always called 'body', but now in this wordless fleeting glimpse, this moment of clarity, the body lit up by awareness is something almost alien, wispy, and only just unstably holding together the idea that it is 'me'.

And we should not ignore the sutta's phrase *viharati ātāpi*, meaning dwell zealously, ardently. This is no ordinary looking at something; this is seriously inspecting/probing. If this were a sport, say, throwing a javelin, the instructor would be saying to the athlete: 'focus on the target, put everything you've got into it!' Here the Buddha is doing something similar, but of course speaking of *mental* effort, with the same seriousness of intent.

When I encounter the flickering, fragmented body-experience 'as body' then it is alien; it is *not* me. This is a crucial discovery that anyone serious about mindfulness may make for themselves—it is just a matter of freeing oneself up, and catching the experience as it actually is. Now do this for yourself, burrowing down to the unfamiliar experience—see on investigation that the 'something alien' is transient or void—and you are well on your way to *nibbāna*, and reaping benefits at different levels. Yes, it's not so easy, but possible.

9.6 Mindfulness of Breathing

To continue the quotation from the sutta, then, the Buddha answers the implicit question: 'How does one approach body in this way in practice?' and he gives us a diverse range of options. He starts with breathing. Again, this requires paying attention to the breathing-motion going on, but not *just* attending but attending in a *special* way, namely, with *sampajañña*. The light has to be switched on. In every detail of the breathing there is understanding. I am not *just* breathing out long or short, but I 'understand' it is just *that* that is happening. I am brightly aware of its nature. Note that the key word is now *pajānāti*, meaning to know, find out, to come to know, understand, and distinguish.[7] But the point is the same: full awareness, clear comprehension.

Eventually there is the insight that breathing does not need 'me' in order to breathe. I am not doing the breathing: the breathing is breathing me, the 'me' that arises and falls.

So, in the last analysis all the seeking of definitions of words is only a useful crutch to assist one now and then. The real point is seeing what the Buddha *is getting at* by doing it. Analysing the words is a crutch, but a lame person is only assisted by a crutch if they are willing to do something: to try to stand up and walk. It is only through the *doing* that one sees how 'wonderful and marvellous' the Buddha's teachings really are.

Full awareness may also be described as non-delusional understanding.[8] *Sampajañña* is a *requirement* for attaining the insight (*vipassanā*) that fully reveals impermanence, insubstantiality and the source of suffering. Clear awareness of the body, in our example above, unfolding and folding to stand and to sit is completely misunderstood if is taken to be intense attention only. Intense attention is vital, but it is not sufficient. It is particularly misunderstood if this practice is aimed at strengthening the sense of discrete self rather than weakening it. The ontological light has to be switched on; the delusion must be revealed. It becomes sufficient (within mindfulness practice) when it points us to the inability to find the discrete 'self', whether as body/matter (*rūpa*), feeling/sensations (*vedanā*), cognition (*saññā*), thought/formations (*saṅkhāra*) or consciousness (*viññāṇa*). (See section 14.2, 'Doctrine of "Aggregates"'.)

9.7 *'Wonderful and Marvellous'*

To conclude this chapter, there is a rather neglected sutta that tells a story about *what it is* that is truly wonderful and marvellous about the Buddha:

> Once, the monks were assembled in Anāthapindika's Park. The disciple Ānanda had just finished saying in mythical terms how the wonderful quality of the Buddha is attested by the magical things that happened in his previous life and his rebirth (such as 'immeasurable light' appearing when he descended into his mother's womb from Tusita heaven). I suspect there might be some deliberate irony in this sutta. For, when Ānanda had gone

through this list of supernormal events the Buddha added what was *really* important and down to earth. He interjected:

... Ānanda, remember this too, as a wonderful and marvellous quality of the Tathāgata: Here, Ānanda, for the Tathāgata, feelings are known [vidita] as they arise, as they are present, as they disappear; perceptions are known as they arise, as they are present, as they disappear; thoughts are known as they arise, as they are present, as they disappear. Remember this too, Ānanda, as a wonderful and marvellous quality of the Tathāgata.[9]

Chapter 10

Right Mindfulness: Insight

10.1 Introduction

We now run through the first three 'Foundations of Mindfulness' with some simple exercises. We shall return to the fourth foundation later. By a 'foundation' of mindfulness is meant a category of those things we can be mindful of. The four are bodily experience (e.g., skin sensations), pleasure/pain experience (e.g., an insect bite, a delicious morsel), the meditational quality of the mind (e.g., whether it is concentrated or not). Fourthly, this is a reflexive evaluation of one's meditational journey and its landmarks (e.g., the struggle with hindrances or the cultivation of good-will).

10.2 Foundation 1: Mindfulness of Body

A crucial part of the Buddha's practice is meant to dispel misconceptions about what we call 'my body'. Some people of a philosophical bent use the word 'body' (and 'matter', 'nature', 'physical objects') as a generic term for all those 'things out there' that comprise the objects of scientific study: human bodies and their parts, earth, water, trees, animals, bacteria, planets, galaxies, and so on. Usually we take it for granted that 'there *really* are physical things' as they present themselves to us, so we do not seriously consider what we mean by this or how such concepts actually function in language. The Buddha did not assume a clear distinction between the 'mental' and the physical or bodily. For him the mental-bodily was more like one experience in two dimensions. Philosophically speaking, he was neither a materialist nor an idealist, and not a dualist. This is a tricky conceptual issue, which I will explore further on. The important point is that whenever the Buddha speaks of the physical or bodily or external, the reader should keep in mind that he did not mean it in the completely separate way we do now in Western languages. I often short-cut this deep and crucial issue by referring to 'the apparently bodily' and 'the apparently mental'.

In meditation we can start by paying attention 'in the here and now' to an apparent sample of 'body' until its very body-ness is challenged. We are not interested in anatomy, physiology or biochemistry as a scientist or doctor might be, since we are not trying to explain, predict or control. We are instead looking very closely, at this stage on the Path, at our *ongoing experience* of 'body'. For example, as already mentioned, it is not the song of the bird that interests the meditator but 'this hearing as it unfolds now'. This approach is not to be elaborated into a philosophy, such as phenomenology, but a liberating inward practice.

In our exercises you have already focused your mind on a candle image, your sensation of breath or your abdomen-motion. We have already considered practices to counter bodily cravings, greed and lust, and so on, and we can now understand these as involving 'mindfulness of body' too. You could mindfully examine your skin, hands, nails, feet, etc., not as objects to pass judgement on such as 'This is smooth and nice', or 'old and ugly', or 'still youthful' or 'getting dry, needs some cream', but rather in the directly investigative spirit of 'What are *the most fundamental characteristics* of this? Is this a permanent and discrete entity; is it *me* or *mine*?' You could also contemplate all the body parts you do not usually see. You could look into the body as it is comprised of blood, lymph, water, fibres, urine, bone, flesh, phlegm, faeces, hair, air, etc., and we could also take a stroll through a cemetery contemplating all the remains.

I realize this could be misunderstood as some kind of morbid preoccupation or even pessimism, but it is not at all. The point is that we have to counter a 'natural' craving or tendency to see only what we want before we can move on to a position of equanimity and wisdom that is far more solid than the 'happiness' of passing pleasure and leisure and of avoiding their (ultimately unavoidable) opposites. To be mindful only of the 'pleasant things' in life would be one form of 'wrong mindfulness'—that is, it would be unhelpful to developing equanimity, peace, wisdom and compassion.

We could pay closer attention to the experience of all those things we conceive as 'material' or 'bodily'. Observe their arising and their passing away. And our ordinary actions will manifest our level of mindfulness. For example, in the meditation hall we do not throw down a cushion, but place it gently with awareness of the action of placing. We do not 'strike a bell', but we 'invite' it. Small signs can imprison us, and small signs can wake us up.

Now we can read about two exercises in mindfulness of body and then mindfully put down this book and *do* them. Before you approach the walking meditation exercise (below) you need precisely to understand the instruction. You need to be mindful of the motion of the left foot only (or right foot only). It is best to focus on one foot because it encourages the mind to stay in one place and be calm, as opposed to switching attention from one foot to the other as you walk.

Exercise 19: *Walking Meditation*

Preferably having removed your shoes (and your socks, if you wish), you should walk very slowly, with short steps. It is well to remind yourself as you start that 'I am not walking; I am meditating'. This is because familiarity is the enemy of mindfulness, and if we think we are walking then we pay attention to all the wrong things, such as: 'Am I walking properly?', 'Am I catching up with the person in front of me?' Pay close and continuing attention to the *experience* of the motion of the left foot—that is, in terms of the characteristics of mindfulness already discussed.

It may help to settle your mind in this experience if you, at first, think the following words to yourself as your left foot goes through four phases of the gait cycle: 'lifting', 'moving', 'placing', 'pressing' (see Figure 3). Say 'lifting' as the foot takes off from the ball and toes; say 'moving' as the foot goes through the air; say 'placing' as the foot settles on the heel; say 'pressing' once as the foot takes the weight on the heel and once again as the weight shifts to the ball of the foot; and then say 'lifting' and repeat the motion. After a while you should be able to drop the words.

There may be a tendency to shift the attention to the other foot as it begins to lift, but resist this and keep the attention on the pressing of the left foot. (Of course, one could do all of this with the right foot, if one prefers.)

The mind will, inevitably, wander into thoughts, anxieties, shoes, and ships, and sealing-wax, cabbages and kings, and why the sea is boiling hot, and whether pigs have wings. Persistently, gently and without frustration, bring it back to attention to the foot-motion in all its detail.

Figure 3: *Walking Meditation*

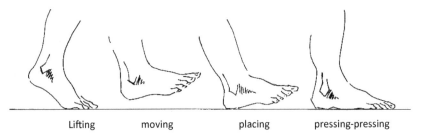

| Lifting | moving | placing | pressing-pressing |

You will not be able to apply the Anchor and Buoy method in this exercise. This exercise crosses the fuzzy line from concentration meditation to insight meditation because, although the foot-motion is one object in so far as it is a *foot*, it is a process of change in so far as it is a *motion* in which different aspects arise and fall. We are watching the ongoing changes that constitute this particular process; not watching casually but intently, picking out shifting detail as much as possible. We could not use such a changing process as an object for the higher levels of concentration meditation because in this case the attention is always momentary, from one arising to the next, rather than fixed.

At the end of this exercise you may feel quite calm, and you may also wonder why you and others spend so much time in unnecessary haste and frustration. The same goes for reading this book. Go slowly, pay close attention, do not think too much, *do* what it suggests.

10.2.1 Cushion or Chair?

Incidentally, you may wonder whether you should be sitting on a cushion or on a chair. The short answer is that generally speaking it does not matter. It is the activity of the *mind* that really interests us, and that is why posture has not been mentioned so far. If you are sitting in a chair then be aware of the folded nature of the body and the pressure on the buttocks; and if sitting on a cushion be aware of the folded nature of the legs and hands. It remains true that wrong posture can hinder meditation and good posture can support it. An account of posture is given in Appendix 1.

10.2.2 Standing Meditation

Much the same that has just been said about walking meditation also applies to standing meditation. The latter is usually only effective when the meditator has practised walking meditation for some time. That is because this form of insight meditation requires a more refined ability to attend to subtle changes. These are changes in the pressure in the soles of the feet and in the tension of muscles around the feet and legs as balance is maintained. Again, due to familiarity, we adults take for granted the small and fluid adjustments we must constantly make just to stay upright. Again, you will not be able to apply the Anchor and Buoy method in this exercise.

Exercise 20: Standing Meditation

Take off your shoes and either in bare feet or socks stand with a straight back and about 25 cm (ten inches) separating the big toes. As you begin, remind yourself: 'I am not standing, I am meditating'. Then pay close and continuing attention to the changes in pressure in the soles. Also note changes in tension in the muscles of the feet and ankles. Breathe regularly and with awareness. When the mind wanders, immediately bring it back to the experience of the tactile sensations in the soles. Continue with this for at least ten minutes, but a 20-minute period is usually more effective.

10.3 Foundation 2: Mindfulness of Pleasure and Pain

Mindfulness of body leads us to the second foundation: mindfulness of pleasure and pain, comfort and discomfort. These states include titillation and itch, orgasm and agony, delicious and disgusting, smooth and rough, soothing and disturbing, the beautiful and the ugly. They also include the neutral, those things we have no feelings about, do not notice or do not pay attention to. During our watchful walking exercise we learned to pay attention to our surroundings using our five senses one at a time. We will have a strong inclination to think that this must be a wholly pleasurable exercise. Now we are going a step further and paying attention to our first 'reactions', to whether we take things to be pleasurable, painful or neutral (using these words rather broadly).

We earlier located the initiation of our reactions in flickering 'signs' to which we attach. Hopefully, you will now see that pleasure and pain have their roots in some initiating sign, some 'contact' or other. This may be a physical sensation or a mental image. On contact with the thirst-quenching soft drink, pleasure arises. On contact with the vinegar that someone put in your soft drink bottle as a joke, disgust arises. The memory of either of these gives rise to mental comfort or discomfort too.

The question is this: Can you note the feeling arising without attaching to it? That is, without making it 'yours', without judging it? It is time for you to find out with an exercise.

Exercise 21: Mindfulness of Pleasure and Pain

Find a quiet place and adopt a recommended posture. For about 20 minutes meditate on the motion of the abdomen, as recommended. After this period the mind will probably be much calmer and ready to attend to subtle sensations in the body. Pay close and continuing attention to 'discomforts' in the body. These may be an itch, a desire to cough or sneeze, an ache in the knees or in the lower back, wind in the stomach or elsewhere. Note each sensation, look into it, inwardly saying 'sensation ... sensation'. After a while investigate its character, its arising and its falling away. Maintain a deep and regular breath. Continue with this for at least another ten minutes, but a 20-minute period is usually more effective (making 40 minutes in all).

Awareness is crucial. Be a 'buddha', for that is what 'buddha' means: 'aware one' or 'awakened one'. As the Buddha said,

> ... *feeling a pleasant feeling, a bhikkhu understands: 'I feel a pleasant feeling'; when feeling a painful feeling, he understands: 'I feel a painful feeling'; when feeling a neither-painful-nor-pleasant feeling, he understands: 'I feel a neither-painful-nor-pleasant feeling'.*[1]

Perhaps the truth of what I pointed out earlier is now clearer: In following the Path, ethics does not really precede meditational insights, for such insights rebound on your ethical understanding and behaviour. There is but one taste of salt.

10.4 Foundation 3: *Mindfulness of Quality of Mind*

Mindfulness of pleasure and pain can lead us to mindfulness of mind itself with regard to its quality. But what is meant by 'quality'? Here we can now see that the 'Four Foundations of Mindfulness' are not just 'foundations' but are *reminders to evaluate* one's movement along the path to *nibbāna*. So far we have evaluated our practice in regard to the apparent body and in regard to the apparent feelings of pleasure and pain (this time including those apparently 'not of the body', i.e., apparently mental).

Now we examine our state of mind as though asking 'How far has understanding progressed?' What are the general changes? Is it more concentrated (less fragmented, agitated)? Is it still wanting something or is it more accepting, more contented? Is it more free and spacious (less clinging or shut in)? Is it more awakened, more still? How marvellous it is that the mind can evaluate itself. Here is a shaft of light showing us where liberation lies!

A passage from the *Satipaṭṭhāna Sutta* shows what the main aspects of quality of mind are.

> And how, monks, does a monk abide contemplating mind as mind. Here a bhikkhu understands mind affected by lust as mind affected by lust, and mind unaffected by lust as mind unaffected by lust. He understands mind affected by hate as mind affected by hate, and mind unaffected by hate as mind unaffected by hate. He understands mind affected by delusion as mind affected by delusion, and mind unaffected by delusion as mind unaffected by delusion.[2]

The same goes for other qualities: contracted/distracted, exalted/unexalted, surpassed/unsurpassed, concentrated/unconcentrated, liberated/unliberated. Finally,

> In this way he abides contemplating mind-objects as mind-objects internally, or he abides contemplating mind-objects as mind-objects externally, or he abides contemplating mind-objects as mind-objects both internally and externally. Or else he abides contemplating in mind-objects their arising factors, or he abides contemplating mind-objects in their vanishing factors, or he abides contemplating mind-objects in both their arising and vanishing factors. Or else mindfulness that 'there are mind-objects' is simply established in him to the extent necessary for bare knowledge and mindfulness. And he abides independent, not clinging to anything in the world.[3]

10.4.1 States of Mind

So far we have spoken of the 'quality' of mind, such as concentrated or not. Perhaps we should extend the third foundation by distinguishing between *quality* of mind and *states* of mind. States of mind have already been approached from another angle under 'Right Effort'. It may help to re-read the discussion of Right Effort. There we explored the efforts that may be made to let go of unarisen and arisen states of mind that are unfruitful, and encourage and nurture unarisen and arisen states of mind that are fruitful.

So we could extend and populate the category of 'quality of mind' with more specific states: 'emotions' or 'emotional tones', moods, character attributes and attitudes (predispositions to react in certain patterns). For example, jealousy and lust are states of mind that fall under the quality of mind of craving/clinging. States of mind can be brief, such as a minor irritation or fleeting desire, or can be long-lasting such as a character attribute (virtues and vices) like kindliness or resentment, exuberance or cynicism. However, brief or long-lasting close examination through mindfulness shows that they are all ultimately unstable and changeable.

States of mind are, on analysis, seen to be fluid blends of pleasure/pain, consciousness, thoughts, images, volitions, and so on. From a higher vantage point there are no separate or independent 'states of mind'. They include a lusty or greedy state of mind, a hateful or angry state, a kindly mind, a deluded or ignorant state (lack of insight), a narrow mind, a scattered mind, a grateful and generous mind, an immature mind, a magnanimous mind, an arrogant mind, a fearful mind, a grieving mind, a gloating mind, a sceptical mind and a cynical one. There is also a neutral state of mind in which there is no particular polarization. What we are looking for in this mental turbulence is equanimity (*upekkhā*), namely, stability and balance—but not indifference.

Could we do the equivalent of a 'watchful walk' (see Exercise 15) through our states of mind in the course of a week? I suggest this in the exercise below. It is not easy at first, because we all tend to 'be' our state of mind. Paradoxically, if I am in a low state of mind I will not feel at all like watching my state of mind! We might call this 'the *To Hell with my State of Mind* state of mind'. Although we do not think of it as something we could observe in a detached way, in fact, most of us do this when we admit that 'I'm feeling low today', or 'I've been happy all week', or 'I feel I want to smash something (or someone)'. Other states of mind (attitudes, character traits) are more tenacious, deeper and hard to acknowledge (e.g., 'I am narrow minded', 'I have a tendency to denial', 'I am a control-freak' or 'I am a pessimist').

What we have noted about the initiating signs of pleasure and pain might also apply to states of mind. Sometimes one small sign will precipitate a change in our state of mind, although often there has to have been a readiness for this to happen. This could be someone's smile precipitating a generous state of mind, or someone's sneer precipitating a hateful one. However, things are often more fluid and indefinable than this.

States of mind also tend to ripple out through groups and even whole societies or historical periods. Fear, even without a clear 'objective' stimulus, can sweep through a whole population. So, keep in mind that *your* smile or grimace may be rippling through someone else's state of mind.

Now you can try to observe your changing states of mind, or the general drift of it, in a detached way, without rejecting it or clinging to it.

Exercise 22: States of Mind Diary

Every so often you could look at your own state of mind. You will notice that this is difficult to do when you are swept up in the normal course of domestic or office events, even though that might be the most productive time to do so. It will be easier to observe your state of mind when you have a moment to yourself, such as waking up in the morning, taking a short walk, having a shower, sitting on the loo, or settling down on arriving at your workplace. What can be more revealing is keeping a 'States of Mind' diary. This is not a diary of events or thoughts and ruminations but quite a different kind. It can be compared perhaps to a mariner's logbook: 'Early morning, sea calm, mild westerly wind, dark clouds in distance...' Keep a small, unobtrusive notebook in your pocket or bag, and whenever it occurs to you during the week jot down your state of mind, and do that whether the state is positive, negative or neutral or indeterminate (indefinable).

I emphasize that this is not an opportunity to pass comment on encounters with other people or to express particular aspirations or disappointments. It is an attempt to capture a general state of mind at a particular point. You do not say, 'I feel X state of mind', and you do not say, 'I feel X state of mind because of Y'. No 'I' and no 'because'. You simply say the name of the state of mind. After a few weeks, flick through the diary and analyse what you find there. Language and states of mind are inextricably co-dependent. So it helps for this exercise to have a vocabulary for describing your own state of mind, so there are some examples below. It will often feel like trying to measure waves on a pond—but try it anyway.

Remember that it should be more than a fleeting mood in order to count as a state of mind, but fleeting moods might be noted too. Try to watch how long the states last—very short, short, moderate, long, enduring. Needless to say, you should honestly note your actual state of mind, rather than what you would like or imagine your state of mind to be, or rather than noting only the 'good', or only the bad, ones.

Finally, do not try to force a neat template onto a state of mind. It is important to note that such states are nearly always vague, fuzzy, indescribable, ungraspable, rising and falling.

10.4.2 States of Mind: Random Vocabulary

Greedy, relieved, hateful, angry, violent, deluded, joyful, ignorant, narrow-minded, scattered mind, immature, resentful, depressed, humiliated, sense of worthlessness, fearful, kindly, lusty, grateful, generous, magnanimous, concentrated, grieving, smug, sceptical, cynical, absorbed in fun, absent mind, conceited, inquisitive, expectant, frustrated, suspicious, equanimity ... and many more.

10.4.3 Examples of Diary Entries

Monday

- Waking up: short irritation, moderate hopelessness.
- Mid-morning: expectation.
- Evening: moderately conceited, smug perhaps.

Tuesday

- Waking up: tedious, moderate hopelessness.
- Meditated: scattered mind.
- Mid-morning: slightly bewildered.
- Afternoon: absorbed in fun.
- Evening: lonely, slightly empty.

Wednesday

- Waking up: anxious, expectation.
- Daytime: excited, hurried.
- Meditation: rejecting state of mind.
- Briefly: irritated, almost angry.
- Evening: neutral state of mind, perhaps boredom.

Thursday

- Waking up: slightly anxious.
- Most of day: absorbed in fun, absent mind.
- Evening: scattered mind, tired.

Exercise 23: Anonymized Shared Reflection

One facilitator and a minimum of ten people are needed to maintain privacy. The facilitator gives an identical piece of blank paper and identical pen to each participant. Everyone meditates for 40 minutes with mindfulness of states of mind, as described above. At the end each person writes down in block capital letters (to maintain privacy) what state or states of mind they observed and folds the paper once, placing it in a large envelope held by the facilitator. The facilitator shuffles the slips of paper to ensure anonymity and redistributes the slips to the participants, one slip to each person. If you receive your own slip it does not matter, and do not say so. Read the slip you have in front of you, and then pass it to the person on your left. Continue reading and passing to your left until everyone has read each slip.

The facilitator now orchestrates a discussion of comments on what is written on the slips. Right speech is observed. No attempt is made to pass judgement or to identify any participant. Do not use 'I', 'you', 'he', 'she'. Only comment on the states of mind as though they were various blades of grass in a lawn. For example, 'The comments were similar'; 'they were very different'; 'scattered mind came up a lot' (or, did not come up a lot); 'even for one person they seemed to change quickly'. The facilitator sums up the findings, with some reference to the 'Three Marks of Existence' summarized below.

10.5 Insight: Three Marks of Existence

What do we learn from doing these mindfulness exercises? Here we enter the very nub of insight (*vipassanā*), an important concept of the Buddha Dhamma. I am not describing here what you must necessarily discover from the exercises, but what you are likely to discover if you persevere in mindfulness of body, pain/pleasure and quality of mind. Note that here we are speaking of mindfulness and not the absorption that may come at the higher levels of concentration. Having mastered a useful level of concentration, our mindfulness will now have developed to a point when following it one can contemplate (Dhamma-directed thinking) on what it reveals about our ordinary but delusory view of human life. We may discover in such penetrating contemplation these three general features of these arisings, as follows.

- *Insubstantiality*. In Pali, *anattā*. Despite appearances the world is not composed of fixed, separate, discrete and independent 'things' or objects'. This applies to me and you, too.
- *Impermanence*. In Pali, *anicca*. There is nothing absolutely stable and permanent in the world; all is unstable, constantly changing, shifting, in flux. This applies to me and you, too.
- *Dissatisfaction*. In Pali, *dukkha*. There is nothing completely graspable in the world, nothing I can hold on to, no secure and completely satisfying thing. You and I 'suffer' dissatisfaction and disappointment (for example) in trying to grasp the ungraspable, and the Noble Eightfold Path is the only way out.

These three marks of ordinarily perceived existence are related. Since nothing that arises is a solid and fixed thing so nothing that arises is a permanent thing, and therefore nothing that arises is secure and satisfying, so we are insatiable and suffering. Ordinary life is the rigmarole of grasping the ungraspable. This is the source of the great human delusion, and the way out is, through meditation and attitudinal change, to accept this truth with wisdom and compassion for each other.

If we meditate deeply on the bodily arisings, pleasure/pain arisings and states-of-mind arisings we shall probably discover these three marks of existence. No bodily thing subsists; all passes away and is passing away and eluding us at any point in time, however short we make that moment. We may wish to hold on to our youthful bodies, our health, our property, our money and belongings, but all these will pass away and are passing away right now. No pleasure and no pain subsists, and both the worst pain and discomfort and the greatest pleasure will pass away and are passing away even as we try to take hold of them or annihilate them. No state of mind subsists, but even the worst fear, the most avid lust and greed, the most burning hatred or aching love will pass away and are passing away even as we try to deny or reject them or hold onto them for ever. It has been said: 'The moving finger writes, and having writ moves on.'

We human beings are ultimately always dissatisfied and bewildered. Something may be satisfying or appear satisfying for a while, but we may lose it any time and even when we have it we may fear losing it. If we can get to the bottom of this fact of 'existence', and accept what we find, then maybe everything will change for us. But can we do so? The Buddha thought we could, but not easily. The rest of this book (Part Three) is a clarification of this truth. Hopefully, Parts One and Two will have prepared you for embarking on the higher road to peace.

10.6 An Anchorless Buoy?

Once you have sharpened your concentration ability, and then your Anchor and Buoy ability, and there is also at least a glimpse of the 'three marks of existence', you could spend some fairly short periods of time in an anchorless watching of arisings. What I mean by this is that you could still your mind and then with equanimity leave it open to anything that arises in random fashion: hearings, seeings, sensings, touchings, thoughts, pains, discomforts, desires, thrills, awe, fears, and so on. What is happening here is that your awareness is being generalized, is growing into a faculty of consciousness that you might not have previously deployed. There is a transition between Part One and Two, now completed. Part Three is now coming up; strive on.

PART THREE

WISDOM

Chapter 11

Right Understanding: Ignorance and *Nibbāna*

> **Right Understanding (Right View)**
> *sammā-diṭṭhi*
>
> This is a holistic understanding or view of suffering, the 'law of kamma', and the release from or attenuation of suffering. The mundane understanding of the Path introduces what is conducive to a good life and its benefits 'in this world'. The full (supramundane) understanding entails the transformation of one's human reality: the *Middle Way* (nondual) dimension and dependent origination (complex emergence). Right Understanding (or Right View) is not just intellectual, but enjoins authenticity and radical honesty.

11.1 Consolidating

We began this book with a brief account of human unhappiness, its basis in craving and rejecting, the possibility of going beyond that craving and rejecting, and how we might change our lives to address that craving and rejecting and open up a deeper level of peace and contentment. In the classical texts these factors are called 'The Four Noble Truths': dissatisfaction, the source of the dissatisfaction in our craving and rejecting, the ending or weakening of that dissatisfaction, and the way to go about undermining that source of dissatisfaction by means of meditation, contemplation and attitude change.

Now we return to the place where we began, but hopefully with the higher vantage point we have attained so far by following the first six factors of the Noble Eightfold Path, in study and practice:

- Practices of Right Speech, Right Acting and of Right Livelihood together with a greater awareness, subduing of ego, subduing of craving and rejecting, and enhanced good-will.
- Training in the tools of Right (mental) Effort, Right Concentration and Right Mindfulness that support that subduing of ego and enhancing of peace.

In other words, we may have reached a point at which we can begin to consolidate the cultivation of our understanding (wisdom) and our change in attitude (compassion), i.e. the seventh and eighth factors of the Path. As we consolidate this Right Understanding we can enhance our wisdom and compassion by continuing on the spiral back through speech, action, livelihood, and mental training, all the time strengthening and deepening our practice, taking it to a new horizon. The path is lifelong.

We now return to the first two Noble Truths, what might be called the two truths of ignorance: suffering and craving. In the following chapters we reconsider the two truths of wisdom: ending suffering and the path to that ending.

11.2 Authenticity

The Buddha and his teachings are authentic. But not because of divine or scriptural authority. The Buddha himself is authentic in the sense that he was absolutely true to himself, he was sincere, completely without pretensions. How could he have been otherwise if he was to dissolve his very sense of 'self'? He was not satisfied to trim himself down to humble personhood, which is already quite a task for anyone. He saw that ultimately the suffering of the world was rooted in personhood itself. He was not afraid to admit to his prior ignorance or delusion.

This means that the Buddha's quest was a 'spiritual' one, the recognition of an absolute boundary on human knowledge and experience. His teaching is made authentic by scrupulously recognizing that boundary and its implications. Furthermore, it is authentic in conforming to things as they really are, coming up against the aporia (mental block) ultimately presented by the nature of the facts, a point at which facts are not enough, an inevitable and irremovable paradox, a logical impasse, and the helpless question 'What am I?' His approach imitates no one else and nothing else. He reached down to rock bottom; he went beyond humility to a place where only silence remained.

11.3 Ignorance and Authenticity

Let us think about ordinary humility first, since it is a necessary stage on the way to 'liberation' which is the letting go of discrete personhood itself. In the Western world humility is now almost unknown, having been sold off to the entertainment and consumer industry, to corporations and their advertisers and gadget-innovators. And as for transcendent peace: for now it cowers in the corners of retreat centres until mass suffering will bring it once again to the surface.

As we look around us at social trends and values it may seem, paradoxically, that we are quite genuine about our inauthenticity, quite sincere about our insincerity to the true nature of life. The self is now so corpulent that insight cannot see beyond the bloated abdomen.

In general, we are not paying careful attention to what is around us. We may pay fleeting attention to the everyday nature of human life, but it is not careful and *aware* attention; it is not a form of attention which places things in a whole-of-life context. It does not see the wider context of things and it quickly turns away from the unpleasant. Most of us are 'uninstructed worldlings'.[1]

When the Buddha spoke of the general condition of humanity as 'ignorance' he was not insulting us, but was speaking honestly and accurately of the general human state of mind and the behaviour that flows from it. He was once in that state himself. Six years of determinedly looking into himself by himself changed that state. (Of course, he also had the benefit of previous spiritual traditions and teachers.) It was not so much a change from one state to another as a letting go of everything that stood in the way of seeing the truth of human life, including his very identity. He had to be strongly self-aware, watching his own conditioning, assumptions, attitudes and reactions, and acknowledging rather than rejecting them.

In short, the Buddha had to learn to be completely authentic, utterly sincere with himself. He learned that there were different methods of doing this, some more helpful than others, and then decided to share these ways with us. What it amounts to is concentrating and calming the mind, penetrating the movements of the mind/heart, understanding their fleeting and insubstantial nature, and eventually seeing directly that none of these movements and attachments need be identified as a discrete 'me' or 'mine'. At this critical point one may be ready for the universal vision (*sammā-diṭṭhi*) of the needless suffering of humankind and what is required to attenuate it, even eliminate it, and the kind of gratitude that transcends mundane thankfulness.

It is delusion (*moha*) or ignorance (*avijjā*) to believe—and live by the belief—that one can grasp the ungraspable, satiate craving itself, and annihilate that which one rejects.

11.4 Three (or Four) Levels of Behaviour

So, one might say, my personal behaviour operates at three levels of sincerity and insincerity. As a child I may be completely sincere, in the naïve way that is based on the assumption that the world is, or at least can be, as I would (reactively) like it to be. Every so often I do not get what I want so I throw a tantrum, a simple instance of craving-suffering. Gradually, I learn that it is not and cannot be as I would like it to be, at least not all the time. I have to accommodate to that fact. So, I split myself into two. I grow a public face to conceal the suffering: I am tensely polite, habitually pretend, act out a role that's not completely 'me', hide or deny my feelings, act out passive aggression when I am frustrated, conform, keep in the running, and generally try to be 'a nice person' in the eyes of others. This is unsustainable.

Arriving home from work, the mask slips, and my suffering face emerges. I can now, supposedly, 'be myself'. I am still in the middle level, in which being myself means following my mood, just being whatever grabs me at the time: kind, cruel, patient, impatient, gentle, angry, helpful, obstructive and so on. This unleashed moodiness is very much celebrated as good and natural in our society. This is not surprising since having to maintain a public face and a social role is stressful, and letting one's moods take possession is such a relief—for a while. And, of course, it may not be such a relief for others in the immediate environment, such as one's family.

The Buddha's Path opens up a third, deeper level. I start to reach out to equanimity. At this level my public/personal split evaporates. I am neither my polite self nor my moody self. I neither have to maintain a false image nor let my jolly and grumpy moods run amok. Somehow I have found a refuge from which I can watch the entire tragicomedy. I sincerely and compassionately watch what my thoughts, feelings and sensations are up to, and get to know them and their primordial ways. Instead of escaping for a while from boredom by attaching to excitement, or escaping for a while from excitement (which I now call 'stress') by attaching to boredom (which I now call 'relaxation'), I now learn mindful release from the merry-go-round of clinging and rejecting. If I am sick on the see-saw, there is a solution: I can get off it. I am not the see-saw itself.

The next step is to try to obtain a better *understanding* of these truths, a higher vantage point. This is not merely an intellectual understanding but one based on one's own experience of life filtered through Dhamma.

One may be on the threshold of a fourth level, rare, purified and peaceful: the sense of a discrete self has gone.

11.5 *Suffering in the Cosmos*

Now we need to go deeper. 'Suffering' is a translation of the Pali *dukkha*. The best way to understand the Buddha's meaning is to consider it in relation to the meaning of the other Noble Truths, namely, the craving that is the cause or origin of suffering, the cessation of the suffering and the way to end the suffering. Clearly the Buddha does not have tooth-ache, boils or rheumatism as his primary concern, painful as they may be. The relation of suffering to craving, cessation of suffering and the way to cease show very clearly that the Buddha's concept of suffering makes full sense only in the context of the Dhamma. The Dhamma view of human life requires an understanding of the 'cosmos'. The 'cosmos' is not the same as the 'universe' as we now understand it. For us moderns the universe is the entire *physical* presence of molecules, trees and oceans, planets and stars, outer space, galaxies, black holes, and biological organisms such as humans, birds, frogs and bacteria. In that modern sense the Buddha's physical universe was much smaller in one way and much larger in another. Smaller because he knew very little or nothing about such things as planets, stars and human physiology; larger because for him that universe was imbued with ethics (morality) and aesthetics. The way he thought was not the way we now think. If we are not very careful his most important point could be lost in translation. This is especially true if his most important point is silence.

For the Buddha the universe was not just working in the right or wrong way according to scientific expectations. The word 'right' may be useful in making my point here, because even in English it has both a moral and non-moral sense: 'the right screwdriver' is not a moral judgement, but 'the right conduct for a president' is. To reconnect the two sides of dualistic thinking in a nondual concept of 'right', where applicable, I invent the neologism 'ethico-cosmos'. That captures the Buddha's widest vantage point. The rightness/wrongness of the cosmos is both ('both' in a special way) an ethical matter and a physical or practical one.

11.6 *Ethico-cosmic Right and Wrong*

Now, to return to the matter of the two truths of ignorance. This ignorance was in the Buddha's eyes ignorance of rightness, that is, of laws which were both at once natural patterns of the physical world and moral patterns of the human world. The distinction between the two, which we now take for granted, was creatively 'fuzzy' in the Buddha's thinking. Thus 'breaking a major law', such as murder, was for him an ethico-cosmic infringement—it was both against nature and against morality, and in the same moment. It is here that suffering arises. It is here too that the cause of suffering lies. The cause of suffering is ethico-cosmic (ethico-natural, if you prefer). Craving, wanting more, thirsting after this or that, is a natural feature of the human condition which is unethical when pushed beyond its limit. Even in today's thinking this is a feature of purely physical law: add a weight to the end of a piece of solid metal and it will bend according to certain physical laws while its integrity is maintained; but add too much weight and it will snap and its integrity is lost. (Note that the term 'integrity' also has both moral and physical uses.)

In ancient thinking, taking too much, for example, from 'nature' (as we now dualistically call it) at once contravenes a natural law, disturbing ecological balance, *and* a moral infringement (greed, craving); and in tribal societies it is a spiritual offence too, requiring apology and appeasement. Suffering would follow, and this suffering was ethico-natural. For us in this century it is crucial for understanding the meaning of 'climate change'. It is not just the climate that has changed, so has the ethical climate, and it is an ethical/climatic change (see Conclusion). It is slowly dawning on us that we all have a moral responsibility for the harm and suffering that is 'climate change'. The challenge for us humans is a change to a renewed form of ethical nonduality, which has to be addressed at the same time as the economic and technological outcome of our boundaryless greed—otherwise, and more likely, change will be *forced* upon us.

The general point about suffering and craving, then, is that in a law-bound ethico-cosmos doing wrong manifests as ethico-natural suffering, and right manifests as ethico-natural wisdom and freedom, as *nibbāna*. The *saṃsāra-nibbāna* cycle is an ethico-natural cycle.[2] There can be no dualistic and absolute separation between *saṃsāra* and *nibbāna*, but only a nondual 'hovering'. That is the truth of the human condition.

11.7 Noble Truth 1 (Unhelpful View)

We ordinarily think that the dissatisfaction we suffer in life is due to an inadequacy in our 'position' and an insufficiency in the things we have.

We believe that we just have to try harder. We may think that 'If only I had ...' more money, a better job, a qualification, a kinder boss, a better reputation, a husband or wife, or no husband or wife, more power, or even a gun, then I would be satisfied, happy, a success and my 'stress' would be at an end. This is an unhelpful view of dissatisfaction and suffering.

It is perfectly true that any of these things may bring some specific pleasure, praise, fame and gain and help us to avoid specific pain, blame, ill-repute and loss. Some security may be gained and some insecurity avoided. However, what will lead to a suffering at least as great as the absence of these satisfactions is the *reliance* on gaining them alone as guarantees of happiness. Man does not live by bread alone. While there is certainly some satisfaction in having made a gain or avoided a loss, there is a false security in the conviction, whether acknowledged or not, that such satisfactions are the *ultimate* in human life.

The lack of balance and moderation that is to be found in an attitude of craving for worldly gains and an attitude of proactive rejection of their opposites sets us up for even greater suffering. Where there is more craving there will be more disappointment and frustration. The man who hungers for gold will suffer his not getting it. The woman who rejects people of other faiths and races will suffer her inability to remove them.

However, the obverse is also true. Where there is less craving there will be less disappointment and frustration, and where there is less rejecting there will be less resentment and anger. The person who has never heard of gold will not suffer not having it. The person who sees beauty in human diversity will not suffer from an inability to live in peace with 'other people'.

Ultimately, there is no greater suffering than the disappointment of not getting, or in losing, or in realizing too late the worthlessness of that which we have chosen to make the anchor of our lives. The Dhamma intimates that we need not coercively hold on to a rock-solid anchor, for (putting it metaphorically) we are already held by the ocean.

11.8 Noble Truth 1 (Helpful View)

So far this is a mundane and purely ethical understanding of dissatisfaction, helpful as it may be. For the Buddha, the real issue is deeper. There is dissatisfaction beyond ordinary worldly dissatisfactions, a dissatisfaction which religions try to address. We might call it 'existential dissatisfaction' or 'alienation' or 'existential angst', or simply a deep-seated bewilderment or sense of futility. Whatever we call it, what is its nature?[3]

It is a dissatisfaction that sometimes shows itself only when the fleeting satisfactions of the world have disappeared and you are left facing the true nature of your life. At those moments you may sense disorientation, emptiness, fear, a loss of meaning that is hard to name but is nonetheless real for that. It is at those times that life may reveal itself as a tiresome trajectory beginning with being inexplicably thrown into the world, followed by a long struggle for a place in the sun, frustration and disappointments, and then a decline and an inexorable loss and ending from which there is no return and no certain second chance.

This is the dissatisfaction of deep bewilderment at existing, of dread at not existing, and the absence of any sign or signal as to what the point of moving from one to the other could be. The world just passes by, taunting me, and I have in the end failed to bend it to my will. I shall be completely forgotten, and even those who remember me shall be forgotten, and eventually all those recollectors and forgetters shall have no one at all to remember or forget them.

I could *invent* a solid prop for myself; and make myself believe in it, but I would know it is my invention, and therefore no more solid than anything else that I might invent or have invented for me. I would be whistling in the dark, knowing that it is nothing but my own anxious whistle.

This is the dissatisfaction that, for the Buddha, is an unnecessary suffering—unnecessary because it rests on a delusion. This root delusion, this profound ignorance, is a dense mist obscuring our true peace. The mist can be lifted, and the Buddha knows how to blow it away. That is the Noble Eightfold Path. For, as we shall consider later, each one may ultimately be 'dissolved' (and is already dissolved) in that from which they came; what the Buddha refers to as 'the unmanifest ... the peaceful ... the deathless'.[4]

11.9 Noble Truth 2 (Unhelpful View)

There are many popular and contradictory beliefs about craving in the ordinary sense. It is often seen as an 'instinct', such as sexual desire, that one can but indulge or an indulgence that ought to be corrected or even punished. This book began with a short account of craving, stating that: 'In a broad sense we are all addicts, feeling a deep lack that we seek to fill with material gain ...'. Now we are in a position to understand this with greater wisdom.

When the Buddha sat under a tree meditating all night after many years of intense practice, he saw that our existential malaise has a broad condition, something without which the malaise would dispel itself. It is a kind of craving, clinging and rejecting, but these words do not capture the depth of the condition. There is a real danger of understanding the condition in only a superficial way.

This is not a craving/rejecting that occurs from time to time in life; it is the craving/rejecting that *is* life itself. It is not something that we can address at once with some ethical moderation, with a period of abstention or with 'common sense'. Common sense—or what appears to be obviously true or desirable—may be part of the problem here.

To give an example: one may crave alcohol, and this may certainly be a self-destructive torment, but what is the craving that the alcohol-craving is trying to satisfy? Is it *just* a craving for alcohol as such? There are surface cravings that depend on a deeper craving: a craving for wholeness, for fullness, for purpose, total security and completion.

This discovery hit the Buddha like a thunderbolt, and from then on he understood rightly.

11.10 Noble Truth 2 (Helpful View)

Craving in Pali is literally thirsting (*taṇhā*). So craving/rejecting is not something that just happens now and then, or even often. It is embedded in the very nature of 'being here'. The Buddha is reported as saying:

> *Now this, bhikkhus, is the noble truth of the origin of suffering: it is this craving which leads to renewed existence, accompanied by delight and lust, seeking delight here and there; that is, craving for sensual pleasures, craving for existence, craving for extermination* [non-existence].[5]

In craving I am reborn in every moment, and so is my world. The craving and rejecting that the Buddha discovered in himself is the manifestation of the assumption that the 'world' is something *apart* from 'myself' that I can grasp, manipulate, make mine or reject. Conversely, the assumption is that 'I' am something apart from 'the world' that is free to relocate, to remake itself, even to be all-powerful. According to common sense, the world is 'out there' and I am 'in here'. The two are apparently separate and of a different nature from each other: the 'material world' on one side, and 'mind' (consciousness, soul, spirit) on the other. This common-sense view is the dualistic delusion that the Dhamma addresses.

But common sense is as wrong about this as it is in assuming that the sun rises in the East, moves across the sky and sets in the West. The sun does not move; we do. (To be precise, the sun also moves within our galaxy, and even the galaxy moves.) Me/world dualism is the *root* delusion, and it is here that our human dissatisfaction has its origin. The failure of popular religion is, for the most part, the failure to expose this root, taking it instead for granted and trying with more or less success to grow existential security from it.

The truth is that there is neither 'material world' nor 'mind' *as we take them to be*. There can be no separation because ultimately there is nothing to separate. This does not mean that the 'mind is really matter' (materialism) nor that 'matter is really mind' (idealism). Nor is it to say that the material world and the mind have no 'reality'. It has been expressed by some Dhamma teachers as a case of 'Not-one, not-two' (see Chapter 13). To put it in a less metaphysical way: the questions 'What *ultimately* is reality?' or 'What is its foundational bedrock?' really have no sense. We return to this Dhamma insight later on.

Chapter 12

Right Understanding: The Horizons Model

12.1 Introduction

With insightful understanding of the first two Noble Truths, namely, suffering and the delusional self-cause of suffering, the very possibility emerges of keeping the delusion at bay, of attenuating the suffering, and considering what more we can do to understand the absolute necessity presented by the silence that liberates. Having dealt with mundane and transcendental (supramundane, ultimate) views of Noble Truths 1 and 2 in the previous chapter we now reflect on the positive Truths 3 and 4, that is, the cessation (*nirodha*) of suffering and path of cessation. Again there are unhelpful and helpful interpretations of these two.

12.2 Noble Truth 3 (Unhelpful View)

The Buddha says of cessation (*nirodha*):

> Now this, monks, is the noble truth of the cessation of suffering: it is the remainder-less fading away and cessation of that same craving, the giving up and relinquishing of it, freedom from it, non-reliance on it.[1]

The 'remainderless' (i.e., total) cessation of craving, which we read about in orthodox texts, is barely conceivable. That is not a criticism, but a conceptual necessity.

It would be an error to think that the 'relinquishing' mentioned in the quotation could mean rejecting, suppressing, forcing down or denying. We should conceive of it instead as letting go, relaxing, removing obstacles, softening, diminishing, attenuating, ameliorating, alleviating, dissolving, and a deep and durable sense of relief and freedom. Craving and rejecting cannot be beaten down, threatened or cajoled; they can only be weakened to a greater or lesser degree. One may reach a degree at which wispy forms of craving are still there (after all, one has to continue breathing and eating) but of little or no importance in the wondrous peace of things. Cessation, then, is an outcome of purifying oneself of defilements—it is not in itself a state, but ideally is the absent of states. We may also recall what was said in 'Right Effort' about the effort of non-effort.

12.3 *Noble Truth 3 (Helpful View)*

What, then, is a helpful way of understanding so-called 'cessation of crav-ing'? For the Buddha, once we sincerely let go of the dualistic assumption of a 'solid objective material world out there' and an 'intangible subjec-tive mental world in here', then I am emancipated. In fact, 'emancipated' here paradoxically means no discrete 'I' to have such an experience. Craving/rejecting then ceases, or is at least significantly diminished. This is because ultimately there is nothing to crave or to reject and no one to do the craving and rejecting. This insight is what the Buddha calls 'wis-dom' (*paññā*, or *prajñā* in Sanskrit), and with it will come compassion for all the anguished struggle of humanity.

The liberation from craving is reported to be *nibbāna*, and this is a good juncture to grapple with the meaning of that.

12.4 Nirodha *and* Nibbāna

First, it is worthwhile confronting a potential confusion. The Buddha speaks both of *nirodha* and *nibbāna* as an ending of the insatiability, of the suffering. *Nirodha* and *nibbāna* are not to be conceived of as *states*, which might leave us with the puzzle of which is 'higher'. That problem only arises if we insist on treating these two concepts as discrete states, rather than two angles on describing the approach to a final peace. *Nirodha* emphasizes the end (3rd Noble Truth) of the suffering (1st Noble Truth) brought about by the craving, clinging and rejecting (2nd Noble Truth) which meditational training (4th Noble Truth) unravels. *Nibbāna* does not directly appear in the simple statement of the Four Noble Truths, and that is conceptually significant. It is due to its role in drawing atten-tion to the way in which meditational training gradually undermines the vitality of craving, clinging and rejecting. All the fuel that feeds the fire of suffering is gradually burned out, so to speak. Unhelpfully conceiving 'nirodha' and 'nibbāna' as states is like an undiscerning reader now treat-ing my words 'ending' and 'unravelling' as discrete states ('The End' and 'The Unravelled') and then puzzling over what kinds of state they are and which is 'higher'. It is not surprising that, with this logical contortion, many people have come to see *nibbāna* as an elevated state of mind that one strives to reach.

The Buddha's model of a heating-up process of craving and a cooling-off process of meditation was appropriate to his time and culture. It would, perhaps, have been fairly commonplace among those he encountered. Still, at this point I could risk innovating a little with some modern models, namely, asymptotes and horizons.

12.5 Nibbāna *as Asymptote*

As a thought experiment, *nibbāna* could be conceived as asymptotic, which is a commonplace concept in mathematics and geometry. In the simplest terms, this means always getting nearer to a place but never quite reaching it.

In the Buddha's time and place there was no notion of the asymptote, that is, a curve that gets closer and closer to a line but never touches it but proceeds infinitely. In the simplest case, a graph of $y = 1/x$, the line approaches the x-axis ($y = 0$), but never touches it. For the ancients, usually anything in the form of an extending line was conceived either as coming to an end or continuing in a cycle. This ancient view is perhaps expressed in the notion of the rebirth cycle in which *nibbāna* is the final ending ('release'), and rebirth is a cyclic return. But another way of looking at *nibbāna* (and *nirodha*) is asymptotic (see Figure 4).

Some readers may instantly accept the asymptotic model of *nibbāna*, concluding that as near as one may get to it—and peaceful and awesome

Figure 4: Asymptote. The curve infinitely approaches the line but never reaches it.

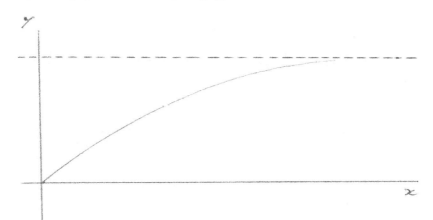

as that may be—one can never *perfectly* complete one's journey and 'arrive'. This interpretation makes sense of the fact that however near you get, there must be some remnant of 'you' to *experience* it. This would seem to make personally worthwhile the whole lengthy journey of the Noble Eightfold Path.

However, there is a cogent objection to this asymptotic interpretation; and Dhamma insight may be assisted by seeing into the nature of this objection. To express it logically: 'I experience *nibbāna*' is a self-contradictory proposition. After all, what defines *nibbāna* is said to be the *absence* of the 'me/world' division. So a better interpretation is that a perfect *nibbāna* would not tolerate the faintest whiff of 'you'. It is the vestigial 'self' striving for a separate *nibbāna* that is itself the final and subtle obstacle. So one must allow that 'you' can indeed 'disappear into' *nibbāna*. Now, how does one make sense of that? Here we need to see things nondually.

12.6 Non-clinging

The Buddha emphasized that there can be no question of *nibbāna* as long as there is striving for *nibbāna*. There is no *nibbāna* as long as one is thinking, 'Ah I have attained *nibbāna*!' The Buddha states clearly:

> And when this venerable one regards himself thus: 'I am at peace, I have attained nibbāna, I am without clinging', that too is declared to be clinging on the part of this good recluse or Brahmin. [Note that the emphasis of 'I' is added by the translators.][2]

Where there is the faintest vestige of clinging there can be no *nibbāna*. This may be regarded as a statement of logic, since *nibbāna is* the complete absence of clinging. It is also a statement of ontology and epistemology, a statement about the fundamentals of reality and human experience.

Still, we must beware of an important misunderstanding. Attaining *nibbāna* is not the *annihilation* of the discrete 'self', or of 'the world', but is rather the most fundamental conception of nonduality itself. That is, *nibbāna* may be conceived (if we must *try to conceive it*) as a kind of oscillating or hovering state of consciousness, a 'realization' in which both self and world are still 'present' but in a completely different manner: an *undivided mirror-like unity. Nibbāna* is not like any sense-based experience, but is rather a *realization*. What we take to be reality is then revealed to be unreal, and in the same flick of the mind the deeper reality reveals itself— and this revelation demands that there is no discrete 'self' to reveal itself to. One might say, it is the lay person in the monk, or the monk in the lay person.

12.7 Nibbāna *as 'Horizon'*

Since so much depends on making some preliminary sense of *nibbāna*, another model may help to explore the concept.

Nibbāna could be conceived analogically as a 'horizon' rather than any kind of place or state of mind. Horizons do exist—I can point to the horizon. Of course, I can never reach the horizon, for it apparently recedes as I move towards it. Let's say I am climbing gently upwards. I could indicate some point on my current horizon, say, a distinctive tree and then decide to move towards it. However, if and when I get to that tree I will see before me another horizon, and an infinite series of horizons. Every time I reach a chosen and demarcated horizon I have climbed a little higher; I am wiser. I look back on all the experience of the horizons now gone, 'behind' me. I am at a higher vantage point, but no horizon has any special reality of its own. It has a reality only from the *specific perspective* in which 'I' stand at any time.

Thus one may think that *nibbāna*, like a horizon, is real but only from where you are standing, your vantage point. Perhaps we could speak of many '*nibbānas*', and they *depend* on where you are in your meditational practice and understanding. Such an interpretation could help one along the way, but eventually it would give rise to other intellectual problems similar to those of the asymptote model.

12.8 Nibbāna *as Non-Vantage Point*

Some readers may go with this simple horizons model. Others might be understandably dissatisfied with the implication that there is no *final* horizon. In their minds, as we have seen already, *nibbāna* has to be complete and final. However, by now we should be asking 'complete and final' in *relation* to what? Let us imagine that there is no 'what' and no 'self' to observe or otherwise relate to a 'what'. For at last *there is absolutely no vantage point* from which that could happen. All vantage points have dropped away, and indeed that process of dropping away is one definition of what the entire Noble Eightfold training is all about: from fixated grip on the I-me-mine vantage point, through diversification of and releasing of intermediate vantage points, to finally the dropping away of all vantage points.

So here is a final model for exploring the concept of *nibbāna*. We deploy this model by asking an intriguing question: what is in a mirror when no one is looking into it? When I am there looking into the mirror a single vantage point is provided ('me') from which various reflected objects appear in the mirror. I shift my vantage point and the perceived objects shift, appear or disappear. But when I am not looking into the mirror, and neither is anyone else, a question arises: is there anything in the mirror? Is there something, nothing or everything? Well, such is *nibbāna*—a vantage-less 'space' in which I am and am not, both am and am not, and neither am nor am not.[3]

12.9 *The Laity, the Monastic and the Arahant*

This is a good place to question further what is meant by 'cessation', 'escape' and the 'remainderless fading away' mentioned by the Buddha. One may have been led to think that *nirodha/nibbāna* is only for monks and nuns, and that for ordinary people only some relatively modest *degree* of softening or amelioration is possible. In other words, those who have left their families, as the Buddha asked of some people, and dedicated their lives to the Dhamma have a good chance of 'attaining' *nibbāna*, while ordinary 'householders' or 'uninstructed worldlings' have little or none.

This distinction is perhaps an implicit foundation of some orthodox Buddhism, and is reflected to some degree in the supposed distinction between the 'Theravāda' way for monastic people and the 'Mahāyāna' for ordinary people. But even Mahāyāna often relies on the distinction, for it too has monks and nuns, and often not only monks and nuns but priests.

It seems to me that such a distinction depends on a dogmatic understanding (as just clarified) of the third Noble Truth, the truth of cessation. The view that only a select few—all of them monks and nuns—could 'reach *nibbāna*' is absurd. If this were true then we would have to accept the pessimistic view that, except for a handful of people (arahants) all of suffering humanity will remain unawakened. In some distortions of the Dhamma the Buddha himself has become that superhuman, reminding one of a similar conviction in certain other religions.

I maintain that to truly understand is not literally to 'leave the world'; it is to remain in the world and go about life with a relatively different attitude, the attitude of the 'vantage point of no vantage point'. The overwhelming majority of people currently have their lives defined by and in a set of vantage points. The arahat is not in that position. However, this should not be understood as a *separation* between arahant and non-arahant or between monastic and lay.

The Buddha felt great compassion for the unnecessary suffering in human lives, and had great faith in the ability of each to bring some light into living. That is why he chose not to pursue a career and worldly possessions but to spend every day of 45 years bringing some deep understanding to others. This selfless life of teaching by wandering about came to an end not when he attained *nibbāna* (an understanding he had attained much earlier) but when he was struck down by a mesenteric infarction at the age of 80.[4]

12.10 Craving as Co-emergent

A wrong notion of *nibbāna* is enfolded in a wrong notion of suffering and craving (Noble Truths 1 and 2). Craving is not just the linear cause of suffering. Instead they are co-emergents feeding off each other. Even the most banal experience shows us that: 'I want a bigger car because I am dissatisfied, and I am dissatisfied because I want a bigger car'. Practising the Noble Eightfold Path I cool off all particular cravings, moving towards the cessation of all craving. Whether there is a *state* of being absolutely 'stopped' is also a misconceived and fruitless question. Ceasing and the Path are also co-emergents, feeding off each other: cooling off I follow the Path; following the Path I cool off. Ceasing is not a disappearance: the awakened ones live on in this world, but their grasping attitude has ceased. Paradoxically they no longer see this world as 'the world' as ordinary folk do.

The Buddha was not primarily philosophizing—he was not turning humble participles into grandiloquent nouns; not turning 'cooling off' into 'The Cooled Off'. He was telling us *what to do*.

12.11 Noble Truth 4 (Unhelpful View)

There is always a strong inclination to interpret the nondual understanding (supramundane) as though it were a variety of the dualistic, the ordinary or mundane. It is also tempting to interpret the Buddha Dhamma in terms, such as religious (theistic) terms with which we are already familiar. Thus, when we are told that the subduing of craving/rejecting is possible we may jump to a wrong idea of *how* supposedly it is possible, and then say to ourselves '*that* cannot be done!', and then reject as the Dhamma what is in fact our own wrong idea of it.

A common error is to think of the Noble Eightfold Path and its eight factors as an elimination, eradication or purging. One hears uninformed opinions about Buddhists trying to eliminate the bad things in life, or eliminate the good things in life, or drop all ambition, or life itself, or eliminate 'God', and so on. It is said by some that Buddhism is life-denying rather than life-affirming. It might be true that some versions of Buddhism wrongly slip into pessimism or optimism, or that followers of the path may occasionally do so. We also sometimes hear of Buddhists supposedly being quite 'unrealistic' in trying to eradicate once and for all bad thoughts and reactions or human weakness and harmfulness, cleansing themselves of all 'sinfulness'. Since this would be a naïve endeavour, it is said that Buddhism is really a waste of time. Well, if this misconception were the Buddha Dhamma, then it would certainly be a waste of time. But it is not. The Dhamma practitioner takes all the arisings and falling conditions of life as teachers, and thereby learns equanimity.

12.12 Noble Truth 4 (Helpful View)

The Path discussed in this book appears at first to have a point of departure and a point of arrival. But actually following it involves reappraising the ordinary ideas and responses of departing and arriving. To use a metaphor: the discovery is that there is ultimately no departure and no arrival—just a floating down an endless stream. In fact, the Path is the realization that your being is simply a fleeting wave in the stream itself.

So, we might say, on this Noble Eightfold Path you know you have 'arrived' when you begin to realize that there is nowhere to arrive. Arrival is non-arrival. In some respects, 'you' are already there and always have been. 'There' is always 'here', and it always has been. A complete change of heart/mind is what is required.

The right understanding of the Path may now be put in a nutshell: you examine yourself in order to understand yourself, in order to lose yourself, in order for realization to 'occur'. This is not in any worldly sense an ambition, or an achievement, or an accumulation of information, or a ready-made path to be followed (despite this book); nor is it a series of gains by which comparisons can be made with others. It is usually and mainly a slow cultivation, but at a certain point there may be sudden insights or illuminations until they add up to a kind of *gestalt*-shift: so-called realization.

The butterfly may emerge at once from the caterpillar, but one should remember that it is a long time a chrysalis.

12.13 Awakening

Some people embarking on the Path ask: 'How will I know when I am enlightened (awakened)?' This is an understandable question, but utterly misconceived. To start with, could one be enlightened and *not* know it? But, look more deeply into this: the newcomer may be looking for a 'marker' or sign that will tell him or her 'Ah! There's that sign—I must be enlightened!' This is a very odd way of thinking about meditation. One is thereby putting oneself *outside* the experience of meditation, like a bird-watcher waiting for the song of a nightingale to know that indeed there are nightingales around here. Nothing remotely describable as enlightenment could possibly arise in this frame of mind; and that's because the 'self' one is supposedly letting go of is quite solidly established as an enlightenment-watcher. One would like to shake this person and announce 'You *are* the "nightingale"'!

It might help to speak of 'awakening' rather than 'being enlightened'. Certainly you may notice that you are changing in some ways, and others close to you may notice too: less anger, more patience, more empathy and care, more generosity and gratitude, and more attentiveness and mindfulness, and a nurturing (or at least less harmful) livelihood. But this awakening is not really a one-off event. Awakening does not have a trademark or logo. You might say it is more like learning to ride a bicycle. A breakthrough moment (or moments) may come when you can keep your balance, you know not how. What joy! But effort has to be made and there will be bruised knees and grazed elbows along the way.

12.14 Not about Me

Despite what has been said above about *nibbāna* and the paradoxical 'vantage point of no-vantage point', without regular and deep practice you may find the great realization beyond your grasp. Actually, it is the 'grasp' that is the obstacle. The major reason that you may still be *awaiting* a deep reorientation at this point is that you may continue to believe and act as though all you have learned is about *you*. Your orientation in life has begun to turn *you* around, certainly, but a 'turned-around you' is only halfway along the Path. Is this really all about you?

It is fairly easy to accept 'mundanely' that I ought not to steal the property of others, ought not to tell lies to others, ought not to sexually exploit others, and so on. For one thing, I do not wish to suffer these things at the hands of others. The You may respond by asking: 'Is it not *me* that now speaks helpfully, *me* that now acts helpfully, *me* that now has a helpful livelihood, and *me* that now meditates and finds tranquillity?' From a mundane point of view, yes, of course. But from the ultimate (supramundane) it all looks rather different. A key moment in the reorientation process is when I begin to see that the mundane reading of ethics is a reading from *my* perspective; it is about *me*—that is, about *my* thoughts and behaviour. But now I also see that even the 'me' is at stake.

The Buddha certainly did think that accepting all of this 'mundanely' is an essential clearing away of the undergrowth. However, one may clear away undergrowth simply because it is a good habit or because one was told to do so or because it is some kind of rule or because a punishment may be threatened, or for some other kind of *reason*. We have seen that the Buddha warned us against trying to reach existential conclusions by 'logical reasoning, by inferential reasoning, by reflection on reasons, by the acceptance of a view after pondering it, by the seeming competence of a speaker, or because you think, "The ascetic [e.g., the Buddha] is our teacher"'.[5]

If you are awakened then you do not stand in need of a reason for love and compassion for others. There is a love beyond mundane love and a compassion beyond pity. It is no longer a case of managing or regulating 'my' relationships with 'others'. There is a vast suffering beyond 'my' suffering, and a vast joy beyond 'my' joy. Now we may ask: what is this 'my'? What 'others'? Let us consider a popular analogy that we find in certain Hindu and New Age conceptions. The analogy is clear to the uninitiated because it expresses in a positive image a teaching that the Buddha only ever really expresses negatively or apophatically.

Metaphor 6: Raymond the Raindrop

> If Raymond the raindrop could have reasoning, then that reasoning would arise from his perception of separateness from other raindrops. He might even have the ethical thought: 'It would be better if we didn't bump into each other', and there would be lots of reasons for accepting that thought. For example, bumping might cause harm, might damage the 'integrity' of another raindrop or of Raymond himself. But as he sees the ocean rushing towards him, a complete shift of perspective may occur: 'Oh, I was so concerned with bumping into each other because I thought we were separate, but we are not. Look at that endless ocean!'

This analogy might be a step in the right direction, but *beware*: the Buddha did not use anything like it, no doubt because the concept of 'raindrop' suggests a discrete 'self' ultimately reuniting with a theistic Great Self ('ocean'), which was the view of many brahmins.

In any case, instead of the ethics of protecting and furthering 'I-me-mine' in relation to others playing the same game, there is a right-angle turn towards selflessness, generosity, gratitude, love and compassion for all. It is still ethics—although 'supramundane ethics' or 'spiritual ethics' sounds rather grandiose, perhaps.

From this perspective, ethics is really about loosening or dissolving the sense of 'I', 'me', mine', rather than just reconfiguring the 'I', 'me', 'mine'. Gradually, I see that I do not have to have a *reason* for caring for others—actually there is no real alternative. Once again, the intellect on its own may give one an idea of this, but it is but a pale shadow of direct insight.

Now, by reorienting yourself into the supramundane aspect of the Path you learn how to challenge 'your' very idea of 'you' at its foundation, strange and paradoxical as this may appear. Here we begin, like Alice, to enter into a Wonderland in which things can be explained only by undermining the terms of the explanation itself. For example, in these pages I am referring to 'you' (the person reading this book) while helping 'you' to question the permanence, substantiality and 'suffering' of the 'you', so that 'you' may let go of your current understanding of it.

This will be like climbing a ladder, only to kick away the ladder once you reach the top. It will be like building a boat to cross a torrent, only eventually to reach the other side (see section 18.1 below) and leave the boat behind while you travel in a pure land that knows no torrents and needs no boats. It will be like learning to swim, only to find that all along you could float. It will be like seeing that what you thought was far away or over there, or maybe somewhere near here, was right 'with you' all the time, but can only be seen *without you*. It would be like the question of the Caterpillar to Alice in Wonderland, 'Who are YOU?', and she replied: 'I ... I hardly know, sir, just at present ... at least I know who I WAS when I got up this morning, but I think I must have been changed several times since then'.[6]

12.15 Meta-horizon

So this is where the horizon-chasing model comes back into its own. It is true that I need to keep letting-go, keep dropping off defilements, keep de-centring, keep moving beyond horizon to horizon; but having thus merely *facilitated* realization then the actual moment of realization is not a horizon but a quantum leap to that understanding in which horizons are seen for what they are, and how they work. That point of view is not itself a horizon but, one might say, a kind of meta-horizon—a view of horizon-making itself. One is free of all limitations, simply by no longer being even that 'one' that is free. To then continue by doing, thinking and saying all things *in the light of* this understanding is serene; it is to live 'the holy life'.

Chapter 13

Right Understanding: The Mirror Model

13.1 Dependence on Duality

The Buddha was approached by a monk who wanted to adopt the 'Right View' ('Right Understanding'). But what is it?

> Then the Venerable Kaccānagotta approached the Blessed One, paid homage to him, sat down to one side, and said to him: 'Venerable sir, it is said, "right view, right view". In what way, venerable sir, is there "right view"?
>
> 'This world, Kaccāna, for the most part depends upon a duality—upon the notion of existence and notion of non-existence. But for one who sees the origin of the world as it really is with correct wisdom, there is no notion of non-existence in regard to the world. And for one who sees the cessation of the world as it really is with correct wisdom, there is no notion of existence in regard to the world'.[1]

13.2 'View' and Insight

These radical statements of the Buddha call upon me to clarify the existence/non-existence couplet. Admittedly, there is a family of concepts at the heart of the Buddha Dhamma which is difficult to represent, not because it is complicated but because it runs counter to our ordinary assumptions about reality. In the truth of meditational practice, members of this family cannot be represented but only indicated by metaphor, models, analogy and stretching language into metaphysical statements. These concepts are aspects of the coherent *conceptualization* of the Buddha's teaching as a 'view' (*diṭṭhi*). That view can support within our intellectual understanding the insights that the Buddha's meditational practice 'subjectively' reveals to us. They are, in potentially misleading English: 'The Middle Way' or 'nonduality', 'not-self' (*anattā*), 'co-dependent origination' (*paṭiccasamuppāda*) and 'the Five Aggregates'. I try to represent (not replace) all of these in terms of modern models. I start with an attempt to clarify 'The Middle Way'. Put another way, the models provide a kind of visual sketch of the way things stand ultimately (supramundanely).

We know that attenuation or 'cessation' comes about by following the Noble Eightfold Path. But it would be obstructive to presume that the Path has no underlying unity, no single direction, and no single epistemological principle to carry one along. One might flounder about from one doctrine of the Path to another, not seeing their connectedness. So it is, I believe, very helpful to understand this unifying principle in a subjective monologue with one's practice. The Buddha speaks of that principle as 'The Middle Way'. Later Buddhists are fond of calling it 'nonduality'. These two terms are just two angles on the same point. To try and clarify this principle I will later in this chapter use another model: the model of a reflection of oneself in a mirror. I call it the Mirror Model. But firstly, what does the Buddha mean by saying that the Noble Eightfold Path is the Middle Way?

13.3 *The Revolutionary Moment*

The Middle Way (in Pali: *Majjhimāpaṭipadā*) appears to be the Buddha's shorthand for the Noble Eightfold Path. But what does he mean? Its importance is highlighted by the fact that the Buddha uses this expression in his very first public talk after his awakening, which is recorded in the sutta called 'The Setting in Motion of the Wheel of the Dhamma' (*Dhammacakkappavattana sutta*).[2] It would be wrong to think the Buddha is only teaching the cliché of 'moderation in all things'. It is true that having just tried self-mortification to no avail he then understood that neither self-indulgence nor self-mortification could be the way to a liberating understanding of the human plight. It was this realization that triggered something much deeper: an understanding of the radical misunderstanding (delusion) of the division of 'me in here' and 'world out there'. He had himself been deluded when he took his own body (part of 'the world out there') as his target, which entailed the mistake of thinking 'body/mind' was a 'real' distinction. In fact such an assumption was the very root of the problem. How could he now explain to others that the key to liberation from suffering was precisely to undermine that assumed division, so deeply was it now becoming embedded in the brahminical, and increasingly popular, point of view.

He was now creating a way, through his teaching encounters and inspiration, to get across that unleashed duality was indeed the bane of human life. The Noble Eightfold Path is nothing less than the record (rather scrambled over the centuries, I fear) of his 45 years of trying to demolish the early Indian trend to a dualistic mind-set. Some listeners would get it immediately, because they were not inclined to dualism in the first place. Others (notably brahmins and wandering philosophers) who were engaged in constructing duality had difficulty: some were in denial, and resisted. The Buddha announced:

> *Without veering towards either of these extremes, the Tathāgata has awakened to the middle way, which gives rise to vision, which gives rise to knowledge, which leads to peace, to direct knowledge, to enlightenment, to Nibbāna.*
>
> *And what, bhikkhus, is that middle way awakened to by the Tathāgata ...? It is this Noble Eightfold Path; that is, right view, right intention [resolve], right speech, right action, right livelihood, right effort, right mindfulness, right concentration.*[3]

This insight was so conceptually radical that no part of the entire swathe of his teaching is untouched by it. This presents the newcomer with a series of puzzles about whether the Middle Way is the same or not the same as, for example, dependent origination, the Five Aggregates, not-self, and so on. The short answer is that all of these are labels for different ways of undermining the divisive 'world/me' ontology and allowing a nondual alternative to emerge. And not just undermining it as an intellectual product but as a lived vision of human life, the experience of being human, the unfolding of life itself. If one re-reads the eight factors of the Path with discernment one has to acknowledge the ubiquitous effort to dismember duality. Even the Right Speech principle is that of speak to 'others' as one would be spoken to.

13.4 Not-One, Not-Two

So far, hopefully, we have begun to discover through meditation what we might provisionally describe as the effervescent arising and passing away of the experience that constitutes 'my world'. We have also noted that at a deeper level these arisings are nondual, that is, there is in the actual experience no separation between the experiencer ('me') and the experienced ('it' out there). 'Experience' shows itself to be questionable, because the very concept of 'experience' implies something (separate) that someone (separate) is having. This is one reason why many Buddha Dhamma texts use the special term '*dhammas*', meaning experiential items, phenomena, subject-object arisings. To take a simple and preliminary example, consider the experience of the sound of a bird singing. Does the bird called-to hear what I (the human) hear? Is the song entirely 'out there' (objective) or is it entirely 'in me' (subjective), or in some way both or neither?

Here is an analogy to soften the natural rigidity of our human minds to the idea that something can be one or two, both one and two, or neither one nor two. Of course, any analogy breaks down on niggardly scrutiny, but the Möbius Strip should serve as our Middle Way debut.

Figure 5: Möbius Strip

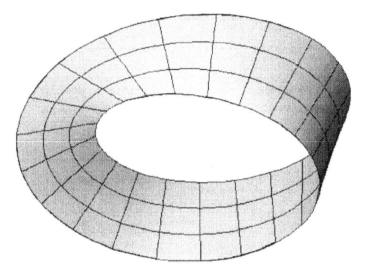

See the Möbius Strip shown in Figure 5. If you take a strip of paper, twist it once and join the ends to each other with tape, then you have such a strip. It looks as though it has two edges and two surfaces. In fact, it has one edge and one surface. You may find this puzzling. How is that possible, you ask yourself? Trace your finger along the edge and you will see that you return to the same place on the edge. Now run your finger along the surface, and you will see that you return to the same place on the surface. There is one surface, and there is one edge. Or are there?

Again, one must remember that the Möbius Strip discussed here is a simple physical *model* only, and as such it has its limitations. Your reaction to this may be: 'Ah, it's because the strip was twisted!'. That reaction would be a case of missing the point of the analogy by giving a physical explanation. The point here is not to *explain* the analogue but see what it *points* us to. Our experience of being is a case of not-one, not-two.

Now we could apply this to all experience or, if you prefer, all 'reality'. It is all something that is and is not, you might say.

This metaphor simply introduces us to the very idea of an appearance of duality with an underlying unity. What looks like two is in truth one. But what is missing from it is any aspect of reflexivity, and that is why we now progress to a better model, the Mirror Model. But first we need to recall what is meant by a 'model'.

13.5 Transcendence and Models

One thing to keep in mind is that a model is deployed because that which it is a model of cannot be directly conceived or 'described' in terms of attributes (properties). The reason for that is perfectly logical. Since the object of our concern is reality as a whole we should consider whether our vantage point on this whole is either outside or inside the whole itself. If it is inside the whole then we have a *limited* vantage (mundane) because one cannot see the whole from the inside but only from the outside. If, however, it is outside the whole then the vantage point itself must be excluded in order to obtain that vantage point, so one's vantage is not of the whole after all. In short, the whole cannot be seen or even conceived. It does, however, manifest itself in non-verbal ways, for example by the models we are using here.

Thus we run into the Horizons Model of *nibbāna* from a different aspect. This receding boundary is also called 'Transcendence' by philosophers and theologians. It is a crucial concept in all religions, spiritualities, mysticism and metaphysics. It is as though one reaches a point in knowledge and experience that one cannot pass beyond, that is, cannot transcend. So we are left with an aporia, namely, a puzzle we cannot possibly crack. We are left with the position that there must be a boundary, but we cannot possibly know its nature or what is 'beyond' it. This sets us up for a 'spiritual' or 'philosophical' or 'existential' kind of craving; and craving (2nd Noble Truth) is the very thing that is the root of deep anxiety. In Buddhism we find the Transcendence issue described in terms of 'mundane' (within the boundary) and 'supramundane' (outside the boundary).

There are a limited number of ways of addressing this ontological issue. But for our purposes we may consider these:

(1) There is no point in wasting time on what is unknowable, so simply turn away. If it is unthinkable then just don't try to think about 'it'. This might look like the Buddha's full response, but I do not think it is.

(2) Recognize that it is unknowable, and remain in silent awe; this acknowledgement itself could be liberating. I think the Buddha's position could helpfully be interpreted in this way, as I explain later.

(3) Whatever is beyond the boundary is in some way the unknowable source or ground of what is within the boundary, and may be
thought of perhaps in human terms as a creative being, 'God'. This is
theism. One version of this view goes with the claim that only 'faith'
in the 'goodness' of an unreachable 'God' is necessary to live a good
life, and another version is that 'God' manifests Him/Herself within
the boundary by the *grace* of various divine signs.

(4) As option 3 above, except that what is inconceivable cannot be
thought of as a 'being' of any sort, for that is to interpret what is
beyond in terms of what is *within* the boundary (the human or other
physical form), which might be termed 'mundane reduction'. Still, it
could be conceived in a more abstract way as, for example, Brahman
(in Hinduism) or mention of 'the Unconditioned' in Buddhism.

One has to be careful that this last view is not actually an attempt to have
one's cake and eat it by eating just an itsy-bitsy piece of it. It seems that
if you swallow it fast enough you will not notice it. It is also as though a
fish that had never been out of water tries to understand what is beyond
water in terms of water, and tries to avoid his own fishy inconsistency by
conceiving what is outside as a very wispy form of water. In truth, this
thinking amounts to the contradiction 'It is *inconceiv*able but here is a
conception'—using a very lightweight and abstract concept such as 'the
Unconditioned'. It is perhaps a variety of what the Buddha called 'eel-
wriggling'.[4] In truth this is a hovering between 'mundane reduction' and
some kind of agnostic doubt.

The craving to achieve completion, where completion is impossible
in terms of the mundane outlook, is one of the subtle and almost irresistible
forms of suffering that the Buddha addresses. For the Buddha, if one lets
go of oneself as the rarefied one who clings to non-clinging then completion is attained (realization).[5]

This leaves us with the matter of what the Buddha says or refuses to
say about certain unanswerable questions, which I leave until later (see
section 19.10).

13.6 Applying the Mirror Model to Duality

The Mirror Model will hopefully provide us with a way of imagining the
enfoldment of duality and nonduality. A question may arise: What is it
that the model is modelling? Well, if one could say with utter clarity then
one would not need a model. The sense of 'me in here' and 'world out

there' (a form of solipsism) cannot be described in terms which them-selves ultimately rest on that division. One cannot describe the nature of dualism in terms of dualism itself. One cannot transcend duality in an empirical explanation but only in an insight resulting from meditational practice supported by Right View. A model of duality/nonduality may assist.

Using a model in these circumstances is to deploy a kind of deliberate mundanity, an image one can hold in one's mind in which one is fully aware that one is using a mundanity, and which one can put aside once it helps one to cross the flood of partial views.

It is a case of 'seeing as'. I suddenly see that the whole of that I am experiencing as reality is *like* the effect of a mirror on an all-embracing scale. The mind has to make a quantum leap and 'see' that as I ('me in here') stand here looking out on the trees outside that is actually a kind of reflecting process. In truth there is no division, there are not two things, there is no discrete 'I' and no separate world 'out there'—just the one reflecting process.

Exercise 24: Mirror of Not-One, Not-Two

Stand in front of a mirror. What is it that you see? Of course *it is* yourself that you see; however, *it is also not* yourself but a reflection of yourself. As you stand there looking, ask yourself: 'What is *this* that is actually looking in the mirror?'

You must ask insistently, inwardly and penetratingly, seeking the 'this' that is *doing* the looking. What do you find? Try this for some time, even if it makes you 'dizzy', for there is a lot of understanding that can be awakened in this way. Do this before reading the next paragraph, because finding out for yourself is so much more edifying than having someone clarify it for you.

Let us assume that the question 'What is this that is looking in the mir-ror?' demands an answer from you. If you persevere you may become quite unsettled, and deeply puzzled. You may want to turn away and return to the familiar. But stay with it.

What you may find is this. The 'this' you are looking for is first found in the mirror. 'That's me', you say, as though it is the most obvious thing in the world. It *is* obvious—that's the problem! It would be tempting to leave it there. But next you ask: 'Yes, but what is it that is *looking* in the mirror right now and *asking* this question?' To answer this question you have to let go of the mirror image of 'you' and be aware of yourself as the 'looking'. There you will find nothing except *the looking* itself. Not a thing, but an activity or process. Stay with that for some time. It will probably be uncomfortable, even disturbing.

You will find that you want to enjoy security in the reflected image in the mirror: 'That *is* me!' But do not fool yourself—it is a reflected image of you. Tap on the glass—that is not your flesh. It is you as you appear in the physical world; it is you as you are *seen*. But you are also the *seer*. If you 'recognize' the familiar image, and like or dislike parts of what you see, then you have made yourself an object in 'the material world' and you are attached to it. But where are you, the *seer*? Where is *that* which is *doing* the recognizing of itself? It would be tempting to think of it as some non-physical ethereal entity, an essential 'you'. The Buddha says No to that temptation.

This shaking up of the deep and almost universal assumption of a discrete separation between the 'real inner me' and the 'real material world' is absolutely necessary if any spiritual understanding is to be attained. Nearly all religions and 'spiritualities' appear at their core to be agreed on this, *in one way or another*. However, in popular and institutionalized form this essential truth is often lost or cast in a mundane or an obscure symbolic form—which, admittedly, sometimes happens in Buddhism, too. (Some readers may take such a view of the analogies and metaphors in this book!) This is why humility and selflessness—letting go of self— have a prominent role in the deeper teachings of all these religions and spiritualities.

Later we shall consider the vastly important notion of 'soul', to be found in some form in just about all societies in all historical periods. The Buddha's way of going about this crucial matter is different from any other approach in history. It puts the Dhamma outside the ambit of theism, atheism and agnosticism. It is this distinctive quality that makes the Dhamma a way forward from the contentious stalemate of humanity's delusional state in the present Age of Blindness.

13.7 *Phases of the Mirror Model*

Taking the apparent relation of subject and object in terms of the Mirror Model we can now detect three phases.

Phase 1: This experience could be represented in a one-sided way: I (subject) see 'me' ('myself', object) in the mirror. This is realism, the naïve way of 'the people'.

Phase 2: However, with contemplation, this perception breaks down. A simple duality emerges: 'I' (the seer; that which is doing the seeing) is not reflected in the mirror but is of a completely different nature. It is only 'my body' that appears in the mirror. The 'I' or 'me' ('self') which knows this is not its experiencing-self reflected in the mirror. Thus arises philosophy's perennial 'problem of dualism', the relationship of mind/body in the face of the impossibility of a relation given their very definition depends on absolute difference (non-relationality). The dualistic philosopher René Descartes (1596–1650)[6] famously could not figure out how a non-physical thing could possibly put in motion a physical thing. This is where we can say, perhaps rather extravagantly, that Western ontology has largely fastened itself for over two thousand years, giving support to a manipulative, self-destructive civilization.

Phase 3: The Buddha, however, does not get stuck in dualism and its tangle of speculative solutions. He 'hovers' in nonduality: What is seen in the mirror is (in a manner of speaking) both the same as and different from that which is looking in the mirror. It is a matter of 'seeing as'. *Seen as* 'my body' it is object (that which is external; 'out there'). From this perspective I am just another thing in the Universal Container. And, *seen as* that which is doing the seeing it is subject (that which is internal; my 'private world', free of any Universal Container). The questions 'Is the world real in itself?' (Universal Container) and 'Is the seer real in itself?' ('the self', mind, soul, consciousness, *atta*) are thus, within the logic of the Mirror Model, malformed questions. Neither a denial of the 'existence of the world' nor the assertion of the 'existence of the self' have any sense within the Phase 3 model. They are questions which can only arise within the logic of the Phase 2 model. Many students of Buddhism have asserted that the Buddha denied the existence of 'the self'; whereas his logic only allowed him to neither assert nor deny it.

13.8 Hovering

You may find yourself hovering, vacillating back and forth between the seer and the seen. Yes, that which *sees* itself is 'real' since *something* must be doing the seeing, but it is 'unreal' because no *thing* is there but the seeing. Yes, that which is *seen* (in the mirror) is 'real', since I see it and recognize it, but it is 'unreal' because it is 'only' a reflection of that which is doing the seeing. As far as 'reality' is concerned, the real and the unreal are one and the same thing, yet two different things. Unity in division:

not-one, not-two. All the main problems of Western metaphysics and theology reside here.

To use another simple model, it is like acting out as an iceberg in the ocean while knowing full well that there is no 'real' boundary between 'me-the iceberg' and 'it-the ocean'. The ocean is fleetingly reflected (through meditational insight) in the iceberg as in a mirror. Iceberg/ocean are not simply one, but not simply two either.

I find myself continuing in the mundane world but now illuminated by the supramundane, frameless perspective. The mundane and supramundane are not one, but not two either. *Saṃsāra* and *nibbāna* reflect one another. If I have this insight then I cannot go on as before; because now I have to hover between two vantage points, living out the 'me' that apparently is and accepting the absence of a *discrete* 'me'.

13.9 A Radical Inconsistency?

It may be thought that there is an illicit contradiction underlying the foregoing kind of talk. You may have noticed that there is the use of the 'I-me-mine' (mundane) terminology even when I am speaking of not-I-me-mine. For example, in the sentence before this one I just wrote 'When I am speaking...', and in fact I just did so again, and again and ... Is there a deep paradox here? The not-me nondual perspective is the claim that ultimately all things/people are connected like waves are connected or knots in a string. It is not saying that one cannot speak of waves and knots—obviously one does speak so, and *even when one is aware* that they are not separate things. Even when one is speaking of not-self in the sense of no absolute separation between all things one is bound to engage in some conceptual leap-frogging. By that I mean that one deploys reified language to leapfrog over itself into a non-reified (nondual) insight. This has been going on, and continues, throughout this book.

The point, it now emerges, is not to jettison I-me-mine in favour of a 'correct' not-I-me-mine. The point is to 'hover' in equanimity between the two. That is Dhamma wisdom.

Chapter 14

Right Understanding: The Reflections Model

14.1 *The Conceit 'I Am'*

In one classical text the Buddha is recorded as saying the following:

> *Ānanda, there are these five aggregates affected by clinging, in regard to which a bhikkhu should abide contemplating rise and fall thus: 'Such is material form, such its arising, such its disappearance; such is feeling* [of pain and pleasure], *such its arising, such its disappearance; such is perception* [cognition], *such its arising, such its disappearance; such are formations* [thought], *such their arising and disappearance; such is consciousness, such its arising, such its disappearance.'*
>
> *When he abides contemplating rise and fall in these five aggregates affected by clinging, the conceit 'I am' based on these five aggregates affected by clinging is abandoned in him.*[1]

The term 'aggregate' is perhaps unfamiliar here. On analysis it means a group of related mental actions, such as conceiving 'my body'. The Buddha is here drawing our attention to five aspects of the delusory experience of 'being me', of I-me-mine. That experience arises by a natural reflection which is conceived (cast into language) in terms of body, feeling, cognition, thinking and consciousness. When the nature of this natural reflection is *exposed* then the common-sense conceit 'I am' is not so much abolished as held in abeyance whilst I live. With this insight, I live in irony, I hover in ambivalence. I am no longer a discrete identity; instead I am 'I', a reflective process. (Note the crucial quotation marks.)

Note three points right away:

(1) It is not a matter of 'my identifying myself' with body, etc., for that would presuppose the very thing that we are accounting for, namely 'me'. There is no discrete pre-existing 'me' to do the identifying. The 'me' is itself an arising and falling away, and its arising is the formation of a number of intertwined conditions doctrinally presented as the 'Five Aggregates' (which I here prefer to call 'reflections').

(2) Speaking of the 'Five Aggregates' in this way also might suggest a view along the lines 'I construct myself out of these five things or

experiences'. This is potentially a misleading view because there is neither a discrete 'I' that is doing the constructing nor a template of one to be constructed.

(3) It might also imply that these five so-called 'aggregates' are all of the same kind of thing. In fact they have little or nothing in common, but are simply a shortlist of possible answers, given by the uninstructed person, to the challenge: 'If there is an abiding and essential "true self" or "me", describe it! Let's analyse it!' The average person comes up with at least five common answers, which the Buddha then knocks down. In a wider context, he is here diverting people away from the brahminical concept of the discrete 'self' seeking immortality as that self.

We now return to this crucial dimension of the Buddha's teaching with exercises.

14.2 Doctrine of 'Aggregates'

The Buddha challenges the newly emerging dualism of brahmins and philosophers by requesting them to examine inwardly, in their own experience, those potential mental actions or groups of actions that they are most likely to regard as (or as evidence of) the 'real inner me'. This is a challenge not just for his followers but for all of humanity today.

To sweep the path clean, let me say that in my interpretation the Buddha himself had no such fixed *doctrine* as the 'Five Aggregates' (which I call 'reflections'), and while Buddhism may consist of doctrines the Buddha in fact has no doctrines (authoritative set of beliefs) whatsoever. All his work is instruction in progress, dialogue, facilitation, analogy, parables, questions, metaphors, similes, disagreements, irony, *reductio ad absurdum*, props and non-attaching to views. Like his Greek contemporary Socrates, the Buddha claimed to be nothing more than a kind of midwife to help bring forth what most people are equipped to understand already even though they do not know it. They just need to identify the necessary skills and deploy them. A midwife does not give birth, but helps others to do so. An experienced midwife has no doctrines, only instructions, advice, tools, support, care and the occasional intuition to offer in the actual circumstances of delivering a baby.

So, the Buddha is not of the view, for example, that 'the self is composed of five aggregates' or indeed four, six or even 500 of anything at all. As we shall see, he speaks more generally in terms of a network of 'conditions'—so-called 'co-dependent origination'.

There is no more, and certainly no less, in this particular teaching than the instruction to adopt your meditation posture, concentrate your mind and then mindfully search for the supposed 'inner me'. Persevere and investigate any of those things that you are inclined to identify as the 'real inner me'. Generally, most people will come up with a few candidates, the five most popular (as mentioned above) falling into five categories something like the following, depending on your native language and culture:

- Body: group of physical things such as brain, nervous system, heart, corpse, etc.
- Feelings: group of pleasures, pains, delights, aversions, comforts, discomforts, etc.
- Cognition: group of perceptions, identifying things, knowing, etc.
- Thinking: group of thoughts, volitions, memories, etc.
- Consciousness: group of self-image, attentiveness, discernment, awareness, etc.

This is a motley bunch of so-called aggregates, but you just have to get the principle behind it, as well as make allowance for linguistic differences between archaic Pali and modern English. Keep in mind too that the Buddha did not think in a dualistic way, with mind on one side and world (matter) on the other. In the popular linguistic ambience of ancient times, a naïve non-dualistic form of thinking came naturally to him. But it was a time of transition in all quarters, and an ontological splitting, a kind of *meiosis* (to borrow a term from cellular biology), in which the dualistic conceptual framework was inchoate or embryonic, just making its debut.

In passing, I may be allowed to speculate here that the Buddha was resisting the tide of dualism arising among brahmins and philosopher-wanderers in his time. It seems he was from a significantly different culture to that of the brahmins of what is now north-east Gangetic India; he was a nobleman of the Shakya (*Śākya*) people, in an area now called Nepal. In English we capture this early ontological splitting (which I model as a kind of 'meiosis') by interpreting the concept of '*dhammas*' as 'phenomena'. In my view (outside the remit of this book), in a certain phase of cultural history we see such phenomena naturally tending to emerge as 'me' (I-me-mine). But there is no absolute necessity about this natural inclination, and that means the Buddha can drive in a wedge, or try his best to do so.

14.3 *From Ignorance to Arrogance*

Here we are in the twenty-first century in which the dominant civilization has allowed the ontological *meiosis* (the slide into dualistic understanding of reality) to reach its self-destructive finality. Living as we do now, in a period in which a scientific and technological conquest of nature is taken to be common sense, the deluded concept of 'me', is much more sophisticated than a mere 'I am my body'. We now hear that 'I am my genes' or 'I am my brain' or even 'my brain-waves'. Instead of 'I am my pleasures and pains', we may have 'I am my sexuality' and 'I am a celebrity' or 'I am a tourist' (or a 'Buddhist pilgrim'). Instead of thoughts we may have 'I am a rational being' or 'a thinking thing'. Instead of 'I am my will' we may have 'I am a powerful being' or 'I am a victim' or 'I have my rights'; and instead of 'I am consciousness' we may have 'I am energy', 'I am information', 'I am an autonomous agent' or a species of 'artificial intelligence'.

The Buddha knows that many people, perhaps most, do not go around *believing* that they have a 'real inner me' somewhere inside, although many people if questioned will refer rather vaguely to a 'soul', 'inner self' or 'true self'. Most people, no doubt, never think about it at all. His point is that this kind of attachment *shows itself* in our human behaviour, relationships, societies, institutions, priorities, way of speaking and thinking, and above all our self-destructive search for happiness. It is the metaphysical bedrock of our global crisis. In the twenty-first century the chickens have come home to roost. It is like a person who walks into a glass door with a resulting mighty crash and a bruised nose. It is not as though this person *believed* that there was an open entrance. They did not believe it was open, did not believe it was closed and did not believe that perhaps it was open or closed. Their behaviour shows that they *implicitly assumed* there was an open entrance.

We behave *as though* there were some 'real inner me' ('ego') that we have to feed, protect and strengthen. We assume it. It is so powerfully attractive to everyone that theologies, including that of the brahmins and their idea of 'self' (*ātman*), are based on it.

Exposed, the 'real inner me' is this self-replicating dissatisfaction that does not know itself. So it is this whole rigmarole of attaching and craving, acquiring and possessing, that the Buddha is trying to loosen up. But beware: he is not trying to replace one literal belief with an equally ridiculous belief that 'there is no self'. He was well beyond 'either there is a self or there is not'. Unfortunately, there are now too many Buddhists announcing that 'there is no self'. It is that which is 'beyond' dualities that this book is attempting to clarify.

So one way in which the Buddha gets us to loosen up this living-a-life through attaching, craving, clinging, aversion and rejection is with this challenge: 'If you think you have a real inner me or soul then identify it!' In this he must have been talking mainly to those of a religious disposition, especially the brahmins and their followers, and it might be very much the same situation today.

However, in speaking to those who do not profess a belief in such a thing, but nevertheless manifest this attachment in their attitudes and behaviour, he has other teaching and learning strategies, some of which are in his ethics, not to speak of his whole lifestyle. That is another reason that the Buddha's ethical teaching and his meditational teaching are on a par. They address the same unhappy and ignorant features of human life. We should note that, although the Buddha has one (unified) teaching, this one teaching is diversely put across and it is largely the Buddha Dhamma teacher's discernment of the learner's propensities and prejudices that indicates which approach to adopt.

14.4 The Ever-present 'Me'?

It is vital to understand at this stage what the Buddha means to do with this type of 'me' investigation. He is not denying that this sense of me-ness is real as opposed to a psychotic image. There is no other 'me' which is the real one. In a sense, this shifting 'me' embedded in experiencing *is* the real me—for there is nothing else to 'me'. There is no contrast with another thing that *is* the real me, for example 'consciousness' or 'soul'. The Buddha is not detaching mental 'aggregates' from what is actually, ultimately and *truly* 'me'. He is intent on removing the very vestige of a discrete 'me', that is, confront what we take to be a reality of separate things in the Great Container of the universe. He is dissolving the mirror *reflections* that come together as 'me' and thereby he leaves us in aporia—in a 'nowhere to turn' limbo. The 'me' delusion is being snuffed out as it reaches *nibbana*. This is not a nihilistic state of 'nothing' or 'nothingness', for that assumes a 'me' that *knows* nothingness by contrast with something-ness. We cannot conceive this 'gone' beyond something/nothing. How could I (*me*) possibly conceive a state in which there is no discrete 'I' to conceive such a state?

Here we are tempted to *characterize* that which is beyond something/nothing. We may think: perhaps it is the *dharmadhātu*, noumenon, 'God',

Brahman, the Unborn or 'universal consciousness', but of course those too would be conceptions, a 'something', even if a super-something or ethereal non-something. Reluctant as we are, we must accept that what is inconceivable is *inconceivable*, no matter how abstract one makes it. On the question of God, etc. we can see now why the Buddha was silent. It is not that he did not know the answer, nor that he harboured the doubts of an agnostic, but that no answer was possible without the inconsistency of implicitly assuming that which one is denying. We are caught in an aporia, a road-block; one is always 'turned back' at one's own consciousness (on Vipassī's Loop see Table 3 and section 16.10, below).

Let us now practise some simple exercises in 'mindfulness of body'. It is probably prudent not to attempt all of them in one day. Take your time if you really wish to learn.

Exercise 25: Am I My Body?

> Adopt a meditation posture, and pay close attention to your breathing until you attain some clarity and tranquillity. This should take 15 minutes or more. Now shift attention to the following parts of the body in turn. There are three pairs of 'objects'. Spend five minutes on each one—that is, 10 minutes on each pair. Between each pair, make a note in writing of anything that results or does not result from your investigation. You will investigate very closely and continuously, penetrating the actual *ongoing real-time experience*, always letting go patiently of other arisings. Look very closely, and ask yourself 'Is this me?'
>
> (1) The contact of the hands with each other; the contact of the tongue with the back of the upper teeth.
> (2) The top of the head; the middle of the back between the shoulder blades.
> (3) The inside of your brain; your genes.
>
> Do not read the next section until you have tried the exercise, if you wish to learn something for yourself.

You will have some reflections of your own on this meditational exercise. So now you can compare notes with my questions, as follows.

(1) In the actual touching of the hands, which one is touching and which one is touched? Which one is a 'me-experience' behind and doing the touching? Or are there now two of you—one behind each hand? In the actual experience of touching, the bare experience, are there hands or just a touching? What is the bare touching attached to—is it just 'suspended in space'? If suspended, where is the 'you' that it is supposedly attached to? Staying intently with the touching, can I

find any trace of 'me'—that is, of something other than the touching itself? And who is the 'I' that is seeking a trace?

The same questions could be asked of the tongue and the roof of the mouth. Which one is touching, and which touched? And so on.

(2) In paying close attention to the top of the head (without touching it with your hand), could it actually be sensed at all? There may be a momentary sensation of movement from a puff of air or an itch—but what about the top of the head itself? Is there anything there at all or is this something else, namely, the *thought* or mental image of the top of the head? It seems the top of 'my' head is absent so at that moment at least it is not the top of *my* head at all; it is at best only 'my' thought of it. Can that which is absent be me? Can parts of me be absent? Can the whole of me be absent?

The same questions could be asked of the middle of the back between the shoulder blades. There may be the touch of clothes or the chair where there is movement, but otherwise? On the top of my head or in the spot between the shoulder blades, where is this 'me' that is so precious?

(3) Is there a sensation of the brain itself anywhere to be found—that is, apart from a thought about the brain or the mental image of one? I certainly may talk about 'my brain' and indeed it is fashionable to explain all sorts of things about myself by referring to it. But I have never seen it and I cannot feel it. If I did see this unsightly lump of lightly electrified porridge I may well think: 'What on earth does that have to do with *me*. I'm not in there!' Well, am I or am I not? If I recoil in horror from identification with the actual brain, why do I not recoil in horror from this physical thing I call my face? Is it just a matter of familiarity? Familiarity, we recall, is the enemy of insight.

Much the same can be said of 'genes'. Look into yourself, investigate. Can you find any trace of these in ongoing experience? Certainly, they enter appropriately and usefully into certain narrow and specialized kinds of discourse and practice, but the limitation of such a view is often not understood. Surely, nothing could be easier to find than the 'inner me', so why should I have to hold the *thought* (or the theory, in this case) of a complex pattern of genes to be 'me'. If it is doubtful that even the buttocks I am sitting on is me, why should I find invisible genes more convincing? And if the genes were made visible in an electron microscope would they be 'me'?

Conclusion: there is no separate 'me-experience' in or of the body.

14.5 'Why Am I Me'?

In discussion groups I have sometimes been asked this related, solipsistic question: 'But why am I *me*?' In another form it is a question about why *I* should be here 'existing' now. A Buddhist answer in terms of the 'coming together of countless conditions' seems too abstractly objective to satisfy. It is a question that can only arise within a *dualistic* mind-set. It is as though I could find an entirely *subjective* answer to an entirely *subjective* question. That's impossible. Once the subject/object division is put aside and one lives out one's 'embeddedness in everything', rather than thinking about it, the question cannot arise.

There is a logical point that the 'why me?' question overlooks: There is no independent 'me' that could have been somewhere/sometime else. That is, the very idea of it being possible that 'I' could have been somewhere/sometime else assumes an essential, independent and discrete 'me'. To put it rather metaphysically: 'You' are this growth point of the cosmos; there is no choice about being 'at' some other growth point. A growth point has no existence outside the cosmic growth. There is great importance in this point, and one should contemplate deeply on it.

14.6 Who is Letting Go?

While considering such paradoxes, and confronting the second possible identification, I should address another question that may arise: 'Isn't the Buddha's letting-go strategy with the so-called Five Aggregates assuming that there is a "me" to do the "letting go"?' Who or what is "letting go"?'

The mind can helpfully be viewed as nothing but an attaching/detaching/non-attaching process. Letting go or detaching is also a natural process (I do not mean dualistically 'physical'), and does not require a detacher, a separate 'me' to 'do it'. Meditational benefits are attained by a vantage-point leap-frogging action in which some aspect of the 'me' delusion is deployed to support or undermine some other aspect. If, for example, I attach to a fear, or detach from the same fear, although I say 'I attach/detach' this does not imply that there is a separate, independent 'I' that is carrying out the action. Detaching from a fear is attained by deploying some other aspect of 'me', for example an image, memory, breathing technique, to dissolve the fear. You might say it is like conjuring up a friendly ghost to dissipate a nasty one, or a nasty one to dissipate an overly friendly and beguiling one.

So the 'I' of 'I attach/detach' does not have the function of a substantive. It is worthy of note that there are some 'tribal' languages that practically have no independent pronouns, such as I, we, he, she. It seems that they belong to the cultures that do not suffer from the conundrums and consequences of dualistic epistemology, ontology and theology. Their lives are radically different, and it could be that there is little or no 'suffering' as we experience now.

14.7 An Immunity Process

To use another analogy, it is not unlike a biological immunity process: either it undermines the harmful entity, or it undermines itself (auto-immune process). Immunity does not have to happen by the introduction of something from outside. It is 'self-organizing'. And so it is in the case of 'the mind': It is either aberrantly self-destructive (e.g., hatred, greed) or it is supportive in acting as barrier or eliminator to the harmful (e.g., dissolving hatred, greed). The biological immune system is adaptive and 'learns' how to respond, but there is no 'responder'. The attaching and the releasing actions of meditational practice are something like that—there need not be either a separate or discrete attacher and/or releaser.

14.8 Scientism

Given that science has itself become a widespread religion of sorts (scientism, humanism, the prophet supplanted by the techno-hero) it is worthwhile dwelling on this for a while. You may take me to be saying that brains and genes are always irrelevant, or even that they do not exist. I am not saying anything so absurd. There are many specific contexts, such as dealing with disease and injury, in which our *conception* of brains and genes and the myriad physical conditions of life is both relevant and extremely helpful. But here we are in a completely different context. Our question here is not within the biological discourse of disease or injury; it is about what I understand myself to be *ultimately* and whether the question itself has any sense—it is an ethical and existential question. If I misunderstand something so fundamental then a deep-rooted sense of dissatisfaction with life (*dukkha*, suffering) will surely ensue.

In the light of the dominance of modern materialistic science it is easy enough to envision oneself as essentially a bodily or material or physical thing. What goes unnoticed, because of this strong attachment, is the question 'what it is' that conceives body as 'body' or matter as 'matter' in the first place. Here is the tangle of dualism, which the Buddha cuts through by the insights engendered by practising the Noble Eightfold Path and contemplation on that insight.

Because science has provided us with so many revealing physical explanations and predictions and so many useful contraptions and shiny gadgets, we are dazzled by it and fail to grasp its fundamental *limitation*. In doing so we tend to fall into 'scientism', which is an ideology with such a strong attachment to physical explanations that we use them willy-nilly, even when they have no relevance to a particular context. One of its prominent delusory aspects is the conviction that science can arrive at a *complete* picture of the universe, which includes of course my suffering.[2] Here is an imaginary scenario:

Parable 6: What's Really on Your TV?

> I am watching my favourite TV drama. The plot is unfolding from last week's episode and I am wondering how a certain character, Mihai, will react to the discovery that his partner is being unfaithful. Will he be violent, or kill himself, or accept it or...? My friend, Jim Brain, is sitting with me and questions my interest in the drama. 'Sssshhhh!!' I exclaim, not wishing to miss a crucial piece of theatrical dialogue. 'You realize', continues Jim, 'that *really* all this that you are watching is electrical impulses in the TV set that are passing down wires, through capacitors, and photons being emitted by...'. 'Don't talk rubbish!' I retort in irritation. 'No, it *really* is nothing but all the complicated electrical activities going on inside the TV set', says Jim.

Is Jim Brain right or wrong? Well, right or wrong is not a helpful way to approach this peculiar situation. Certainly, everything that appears in the shifting pattern of pixels on the TV screen is in fact caused by all sorts of complicated electrical and electromagnetic things physically going on in the TV. We know this is so because, for one thing, if a capacitor were to burn out or a short circuit to occur, then there would be effects appearing on my screen. My watching of the drama might be seriously disrupted. It is in *that* sort of situation that *it is relevant* to refer to capacitors and wiring and call on the expertise of a TV electrician to fix the problem inside the TV set. However, that does not resolve Mihai's problem of his partner's infidelity. My *understanding of what is going on in the drama* has nothing whatsoever to do with wiring, capacitors and photons.

In this case the irrelevance is plain to see (I hope), which is why I chose it as an analogy. Unfortunately, such irrelevant explanation is all-pervasive in our 'modern' culture, and no more so than where it is more difficult to draw the line between relevance and irrelevance.

We now go to the second identification, approaching it from the angle of 'mine', which would seem to imply a 'me-experience' to which the pain belongs.

14.9 Who Suffers?

In view of what we have learned about nonduality, what can be said about the notion of 'my suffering'? Surely, if anything is mine, it is my suffering? Suffering is subjective: it always belongs to a person, to a self, a 'me'. 'I suffered a lot when ...' is a phrase we hear quite a lot. Earlier in this book I spoke directly of 'suffering', the first Noble Truth. Now, it might seem, I am saying there is no 'self' to suffer. Does this make sense? In view of my models of the Mirror, Waveform and Emergence in this book (see Chapters 13, 15 and 16), how do we now understand this *dukkha*? The first answer is contained in the Mirror Model (nonduality). Here we return for an answer to our previous discussion of the Mirror Model and especially the five reflections (so-called Five Aggregates). In that discussion a Dhamma-oriented reconsideration of suffering would, in large part it seems, fall under the category of 'feeling' (*vedanā*): the group of pleasures, pains, delights, aversions, and so on.

If you do have a pain (back, knee, hip, etc.) then ask yourself, 'Is there here any evidence for an independent me-experience?' Although it is not wrong to speak of 'my pain' in most ordinary contexts, the meaning of such an utterance does not function by drawing attention to an independent, substantive 'me' or 'self'. I should add immediately that this does not imply that there is no cause of the pain requiring medical attention. On the other hand, being able to mentally detach from the pain can be very effective in softening or even eliminating some aspects of pain.

The *attitude* to the pain makes a difference, even a huge difference. There are so-called 'psychosomatic' effects by which the pain is subdued or even eliminated, as though it were something separate from me. If you already have significant pain then try shifting attention to a non-painful part of the body and imagine it warming up or cooling off; or imagine your pain leaving your body and sitting in a chair opposite you. The fact that this can be done does not imply an independent, substantive 'me' that can do these things with the pain. It is another case of 'leap-frogging' to see how a vantage point looks from another vantage point. One might speak less misleadingly of a learned self-adjusting response—and that is sufficient.

Also keep in mind that rather than the mind tricking the body, it also works the other way round: the body habitually 'tricks' the mind, in an example signalling to an amputee that the limb still exists and can be felt and carry pain. This is known as phantom-limb syndrome.

The same could be revealed about pleasure: which our modern society tends to treat as wholly good. Of course, that which is so treated is that which is designated 'pleasurable'. One cannot conceive of objects which are pleasurable *in themselves*. Our consumer civilization is now founded on an aversion to the slightest discomfort, and craving for pleasure, clinging to pleasure, making it real, to be got as much as possible and to be enhanced through science, technology, flying about the planet on 'holidays', inebriation and re-arranging a lot of furniture. Yet we vacillate in the same way: it satisfies, and then eventually it is lost, and then comes dissatisfaction and craving for more—on/off, on/off, on/off—and a futile desperation to make it all 'on' and no 'off'. There is in fact nothing about pleasure that entails an independent 'me' to attach to it—there is simply a natural reflection—as the nature of addiction, fetishism and obsession shows us. Also, we should recognize by now that none of those things are traits of a 'bad', 'evil' or 'difficult' person. Instead, take a leap-frogging vantage point on them, and be detached.

14.10 Cognition, Thinking, Consciousness

We may consider the three remaining identifications together. Like 'body' and 'feelings' they cannot do service as an independent, discrete, enduring and nonphysical entity which is my true or inner self—a self which in principle can leave the body, which in some way supposedly 'contains' it. They all suffer from the same ineradicable problem: they are not enduring things at all; they are the active conditions that constitute the appearance of 'me'. There is no 'true' me besides their formation— their coming together emerges in the appearance of me. It is, you might say, a real appearance. Like the actors on a stage that come together in a situation, knowing, thinking, willing and consciousness are 'real', but they are real *actors*.

I repeat: The Buddha is not detaching 'identifications' from what is *actually* or truly 'me'. He has no aversion for the 'me' that *appears*. He is intent on removing the very vestige of an *independent* 'me'. Thereby, he destroys brahmanism, destroys all theism, and destroys all atheism—at least as they are popularly understood. This is precisely what makes the Buddha a world-historical figure.

14.11 Consciousness—a Special Case?

In present times there is a strong inclination to put forward 'consciousness' as the true, real, eternal 'me'. If this were the case, then surely it would be a strong theme and figure as a powerful conclusion in the *Tipiṭaka*. But that is not what we find. Consciousness is not a special case. It is worthwhile dwelling on this for a while.

If I close my eyes, then my eye-consciousness stops. That is, I am no longer conscious of the cup before me as I was before. With eyes closed, I may say 'I am still conscious of the cup', and this is actually affirming a memory of the cup. What I am now conscious of is a memory, perhaps a mental image. If the memory disappears, then memory-consciousness stops. The same would go for touch-consciousness, smell-consciousness, taste-consciousness, hearing-consciousness, thought-consciousness. In other words, there is no consciousness which is *nothing but* consciousness that could lead an independent existence.

When I am conscious that I am looking at a cup, I comprehend the looking as that which belongs to another; I have made 'I' another one of myself and another to myself. But this cannot be done except in conjunction with an actual looking, hearing, tasting, and so on. In truth, there is no such other. It is as though instead of using a screwdriver for screws, one were to bend it double so that it touches itself. What would it find? It would certainly not find a screw, so it would have no screwing to do. It would find itself, and (if it were alive) it could take this to be something other than that which is doing the touching of itself. When I turn my hand to scratch my shoulder), does that sensation have a life separate from the hand and the shoulder? No.

This is how we are able to be mindful. We raise our awareness (consciousness) of our moving, eating, thinking, desiring, rejecting, seeing, hearing, and so on. Imagine the screwdriver is doing its usual job of screwing in a screw (i.e., seeing, hearing, thinking, and so on) but every so often bends double to touch itself to 'see' what it was doing. Of course that would interfere with the doing itself, which is exactly what mindfulness does. Mindfulness of anger subdues anger, mindfulness of craving subdues craving, and mindfulness of pleasure subdues pleasure.

These considerations about mindfulness or consciousness do not, therefore, privilege awareness as though it were some special mystical power or an ether pervading the universe. Unfortunately, some Mahāyāna Buddhists have gone in that direction, as have some other spiritual doctrines.

14.12 *The Mirror Reconsidered*

In considering the letting go of the five reflections such as body, we may wonder here about the role of the 'Mirror Model', which I earlier (Chapter 13) presented as a model of nonduality. How does the self-generation (*autopoiesis*) of mindfulness relate to the mirror-reflecting? Without the reflecting capacity the detaching techniques could not work. In fact, this is one way of looking at the nature of attachment. It is reactivity in the absence of any reflection. To return to our 'immunity' metaphor: it is just as auto-immunity could not work without (reflexive) feedback loops. In the *Dhammapada* (a book in the *Tipiṭaka*) we find it said:

> *Fore-run by mind are mental states,*
> *Ruled by mind, made of mind.*
> *If you speak or act*
> *With corrupt mind,*
> *Suffering follows you,*
> *As the wheel the foot of the ox.*
>
> *Fore-run by mind are mental states,*
> *Ruled by mind, made of mind*
> *If you speak or act*
> *With clear mind,*
> *Happiness follows you,*
> *Like a shadow that does not depart.*[3]

This can be seen as another version of Vipassī's Loop (see Table 3 and section 16.10, below). Nothing goes beyond consciousness, in the obvious sense that every investigation—however scientifically well-evidenced, objective or abstruse—is ultimately a conception, the result of *conceiving*. That truth, that general background reflection, indeed that human capacity, is not a discrete 'me' or any kind of substantive thing. It is the embedded potential to reflect and is precisely what we referred to as the mirror. It is also a natural loop of activity, a feedback, a turning back. (And for that reason this account here is a meta-conception. Trying to explain at this level one's only option is to deploy a conceptual model.)

How can one assert that mind foreruns or shapes objects and at the same time it is possible to detach mind? There is nothing there that qualifies as some kind of discrete substantive thing, 'the mind'. This should be clear if one has grasped the explanations about nonduality. Still, it might come as a surprise, considering how many times this book has already mentioned 'mind' and even given it prime place in some explanations of the Noble Eightfold Path. It might be asked: 'How can we even speak of Right Understanding or View when there is no mind to do the under-standing or viewing?'

14.13 Consciousness

What if we scrutinize the nature of the 'mirror'? That is, if we put up the mirror to the mirror? When a mirror reflects another mirror there is nothing to be seen in it; nothing *can* be seen in it; it is empty. And what about 'me'? The Dhamma argument for consciousness not being me (a 'self') is that 'me' arises only in the *relation* of reflector to thing reflected. In our reflector-model, 'me' is a delusion, but only in the sense that it is what appears in the mirror and is nothing in itself. The seer cannot be seen.[4] Both the seer and the seen have no definable, discrete existence.

Now the question is why should acceptance of this rather cold and contorted epistemological/ontological explanation of the experience of 'being me' make any difference to how I understand my life, understand what is important in my life, dissolve suffering and live my life peacefully no matter what? So much for Right Understanding; perhaps a dose of Right Resolve will help. We come back to this in the last of the eight fac-tors of the Buddha's path of peace (see Chapters 18 and 19).

Chapter 15

Right Understanding: Self and the Waveform Model

15.1 Introduction: Water and Foam

The Buddha did not spend all his time in forests and parks. He wandered about and taught in the watery world of the Ganges plain. Every year it would become flooded. Water cascading from above, water gurgling from below, gushing from left and right. Often, crossing from one place to another was a challenge, and people died trying, as they still do. 'Crossing the flood' became the Buddha's metaphor for non-dually surviving the setbacks of life. He said paradoxically: '*By not halting, friend, and by not straining, I crossed the flood*'.[1]

He must have observed many features of water: waves, foam, raging torrents, streams and rivulets, mist, sudden deluges converging into mighty rivers, drowned bodies, quenching of thirst, washing of robes, fish-eating birds, and children splashing about. It is no surprise that aquatic models of thought are scattered throughout his teachings. Here is another:

> *Bhikkhus, suppose that this river Ganges was carrying along a great lump of foam. A man with good sight would inspect it, ponder it, and carefully investigate it, and it would appear to him to be void, hollow, insubstantial. For what substance could there be in a lump of foam? So too, bhikkhus, whatever kind of form [matter] there is, whether past, future, or present, internal or external, gross or subtle, inferior or superior, far or near: a bhikkhu inspects it, ponders it, and carefully investigates it, and it would appear to him to be void, hollow, insubstantial. For what substance could there be in foam?*[2]

One cannot grasp foam. Trying to grasp it results in an empty hand. It is ever-changing, and adopts any form but fleetingly. It dissipates and disappears as easily as it forms. It appears to be something, and we speak of it as such, and yet its substance is uncertain, its existence nebulous. Water itself transforms between solid, fluid and gas. Water also serves as a model of nonduality, both subject and object; as object you are water (about 60%, and can live only three days without it), and as mind there are fluid waves rising and falling, and it is both the source of our thirst (2nd Noble Truth; *Taṇhā* = thirst, craving) and the quenching of thirst (the intermingling flow of the factors of the Path).

We are invited to hold this shifting model in the mind, and then blow it up into a vision of everything around us, even one's own being.

Modern science tells us that everything around us is, in one way or another, a wave or a wave of waves. Not only do fluids exhibit waves but solids are, at a subatomic level, waves; you are nought but waves, and so am I, according to science. Again, we are not doing physics here but using a powerful model, adapted from what is now common scientific knowledge, in order to 'see' our human reality-making from an ultimate (supramundane) vantage point.

The Buddha taught *anattā*, or not-self, by which he meant that the notion of a discrete, separate entity is always delusory. Putting it metaphysically (which the Buddha did not), 'All is One', but presents itself as a vast multiplicity of objects or 'things'. Here is the nonduality of 'the One' and 'the many'. Mundanely, this appearance may be supported by a vague image of the cosmos as the Universal Container, a mixing bowl full of diverse beans and peas, seeds and berries, and other bits and pieces, including you and me. The Dhamma alternative is quite different: no thing exists *in itself*. To see this is to abandon the picture of reality in which ultimately there is the Universal Container of Things viewed by the non-physical entity we call 'the mind' (subject, consciousness, 'I', 'me', the mental, the spirit, the soul). With its abandonment, 'I-me-mine' is subordinated to a wider and unified view in which the grasping and suffering of 'I-me-mine' cannot be sustained.

15.2 Existence, Non-existence

We read earlier that the Buddha once explained to *Kaccāna* that the very notion of 'this world' (universe, cosmos) 'for the most part depends upon a duality—upon the notion of existence and notion of non-existence'. But this notion lacks any wisdom.

Once the boundaries between things are shown to be (useful) constructs of language one can no longer distinguish absolutely between what exists and what does not. The world exists in so far as we conceive it through the innumerable boundaries of language, and does not exist when we see into the working of those boundaries. Put graphically, it is rather like this: the iceberg exists when we see its icy walls; it does not exist when we see it as just water.

Once I understand the mirroring nature of reality, with 'me' embedded in that nature, I feel uncomfortable with my 'uninstructed worldling' outlook. From that discomfort arises the resolve to find a vantage point which is less uncomfortable. I resolve to adjust my viewpoint. It is as though someone awakes in the night and finds her arm is aching because it is twisted under her own body. She, unwittingly, is the cause of her own discomfort. Awakening to this, sleepy as she is, she resolves to change posture, and release the arm. A peaceful sleep follows.

Our existential trap, and our suffering, reside in the apparent 'thingness' (reification) of the world, of its representation as a mega-aggregate of objects including 'me'. The Buddha counters this misleading metaphor with the concept of *suñña/suññatā* which has been translated into English as 'emptiness'. The Buddha was questioned about this concept by his follower Ānanda:

> Then the Venerable Ānanda approached the Blessed One ... and said to him: 'Venerable sir, it is said, "Empty is the world, empty is the world." In what way, venerable sir, is it said "Empty is the world"?'
> [The Buddha replied] 'It is, Ānanda, because [ultimately] it is empty of self and of what belongs to self that it is said, "Empty is the world".'[3]

I believe that the English term 'emptiness' has had dire negative consequences for any ordinary person's understanding of the Buddha Dhamma. A positive rendering of his critique of the 'thingness' view of reality is best confronted with a positive alternative (which, admittedly, has its dangers of literalism too). I suggest the Waveform Model. It is my guess that if one sees in terms of this model then not only will the meaning of 'emptiness' be clear but the resolve to change one's outlook will emerge naturally.

15.3 *The Waveform Model*

In any waveform, as we shall see below, there is always at once both fixity and change. Consider a wave of water: the molecules in the wave are in a fixed cyclic motion but do not move forward, and yet the water moves forward as a series of waves. This represents the emergent relation between closely related phenomena. They appear as separate things (discrete waves) but there is a continuity of energy and motion within each wave which links them. This goes for all apparent objects including myself regarded as object.

Figure 6: Waveform

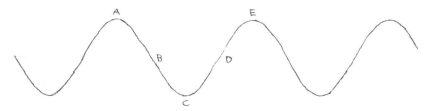

If our way of seeing the world as a kind of container in which there are objects, among which is 'me', it then seems we must proceed by preserving and strengthening ourselves. However, there is an alternative.

Exercise 26: Wave Motion

> Look at any wave motion. It could be on the surface of the sea, a river, a lake or pond, a swimming pool or even in the kitchen sink. If we look, for example, at waves on the sea they appear as identifiably distinct and different 'things'—to which we can give a name: 'wave'. One wave is different from another. One wave might capsize your boat while another does not. As you look at the waves ask yourself: 'Are these separate and independent things?' In what ways could they be described or not described in that way?

In Figure 6 we have a diagram of a typical wave motion. At B a wave is disappearing, at C it has gone but another is about to reappear, at D a wave is growing, and at E it has reached its climax. And so it continues. What is the relationship between the wave at climax A and that at climax E? If we were of a poetic disposition we might say E is A 'reborn'. There is no essence that has independently moved from A to E (like some kind of 'wave-soul'). And yet there is 'kinship' between A and E, because E emerges from A and is *dependent* on it and there is nothing in E that is not in A and the waves before it. We could say A and E are 'not-one, not-two'.

A wave, then, is *identifiable*, it is not nothing at all, and one can rightly say 'Look, there's a wave, and there is another one following it'; still, it is also true (without contradiction) that it is *not a discrete,* separate thing like a ball on a field or a rock in a bag.

The image in the analogy serves to help us let go of another delusory image, the image that has captivated and dominated humanity for thousands of years, one in which the self or soul is of an *entirely* different nature from 'matter' or 'body' (just as the lump of ice might be regarded as of an *entirely* different nature from the water it floats in). In the Buddha's way of expressing the matter, every object is, with insight, seen as *empty* of any 'self', self-existence, essence, discrete core, separateness or independent reality.

15.4 *Slipping Knot*

Here is another analogy, which takes advantage of the appearance and disappearance of the same slip-knot. This is most effective if you treat it as a physical exercise.

Exercise 27: Slipping Knot

> Tie a simple loop knot in the centre of a string, as in the top image of Figure 7. Imagine that you (or indeed any other *thing*) are that knot. It certainly appears as a distinct, separate, independent 'thing' of sorts. I can identify it and name it as a 'knot'. Now I start pulling on both ends. The knot becomes smaller and smaller until in the bottom image it has disappeared. Where is the knot now? Has it gone (non-existent, dead) or is it still there in the string (alive, existing)?

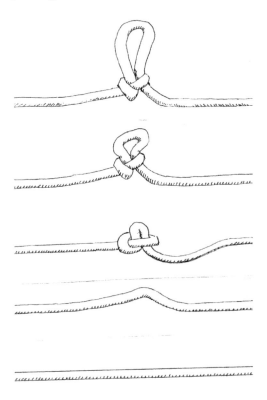

Figure 7: Slipping Knot

There is nothing in the knot that is not in the string. So we cannot say that the knot is independent of the string. Yet the knot appears to have had an identity and existence of its own. When we tied the string the knot emerged—it was 'born'. When the string was pulled the knot 'died'. And yet nothing, at bottom, has changed. So it is with birth and death. In a sense, you cannot die and that is so because you were never born. Our ordinary common-sense way of understanding is not wrong; it is just shallow. It is much less than wise, and from that position compassion and peace cannot fully arise.

I earlier mentioned the relation of iceberg and ocean (see section 13.8). I now present an exercise based on that idea.

15.5 Ice in Water

Another analogy is provided by the relation between ice and the water that it floats in. Again, it is best considered as a physical exercise.

Exercise 28: Ice in Water

> Take some lumps of ice from the refrigerator. Place them in warm water. At first the lumps are things in the water—that is, different from the water— then they gradually melt and we see that they are nothing but water. We could refreeze the water, and new pieces of ice would appear.

Are the new pieces the same or different from the previous pieces of ice? They are different in some ways, but then they are still the same thing, water, and it is all one. When the ice lump melts is there some non-physical essence that waits around invisibly, waiting to re-emerge in the new freezing water? Of course not.

I know that there will be readers, understandably fallen into the jaws of scientism, who will immediately give physical or mathematical *explanations* for the Knot, Ice and Möbius Strip models. These explanations may be true, but are not relevant here. I will say it again: these are analogies for *insights into the nature of ultimate questions*, not physical experiments for the purpose of causal explanation.

15.6 On Not Pinning Things Down

What the Buddha means is that it is a misconception, and a misconception that leads to craving, attachment and clinging, to understand what is around us as a collection of separate, independent, self-subsisting things, each with an existence of its own. He is not saying that the world is empty in the sense of containing nothing. He is not saying that ultimately there is nothing. He is not a nihilist. He does not really want to discuss the futile question of whether the world is ultimately full of something or ultimately empty of anything. Our own meditative investigation shows us that we cannot pin anything down, not even our very selves, as having any separate existence. He is not saying that they have no existence in the ordinary context, but rather that they do not have the independently individualized kind of existence we *assume* that they do, an assumption manifested in our behaviour.

The Waveform Model is logically similar to the Mirror Model in the way it deflates duality. Substantiality is entailed by duality, for in the duality view things are either physical (substantial) or mental (insubstantial), either object or subject. 'Emptiness' is shorthand for the actual non-substantiality of anything one takes to be a self-subsisting external substance, a discrete entity in the universal container. Not-self, for example, as I said before, does not mean 'there is no self' in the sense that 'self does not exist', for that is misleadingly to cast the nondual point in terms of dualistic language.

I too have perhaps presented the matter rather too metaphysically here, and we must be careful because the Buddha is not in fact presenting us with a 'theory of the physical universe' or something of that kind. He is, as he repeatedly reminds us, trying to do only one thing: get to the root of our perennial dissatisfaction and bewilderment. It is peace he is after. In brief, it is a lifetime of frustration to try and fixate an unfixable world and an unfixable life. However, the frustration ceases when we cease trying to fixate or overcome them without awareness of the underlying truth. It is subdued to the same degree that the fixing is subdued. There is nothing more in 'emptiness' than this, and that is more than enough to accept, understand and live by.

15.7 No Soul?

Many people would perhaps recoil in horror at such a claim as 'there is no self' or 'there is no soul'. The fact is that it is not simply a case of there being one or there not being one—this dichotomy arises only if we insist on dividing experience into things that exist (independently) and that do not (at least not now or yet). Exercise 25: 'Am I My Body?' above may have led the reader to the unsettling conclusion that if there is no substantive 'me' then nothing matters—I can do whatever I like! So it will be a relief to know that that is not what the Buddha taught, as we have seen. What does this idea of insubstantiality or emptiness entail for the very Western concept of 'soul'? What, indeed, does the Buddha say about 'soul'?

Classical text: The Middle Way

The Buddha says:

> If there is the view, 'The soul and the body are the same', there is no living of the holy life; and if there is the view, 'The soul is one thing, the body is another', there is no living of the holy life. Without veering towards either of these extremes, the Tathāgata teaches the Dhamma by the middle: 'With birth as condition, [there are] aging and death'.[4]

What does this text mean? Let us deploy the foregoing analogies. We could start by taking the ice-in-water metaphor to clarify the Buddha's critique of the common-sense 'inner self' or 'inner me' or soul or mind. (I realize we could make fine distinctions between these, but for our purposes we do not need to do so.) The question we ask is whether the lump of ice and the water of the ocean are the same or different, or perhaps both the same and different, or even neither the same nor different. The most important point is that, while the ice lump is clearly distinguishable from the water, it is in fact nothing but the water. There is nothing in the ice lump that is not in or of the water. Equally, there is nothing in the water that is not in or of the ice lump. We might say that ice is potentially water and water is potentially ice.

Now, what if there were people who assumed (not having really examined the matter) that the ice lump is quite a separate kind of thing, independent of the water? What if they were puzzled by the disappearance of the ice lump as the water warmed up and concluded that the ice lump then existed somewhere else, perhaps as an ice-ghost or in an ice-world beyond the physical world we know? We could understand their puzzlement as well as the speculations offered. But they would be based on a misunderstanding and, more importantly, based on a deep fear. It is the fear of death, of annihilation. If the ice lump could speak, it would speak of its dread as the sun begins to shine.

We could ask similar questions about the knots in the string. If one knot disappears and another reappears, is there an independent non-physical essence that passes from the first knot to the second? That would be reincarnation of a sort. But it is a muddled view. I suppose one could say that the first knot is 'reborn' in the second knot in the sense that they are both nothing but rope; they have an affinity with each other. Perhaps this is what the Buddha meant by 'rebirth', as opposed to the reincarnation of the brahmins ('Hindus'). But I think it could be misleading to speak about 'rebirth' nowadays since it has come to be widely interpreted as 'personal reincarnation' even within most of Asian Buddhism.

The analogies are meant to help us see that there is an alternative way of looking at this question of birth, death and the 'soul', a way in which all our puzzlement and fear may disappear. For there is a completely different way of seeing in which it is not the case that something (e.g., 'me') is mysteriously created in the world and is then annihilated.

If one would like a positive image of this state of affairs, here is one. Instead of a container, imagine an endless ocean full of swells and currents, in which the only apparently different 'things' that appear are *of* the ocean itself: waves, ice lumps, sea spray, mist, fog, rain, whirlpools, hail, snow, sleet, slush, icebergs. All of this is one thing: just water, nothing but water. Everything appears and disappears in the way a lump of ice in water does. That is, it does *not* disappear and appear as we ordinarily think! In a sense the ice lump was always there and always will be there; as a 'potentiality', if you like.

Chapter 16

Right Understanding: The Emergence Model

16.1 Emergence

The Buddha tries to show us *how* the dualistic ontology of I-am/It-is ('me' and the 'world out there') is sustained and replicated. His account, which no doubt generations of Buddhist scribes have constructed and reconstructed in the doctrine of 'co-dependent origination' (Pali: *paṭiccasamuppāda*), is intended as an account of *how* ignorance of the mirror of suffering is perpetuated. The 12-linked form passed down to us is an ingenious model for its time. It has survived 2,500 years but it is not directly intelligible in *present* cultural circumstances, certainly not more intelligible than some of those ontological accounts given by early Greek philosophers such as Empedocles.[1]

I think the best approach is to 'get' what point the Buddha was making with this teaching, and then apply it in life. After all, the reason that this account is important is wholly practical: knowing even roughly how the delusion emerges and is sustained shows us the way to undermine the replication of the delusion and suffering. All the meditational and contemplative methods of the Buddha are aimed at dislodging links in the chain of emergence and dissolving the I-me-mine delusion. You might say it is *all* co-dependent origination. What a brilliant model in the cultural circumstances of the late Iron Age!

The general point being made by this 'chain of conditioning' is that 'one thing leads to another' in our construction of a sense of separate selfhood. What exactly leads from one to the other is mostly up to you to find out by meditation and mindful living. It is rather like this: take out any stretch of wiring in an electrical circuit and the electrical power stops (*nirodha*), the electrical machine grinds to a halt, and peace reigns. Since there were no man-made electric circuits in the Buddha's time we could revert to his own analogy: stop putting fuel on the fire, and the flames come to an end. Reduce and stop self-centred words, thoughts and actions and then the energy in the circuit of suffering life comes to a halt: *nibbāna*. Co-dependent origination has no other purpose, and it is certainly not a theoretical whim.

Since the Buddha is not a dualist, but a rather inchoate nondualist, he does not distinguish elaborately between subject and object, as I mentioned earlier. This means that it is never wholly clear to us, as habitually dualistic moderns, whether his account of co-dependent origination is about 'objective' psychological or physiological or even cosmic factors interlinked in a chain or network, or about purely *conceptual* (or mental) linkages. (This is not meant to be a negative judgement on the Buddha's thinking—quite the contrary.) No amount of analysis of the *Tipiṭaka* will resolve this for the simple reason that the Buddha's entire thought-world was *meiotic* (see Appendix 2: 'Glossary of Neologisms'). The Dhamma is Natural Law, meaning, as mentioned earlier, that the cosmos is not just a physical entity but a morally charged one, an ethico-cosmos. We see this clearly in his account of co-dependent origination.

16.2 Classical Version of Co-dependent Origination

The chain of links in their most common English translations (Pali originals in brackets) are:

1. Ignorance (*Avijjā*)
2. Volitional Formations (*Saṅkhāra*)
3. Consciousness (*Viññāṇa*)
4. Name and form (*Nāmarūpa*)
5. Six senses (*Saḷāyatana*)
6. Contact (*Phassa*)
7. Feeling (*Vedanā*)
8. Craving (*Taṇhā*)
9. Clinging (*Upādāna*)
10. Existence/Becoming (*Bhava*)
11. Birth (*Jāti*)
12. Ageing and death (*Jarāmaraṇa*)

16.3 One Thing Leads to Another

The important thing is to see for oneself that, taking for example links 6–10, *contact* with the pleasant (e.g., sex and chocolate) results in pleasant *feelings*, the feelings feed *craving* for more of them, which in turns leads to a *clinging* to them (and the potential pain in being deprived of them), which sustains the continuing growth (*bhava*) of the cycle of dissatisfaction (*saṃsāra*). Being aware of such a cycle in all its epicyclical diversity gives one the potential power to 'pull out a plug'. For example, pull out the 'contact' plug (perhaps by withdrawing into rigorous monastic practice as a monk or nun) or let go of the 'clinging', and the cycle falters and flutters and eventually disappears in a vanishing point.

16.4 *The Emergence Model*

The modern scientific methodology known as Complexity Theory,[2] and its concept of 'emergence', presented here in broad outline, might provide some readers with a clearer picture of the network of principal conditions underlying the delusion-making cycle of *saṃsāra* than the unwieldly doctrine of 'co-dependent origination' in its standard account. This new exposition hopefully pitches the Buddha in a new and refreshing light. I would go so far as to say that, in a way, the Buddha was millennia before his time when he presented the linkage of the fundamental conditions of human self-destructiveness, not in terms of reductionist causality—so favoured by centuries of dualistic scientific endeavour in the West—but in rudimentary terms of *complex emergence*. This is a methodological approach which is fairly new in modern science, but I think it resonates with the Buddha's method of laying bare a linked series of co-conditioning that unfolds in delusion and suffering.

The main point of complex emergence is that when large numbers of simple conditions come together ('aggregate' in Buddhist language) they may generate patterns which emerge as more complex units that have properties *quite different from the original units on which they depend*. There is no simple linear causality here, but rather a networking and dynamic formation, the emergence of something new, something that cannot be reduced to the components. You might say, the emergent entity is greater than the sum of its parts. As a result the emergent entity appears to us to have mysteriously arisen (been 'born'), steeped as we moderns now are in our ways of simple cause-effect thinking.

It is true that complex emergence is currently finding its major applications in the sciences, such as biochemistry, genetics and nanoscience, which still largely suffer from the limitations of dualistic and reductionist thinking. Meanwhile, the Buddha's rudimentary version of the layered emergence model takes *nondual phenomena* to be the conditions interacting in complexity. I believe that the perennial difficulties that commentators have had in understanding origination (or 'arising') are largely cleared up if we apply the complex emergence model of understanding—as long as we do not slip back into dualism.

16.5 Transformation

While some Buddhists habitually repeat phrases about the 'rise and fall' of phenomena, what is often forgotten is the sudden transitional or *transformative* phase that can come with a 'rise', or indeed with a fall. This direct observation from meditational practice connects complex emergence with the Waveform Model already discussed. It also helps us to make sense of 'rebirth', not as 'reincarnation' (in which the *same* appears) but as re-becoming (*punabbhava*) or resurgence, which is a matter of a phenomenal entity self-transforming (emerging into) the novel and more complex, sharing sameness and difference; not unlike an acorn self-transforming into an oak.

We can access the idea of emergent transformation from one form to another via the simplest of the Buddha's teachings: closely following the breath. One might, without much thought, conceive the in-breath as one unit and the out-breath as another. It is as though they are two separate events that somehow miraculously remain linked for a lifetime. However, there is no miracle if we practise what I call the Transformation Exercise and see what is happening.

Exercise 29: Transformation

> Now practise mindfulness of breathing as set out earlier (see Exercises 8 and 9). For some minutes pay close attention to each in-breath and each out-breath, one at a time, with clear comprehension of what is going on. Then, we shift our attention slightly but significantly to the moments of transformation in which in-breath becomes out-breath and vice versa. This not easy to do at first. So begin with just one transformation: in-breath to out-breath.
>
> a) Take a deep in-breath, and then hold it, paying intense attention to the process and feel of holding it. There is a build-up; a craving for the out-breath begins to get stronger, dissatisfaction appears. What is this craving? Look into it. The lungs have expanded. The muscular tension which sucked in the air, making the in-breath possible, has now become 'the problem'. The tension has grown and is now 'too much', and relief comes with release of that tension. But that release *is* the out-breath. The out-breath was 'embodied' in the in-breath all along; it was a potential that has now been actuated. There is an inherent continuity between in-breath and out-breath.

b) We could do the same with the transformation from out-breath to in-breath; the latter is contained in the former. The out-breath is an expelling of air, and now that moment of transformation reveals itself. The out-breath and expulsion grow into 'the problem'. Yet the problem is its own solution, for without that uncomfortable and dissatisfying out-breath moment, the very driver of the in-breath could not emerge. The in-breath and the out-breath are co-dependent arisings.

The conclusion we may draw is that there appear to be two events, but at a deeper level there is one. On mindful examination there is no in-breath as a discrete entity or separate event, and likewise with the out-breath. There is a continuously flowing process (a 'becoming', in Pali: *bhavana*) of arising and falling.

16.6 Rebecoming (Punabbhava)

The simplest way to approach the sometimes confusing matter of 'rebirth' is to divide it into two quite different concepts: one is 'reincarnation' and the other is 'rebecoming' (Pali: *punabbhava*). Reincarnation is the personal reappearance (of the *same* person) in this world according to that person's ethical performance in life, and is a view associated with some non-Buddhist traditions. It is inconsistent with the Buddha's teaching, according to which there is no *discrete* object (the 'self') which can re-appear. Re-becoming, however, is a general principle applicable to life and is a manifestation of living things' affinity with each other. In the case of human beings this affinity also includes our ethical behaviour in two ways.

Firstly, since my action is nondual, whatever I do is immediately reflected in the present mundane 'me'. For example, if I am angry or greedy I suffer the greed or anger at the time of attaching to it. The greed or anger I express apparently towards some 'external' object or person is in truth (ignorantly) suffered in the mundane 'me'. There may well be 'external' consequences too, but the lesson of life is to be found not out there but in my own inherent suffering behaviour. The same applies to moral goodness. My generosity or calm is good for other people, certainly, but they are always good for me, my peace and wisdom.

Secondly, my actions influence other people, both those around me and future generations. It is my intentional *actions* that re-become, not an identical copy of 'me'. Thus, one generation influences another. Furthermore, a culture is sustained by its values, customs and ethical norms—until there is an emergent transformation.

'Re-becoming' is a general principle of understanding the affinity and inter-connectedness of all living things, which includes the 'ethical' dimension in the case of human beings. Re-becoming can be fleshed out in terms of the 'emergence' concept of complexity, which is what I try to demonstrate below.

Concerning my own behaviour: every day I have the choice of becoming anew or replicating my old anxious self. How far events 'on the outside' determine my mundane frame of mind is a measure of how far I have taken on board the Buddha's teaching on the path of peace. However far that may be, it is a relatively good thing.

On the malformed question of 'what happens to me when I die?' see sections 19.2–19.3 below.

16.7 Aspects of Emergence

Emergence may be regarded as the phased movement of formation–transformation–destruction–transformation–new formation, and so on. The Buddha, it seems, was indeed speaking not only of arising/forming and falling away/unforming, but of *transforming*—like the transforming of in-breath into out-breath, molecules into crystals, of an embryo into a foetus, the seed into the tree, or the emergence of the butterfly from the caterpillar. These are natural transformations of the change and growth we see all around us. Such a model would have appealed to him very directly—as he lived in a largely verdant rural society, slept under trees and leafy canopies bearing fruit and birds, and witnessing day-by-day and season-by-season the cycle of destruction and renewal fuelled by the mighty Ganges.

Other features of complex emergence, indicated by current non-Buddhist theorists in the field, also make good sense of Buddhist co-dependent origination: features such as holism, criticality, non-reducibility, and self-organization. I now take these one at a time.

16.7.1 Holism

To see complex emergence at work one needs a more distanced or holistic view of the changes one is examining. The dualistic scientific (physics-modelled) approach is often too close up, and works on the premise that the closer the view the nearer we are to the 'true workings' of an entity or process. It is as though the analytical revelation of more and more refined bits will ultimately reveal the nature of the whole. To take a recent example, physicists having supposedly discovered the Higgs Boson (the 'God particle') and the search is now on (at even greater expense) for 'something' smaller and more 'fundamental'. In my view, however, this whole reductionist approach is a misconception. Very often we need to adopt a wide-angle gaze in order to gain the understanding which a 'microscopic' view cannot produce. The forest is not directly visible in one leaf to one who has not paid attention to the forest before.

The Buddha excelled at taking the bird's-eye viewpoint, a panoramic view of human life and suffering: His awakening that first 'turned the Dhamma wheel' (section 13.3) was a superb holistic insight. The holistic framework of the Four Noble Truths and the Noble Eightfold Path immediately appeared with that transformation of mind. He guides us ultimately to a paradoxical and perspectiveless view, a vanishing point, a point beyond horizons. The long-term wide-view reveals that even the subtlest effects of changes to a process may amount to irreversible novelty. A system is always a process, with subtle changes (*annica*) interacting in apparent stability, but is often poised between stability and instability and only needs a nudge to collapse and transform.

16.7.2 Holism

Criticality is the point in a changing system or process at which there is a sudden, often completely unexpected, change in the properties of the system. It is not just unpredicted but unpredictable. For example, just one molecule may trigger cancer, if other conditions are in place. On the positive side, Dhamma awakening itself happens just like that—in a 'realization'.

16.7.3 Non-reducibility

'Non-reducibility' means that an apparently stable process cannot be wholly accounted for by analytically laying bare and stacking up all its parts. Somehow the process goes beyond its parts.

For example, consider the segment of co-dependent origination: 'contact–feeling–craving–clinging' (see Table 3, below). Craving is not just a collection or aggregate of feelings. Craving is a transformation of an apparent collection of feelings into something new in experience.

While it is true that taking away a link and the whole may collapse, that is too simply expressed. Take away links and keep taking away links and the probability of a collapse increases. And remember the collapse aimed for in the present context is the dual 'me/world' delusion, which is a very great matter. (This collapse also requires the stability and guidance provided by a good teacher and a peaceful, cooperative environment.)

Table 3: Vipassī's Loop

CONDITION	MEANING	PALI WORD
1 Consciousness	Knowing, cognition	*Viññāṇa*
2 Mind-body	Mentality-materiality, individuality, personhood	*Nāmarūpa*
3 Sense-bases	'Six sense-bases' of seeing, hearing, tasting, touching and smelling, plus 'thinking'	*Saḷāyatana*
4 Contact	Between senses and 'outside world'	*Phassa*
5 Feeling	Pain, pleasure, neutrality (not 'emotions')	*Vedanā*
6 Craving	Wanting, lusting, desiring, greed	*Taṇhā*
7 Clinging	Grasping, holding, seizing, gripping	*Upādāna*
8 Becoming	Coming into existence, emerging as real	*Bhava*
9 Birth	Appearing in the world, arising	*Jāti*
10 Death	Ageing and death: decaying, passing away	*Jarāmaraṇa*

But there are many smaller collapses along the way, and many of them are conducive to a more wise and peaceful life.

It is the same with, for example, pleasant, unpleasant or neutral 'feeling'. One cannot reduce the experience of feeling simply to a concatenation of mere contacts. Feeling itself is not to be found anywhere in one contact or even a thousand. But, somehow, pile up the contacts and then feeling—a completely new experiential pattern—will probably emerge.

16.7.4 Self-organization

Self-organization is also a defining feature of complex emergence. That is, there is change in the system/process in which the internal dynamic proceeds on the basis of its own internal principles *without external* direction or determination. Often internal feedback loops are at work. In the realm of science we find accounts of the emergence of a unique snowflake-formation 'from within', or the chemical self-assembly familiar in nanoscience, or the development of the embryo. These are all objective examples. What about the Buddha's nondual subject-object process?

Not only is the human individual's life process inherently self-organizing from the embryonic or infantile level, it becomes *consciously* self-constructing at a certain point, that is, I deliberately go on feeding the sense of self. I cling to my existence, to my I-ness. Self feeds self. Clinging self-organizes into 'becoming', into the proliferation of existence. Nothing external perpetuates this self-solidification. And nothing external brings about its inevitable dissolution and death.

At the highest level of abstraction, in the Buddha Dhamma there is no need for an independent and separate Supreme Being to create, manipulate and sustain the cosmos. Alternatively, we might say in poetic language that the infinitely self-organizing (or autopoietic) development of life forms *is* the Supreme Being.

16.8 The Diverse Relationship of Emergent Factors

Complex emergence does not assume that the relation between one level of emergence and a higher or lower one is structurally always the same. The same point applies to the specific case of the Buddha's co-dependent origination. There is not necessarily a commonality of structure—other than the abstract principles of complex emergence already outlined—between one factor and the next factor. For example, the formal relationship of 'contact' and 'feeling' may not be intrinsically the same as that of the relationship of 'craving' and 'clinging', even if complex emergence is a more accessible way of understanding both relationships. The Buddha only needed a depth or degree of analysis of the factors that was sufficient for his practical purpose of revealing what condition (or aggregate of conditions) was a necessary condition for a higher condition (or aggregate of).

As mentioned above, our liberation comes with the capacity, with the freedom, to cut off the depended-upon and so extinguish the dependent. Thus he had discovered a mental technique for undermining or eliminating suffering (or, in the opposite direction, enhancing the movement towards the peace of non-dependency). What he may not have explored is the possibility that while snipping off links, large and small, in the network may cause the desired cessation of a higher-level dependent, it may also stimulate new connections or activate nascent ones—but not necessarily what one requires. For example, a mindfulness technique applied out of its wider context may possibly solve one problem and create or exacerbate another.

16.9 The Emergence Model as a Whole

Here I make the decision to drop the 12-linked cosmological version of co-dependent origination and adopt instead the 10-linked version said to be stated by an earlier Buddha called Vipassī. It is set out with short comments in Table 3, above. The 12-linked version starts with ignorance (*avijjā*) and ends with ageing and death (*jarāmaraṇa*). Since this is now usually presented in Theravāda Buddhism as a cycle involving 'rebirth' across three lives it leaves us with the question of how one moves from ageing and death back to ignorance. This question has led many, Buddhist and non-Buddhist, into metaphysical theorizing about personal rebirth from one life to another, with the gap being filled by a so-called 're-linking consciousness' (*paṭisandhi-viññāna*).[3] Not wishing to fall into fruitless debate myself, I prefer to lay it aside and present a simple and coherent view of dependent origination, and then cast it into a modern model of 'complex emergence'.

A simple view was provided, according to canonical sources, by a buddha that came before *the* Buddha (Gotama), a buddha called Vipassī. His 10-linked version enables us to focus on a coherent trajectory of self-formation and de-formation (dissolution) in a single human life, a version that is wholly compatible with the core concept of not-self (*anattā*).

16.10 Vipassī's Loop

In what may be the oldest of the *Tipiṭaka* texts on this issue, the Buddha relates to his followers how an earlier buddha called Vipassī had become awakened in a secluded spot when contemplating the sorry state of humanity.[4] What is of greatest significance in Vipassī's Loop, I think, is the role he gives to consciousness (*viññāna*). Suffering, attending to suffering and the end of suffering are all in (or 'of') consciousness. Even if I try to give a scientific account of consciousness still that too is apparently a product of, or situated in, my consciousness. This gives consciousness a special role in deploying meditation techniques, but it does not put consciousness at the top of the tree. For we have already found that I am not-consciousness, and that too has dropped away in *nibbāna*. Consciousness is where we have to 'turn back', as Vipassī realized, for consciousness taken as something in isolation from all else actually ceases. Consciousness is itself a condition for all the other conditions listed. We have discussed 'contact', but it seems here that consciousness is a condition, a without-which-not, for contact. Contact emerges, via some other conditions, from consciousness.

In Vipassī's model there is no reference to the 'ignorance' (*avijjā*) and 'formations' (*saṅkhāra*) we find in the traditional 12-factor model. The picture of conditionality is therefore, in my view, clearer and more consistent without them, and then we are not led into cosmological speculation and religious promises of self-centred personal rebirth.

16.11 Downward Counter-flow

Here we run into an important point about emergence: while we see it in a primary function as developing upwards, in fact secondarily it develops downwards too. This is one reason why the model is called *co*-dependent. (This has also been called 'downward causation' by complexity theorists.) In two simple examples, the character of individual snowflakes determines the character of the accumulating snow, but as the snow accumulates it has a reverse influence on the character of the snowflakes of which it is an 'aggregate' or 'formation'. There again, distinctive individuals are conditions for the development of a family or society; and, once formed, a family or society has its influence on the distinctiveness of those individuals. So in this Dhamma example, consciousness is a condition for contact, but contact has a (sometimes retrograde) influence on consciousness.

In the subtle counter-flow: the becoming of 'me/world' as two (apparent) existents expands, strengthens and ultimately transmutes the clinging; the clinging expands, strengthens and ultimately transmutes the craving; the craving expands, strengthens and ultimately transmutes the feelings; the feelings expand, strengthen and ultimately transmute the contact; contact expands, strengthens and ultimately transmutes the six sense-bases; the sense-bases expand, strengthen and ultimately transmute the individuality; the individuality expands, strengthens and ultimately transmutes the consciousness.

Looking at the whole 10-linked chain of upward conditionality we now see that there is an influential counter-flow, generating a feedback loop that is driving our explosive mania for pleasure, possessions, plastics, power, prizes and prominence.

Thus the delusion of 'discrete self' rests on certain conditions, but once formed it has a reverse influence on those conditions, and this feedback proliferates in personhood and ultimately in society. The ultimate source of our current economic, political and environmental woes thus lies exposed. What excuse do we now have for continuing as we are?

It seems that seeing this fact about conditionality is what woke up Vipassī! The Buddha gives the following account.

Classical text: What Vipassī thought

Then he [Vipassī] thought: ... 'Feeling conditions craving'... 'Contact conditions feeling'... 'The six sense-bases condition contact' ... 'Mind-and-body conditions the six sense-bases' ... 'Consciousness conditions mind-and-body.' And then the Bodhisatta

> *Vipassī thought: 'With what being present, does consciousness occur. What conditions consciousness?' And then, as a result of the wisdom born of profound consideration, the realization dawned on him: 'Mind-and-body conditions consciousness' ... 'This consciousness turns back at mind-and-body, it does not go any further'.*[5]

It is important to acknowledge that this 'turning back' is wholly consistent with the statement in the *Dhammapada*, mentioned earlier, that 'Mind precedes all mental states' (section 14.12).

In our discussion of Right Effort we spoke of unarisen fruitful and unfruitful states, which become arisen when certain other conditions are present. This is not because they *already* exist somewhere ready-made and concealed in us. We might call it instead a pattern of emergence. They manifest as 'tendencies' to anger, envy, pride or patience, love and humility in certain situations and not in others. In making an effort to follow the path we have to learn to acknowledge, recognize and work with these unarisen states and counter-flows, which in fact simply means allowing or not allowing them to emerge where they are potential.

16.12 Ten Links are Enough

In the light of the two-way traffic of emergence (i.e., downward causation as well as upward) we do not have to regard the 'co-dependent origination' doctrine as a cosmologically cyclic process at all. It is much more common sense and connected with actual meditative practice than that. Here is a 10-link schema—what I call the Emergence Model—of how defilement proliferates itself upwardly and consolidates itself downwardly in any mental/physical act. The entire practice of Buddha Dhamma purification is in this small schema.

As I already mentioned, the Buddha was not a biologist or sociologist or historian; he was concerned with the experience of suffering (dissatisfaction, anxiety) of each one of us in our here-and-now ignorance of the way things are. Given his starting point, it was irrelevant to posit something before consciousness, because we would then be trying to give a temporal (time-based) account of things, and thereby falling into the objectivity that accompanies dualism, putting an obstacle in the path of the awakening of others.

The early account of the ten links in the *Dīgha Nikāya*, as an abbreviated account of the Buddha's teaching on emergence, is complete in itself; it does the job. In my view, we find in the *Tipiṭaka* a later mundane attempt to improve on it with another two links. In fact it undermines the very point of his account: meditative insight.

Through duality we attach, and through attaching the impermanence of all things manifests itself, and thus we suffer since impermanence conflicts with our common-sense misunderstanding of reality and our craving for and clinging to solidity and security. If we understand this, then we may try not to attach (ethics); but helpful as that is, it will not go far enough so long as our understanding remains dual and there is no change of heart.

The insight, the key to understanding, is thus the Mirror Model of non-duality. First we must see and acknowledge impermanence (insight meditation), then we must retreat to non-attachment (renunciation), then we shall be in a position to let go of the 'me/world' duality (renunciation of the world is ultimately renunciation of myself). In this deep understanding, a deep level of compassion for myself, for others and indeed all beings is inescapable.

16.13 A Sample of Emergence

This is not the place for an in-depth complexity-analysis of all the principal Dhamma conditions of emergence, were it achievable.[6] But here is an example: the segment of the co-dependent chain of conditions linking the six internal and external sense-bases, 'contact' and 'feeling', may be cast in terms of the principles of complex emergence. In the simplest logical terms, each in this series is the 'without-which-not' (*sine qua non*) of the next, for example if no sense-bases, then no contact and if no contact then no feeling. Moreover, contact *emerges* from sense-bases, and feeling *emerges* from contact in the sense of 'emerge' which we have just discussed. That is, contact *is* sense-bases self-transformed—it is a re-becoming or resurgence. In this transformation we see non-reducible novelty, a top-down holistic approach and self-organization. That is, feeling as such (pleasant or unpleasant sounds, tastes etc.) has qualitative features (pleasantness/unpleasantness) not to be found as such in contact, and contact has qualitative features (especially the duality of contacter-contacted) not to be found in sense-bases. Who could have predicted that contact could or would transform itself, by itself, as its complexity intensified, into feeling? And the same goes for sense-bases self-transformed into contact.

Once we already have contact then, looking top-down, we can see its dependence on sense-bases. But we could not have *foreseen* in the opposite direction, namely, how sense-bases can (and will, as we now know) transform into contact, and contact transform into feeling. In each case the transformation itself takes place all of a sudden, relatively speaking.

Then there is counter-flow: 'feeling' once *established* will have its retro-influence on 'contact' and 'contact' will have its retro-influence on the senses.

This is why in meditation, following co-dependent origination techniques, the well-practised meditator may still be taken aback by the suddenness of his or her joyful insight or aversion and anger under certain conditions, and also be aware of the against-the-stream effort required to nurture or undermine such transformation. Transformations, such as joyful insight or contempt for another, do not depend on the joyful-one or the contemptuous one. They are self-sustaining (autopoietic).

16.14 From Conditions to Assumptions

With sustained practice we have by now understood enough to see how suffering and abiding dissatisfaction arise because of the under-development of a self-organizing dynamic, namely, self-aware mental actions to undermine craving and support freedom-from-craving. But we may wonder why this ignorance is so stubborn and how it sustains itself, going on and on through a life, through millions of lives, through self-destruction, through cruelty, torture and wars, through centuries, through millennia, on and on.

Here we may speak of the DNA of Ignorance. Just as biologists tell us that the living organism replicates itself by means of DNA, so the Buddha tells us that ignorance and suffering are replicated by means of a linked series (or, rather, a network) of conditions. However, I suggest that there are autonomous, semi-autonomous and near-autonomous conditions. Conditions that can be 'wilfully' changed, I prefer to call 'assumptions'.

Once feeling is transformed into craving, craving to clinging, clinging to becoming, we enter the realm of *conscious elaborations* of wants and aversions, which settle into *mental* habits. What emerges is a web of assumptions resting one upon another. Craving, clinging and becoming (entering existence; being viewed as 'real') are more accessible, more responsive to dissolution by conscious understanding and effort. These transformations are slower and are the product of socialization, imagining, metaphor-making and sharing, and conceiving. In short, these conditions are a network of *assumptions*. They are still conditions, as we have already considered (*sine qua non*), but at a higher emergent level, now taking the form of mental attachments, assumptions. A closely attached assumption (belief, dogma, expectation) can be as strongly glued to an I-me-mine identity as a sound-sensation or a sense of contact with the 'real'. This is why the Buddha's meditative efforts are mainly concentrated in this more accessible area: the practices of mindfulness, five reflections and five hindrances.

These assumptions are not meant to be understood as physical or material conditions; it is not a physical process in the dualistic sense. It is a case of one basic *assumption* in the common-sense understanding resting on another, usually implicit, assumption. It is a house of cards in which each card is a common-sense assumption. We dwell in this house of cards and try to make ourselves secure there. This does not and cannot work very well, for it is fragile, shifting and unstable.

16.15 Strange Shopping

The assumptions manifest themselves in the fundamental features of our behaviour. They are not explicit beliefs. Before we examine the Buddha's account, let us consider a simple and mundane example. Remember that, like all metaphors and analogies, it has limitations and should not be taken too seriously. Next time you go shopping, try to spot your own very basic and common-sense assumptions—in fact, you could do this in any situation at all. It helps to break down the familiarity (reality) that is the enemy of meditation.

Parable 7: Strange Shopping

> I feel hungry. I look in the fridge and it's nearly empty (I assume there is a fridge where I last saw it, and that it contains food and that the whole complicated system by which food arrives in my fridge will continue). The fridge having food in it immediately depends on my putting food in it, so I go for food to the supermarket. (I assume there is a supermarket and that it is open.) I enter the supermarket and seek my usual items. (I assume these are still in the supermarket and in their usual places.) I collect the items and go to the cashier. (I assume there is a cashier.) I show the items to the cashier, she tells me the cost and I give her money. (I assume money still works, and that she will price the items and take my money.) I then put the items in a bag and head for the door. (I assume there is a bag, that I am allowed to do this, and that I won't be stopped.) When I get home I open the food and start to make a meal with it. (I assume that it is edible and non-toxic.)

Familiarity is the enemy of mindfulness. If I could be fully mindful I would be aware of layer upon layer of assumptions. Ordinarily, without them I would be at a loss—I find myself very reluctant to 'let go' of them or too many of them.

Let us imagine too, for a moment, that some of my shopping assumptions are wrong. I go again to the supermarket. This time the cashier will not take my money and she will not give a reason for this. (I assume that she ought to give me a reason.) Or, this time, on the way out, I am stopped at the door and my food items are emptied by a security man onto the floor. I note that he does this with all the customers, who don't mind this but simply walk out of the store without their shopping. 'Of course, you can't take them out!' he states with a bland smile. When I object, he replies as though I am a space-alien: no one is allowed to take out their food items. There is no reason for this; it is just not how things are done. Or, when I open my food items at home I find that they are all made of plastic and *papier-mâché*—there is nothing edible in the bag. Outraged, I take the bag of shopping back to the shop, but the manager and assistants look at me with a condescending grin: '*Of course* they are inedible—what did you expect!'

This has the feel of a bizarre nightmare. An interconnected series of assumptions has failed me. Yet, it never occurs to me that this world, this 'me', and this division between the two also form an interconnected series of assumptions and are also dream-like. They may also fail me when I least expect it; or I may let them go in meditation and discover impermanence, insubstantiality, the stress and insecurity of holding on and the nonduality of the mirror.

16.16 The Chain of Ignorance

We may notice some aspects of the shopping analogy. First, it is set out in a simple serial order. In truth the situation is not like that, because many different assumptions are interlinked in different ways and at different levels. They form a net, not a chain. Second, 'assumption' does not always mean the same thing, and there are many different kinds of assumption that serve to hold everything together in an impermanently coherent picture. Third, if we penetrate through the layers of assumptions we reach a point at which a further assumption cannot sensibly be found. In the dream-like shopping analogy, no one ordinarily asks the supermarket cashiers why one has to pay for goods, and if the cashiers were asked they would be much more likely to suspect they were dealing with a deranged or joking customer than that a serious reply were required.

It is as though at that point my understanding is blocked. I am up against an unanswerable question. Here is the limit of philosophy, theology and science—and arrival at the departure gate of insight.

I suspect that when the Buddha was asked a question such as 'What is death?' or 'What happens to me when I die?' he then gave his account of a net of underlying assumptions, if he thought the listeners were ready for it. What he did not try to do was give a 'sensible' answer, for he knew that the question itself went beyond the assumptions that give sense to questions.

16.17 Beginning and Conditionality

The question 'What is the beginning?' is unanswerable in the context of existential insight. We are embedded in a loop of conditions and assumptions; we are nought but conditions and assumptions. That loop is the cycle of human suffering engendered by our own ignorance of the loop itself. The consciousness assumption brings us up against this enclosure, but it is not itself the beginning or the foundation (as idealists maintain); the chain of ignorance is really a net, not a series. We can therefore understand what the Buddha means when he says that this cycle of suffering (*saṃsāra*) has no discoverable beginning. The concept of 'beginning' does not apply.

The Buddha is reported to have said:

> ... this saṃsāra is without discoverable beginning. A first point is not discerned of beings roaming and wandering on hindered by ignorance and fettered by craving. For such a long time, bhikkhus, you have experienced suffering, anguish and disaster, and swelled the cemetery. It is enough to experience revulsion towards all formations, enough to become dispassionate toward them, enough to be liberated from them.[7]

This insight that there is no discoverable beginning also undermines our common-sense notions of birth and death.

Chapter 17

Right Understanding: Self-Evaluation

17.1 Self-evaluation

In order to evaluate your own personal development of the movement towards the realization of *nibbāna*, you may now take advantage of the fourth Foundation of Mindfulness. It provides us with a self-evaluation tool. (The reader may recall that the first, second and third foundations are discussed in Chapter 10.)

17.2 Transcending

If the Path is not 'all about me', what is it about? The fourth Foundation of Mindfulness provides us with the opportunity of *evaluating* how far we have gone between assuming 'me' (an 'assumption' in the sense mentioned earlier) and letting go of that assumption. Be careful: there is not a 'not-me' (*anattā*) which contrasts with 'me', for that would make the mistake of assuming 'not-me' to be another thing on a par with other assumed (conditioned) substantive things which include 'me'. Despite the impression given in some quarters, there is nothing more to 'not-me' than letting go of an independent discrete 'me'.

The concept should be easy to grasp, but letting go in this case is very hard—even for dedicated monks and nuns—for it is a letting go of a consolidated boundary-assumption, an assumption upon which all other assumptions rest. This boundary cannot be crossed in the way smaller assumptions can be, but can be *acknowledged* and its implications can be acknowledged and conclusions drawn, for example that physical science is epistemologically incompletable (see Chapter 14, note 2). This is a case of having *insight* into that boundary, of acknowledging its necessity in *any possible view* of a 'world out there', and is prior to any knowledge of what things there are in the world. The evaluation provided by the fourth Foundation assists us in attaining that insight, because it takes us back through the main aspects of the teaching in a manner engaged with our principal meditational practice. For a lay person one may now at least learn to *hover* between me and not-me.

17.3 The Fourth Foundation of Mindfulness (*dhammas*)

Let us go a step further, into the fourth Foundation, which is usually called 'mindfulness of all *dhammas*'. This does not mean mindfulness of anything and everything that arises, or 'all phenomena' (as some have assumed), but means mindfulness of the natural sub-laws of the encompassing natural law known as the Dhamma—the cyclic replication of suffering and the release from it. The point of practising in this leap-frogging way is that it is one very effective way of dissolving the veil between 'me in here' and 'all that out there'—a veil which is elaborated as 'the problem of dualism' by philosophers and theologians.

Mindful awareness, we have discovered, can evaluate its own progress to liberation. This is not a passing of judgement in the negative sense, but a form of self-learning. Long exercise in the Buddha Dhamma, from many of its angles, reveals to us the Dhamma itself in its most unblemished and translucent facets. In the fourth Foundation (or root) of Mindfulness we find set out the most significant of these facets of the Dhamma itself—the Dhamma as it is lived when we actually practise it, firstly dimly, then fragmentarily, and finally holistically. It is useful to have labels or titles for new discoveries, since most people will hardly grasp what you are pointing to without them.

17.4 The *dhammas* of Self-evaluation

Self-evaluation of the practitioner's understanding of the Noble Eightfold Path is provided for by revision and contemplation of five essential categories of the Buddha's teaching, much of which we have already covered. These are as follows:

- The Five Hindrances
- The Seven Factors of Enlightenment
- The Five Reflections (so-called 'Five Aggregates') Subject to Clinging
- The Six Internal and External Sense-bases
- The Four Noble Truths.

We now undertake our revision of the Path by examining these one at a time, one section for each category (17.4.1–17.4.5).

17.4.1 The Five Hindrances

The doctrine of Five Hindrances were covered above in section 4.5 'Unfruitful States'. Now we see that being *mindful* of the arising of the five hindrances of desire, ill-will, laziness, worry (restlessness) and doubt is to be *aware in oneself*—as an inner knowledge—of the natural inclination to undermine or oppose the inner changes necessary to move towards an awakening. The 'Five Hindrances' is not just a doctrine or set of rules; it is *resistance* to letting go of 'me'. It is clinging to 'me'. It is an experience of the boundary itself. We see that each hindrance is not a matter of choice but a human tendency, a natural tendency, a condition shared by all human beings. It is not 'you' that is clinging—clinging happens. Now with mindfulness and an understanding of conditionality and emergence we see for a fact that the 'hindrances' *will* arise given half a chance. We see too that if we go with that tendency it will multiply, and suffering of some kind will follow sooner or later.

17.4.2 The Seven Factors of Enlightenment

With our new understanding we get a higher vantage point and watch ourselves countering the hindrances with the Seven Factors of Enlightenment (Awakening), namely, mindfulness itself, keen investigation of the arising *dhammas*, effort or energy, joy or happiness, calm, concentration and equanimity or balance. This is the positive side of letting go of 'me', sprouting positive experiences of the freedom and peace of not-clinging—of the buoyancy of a fish, of the gliding of a bird. More precisely, in this experience I am hovering, for it is still 'me' that is enjoying the release and the freedom. However, it is a dispersing, liquefying, out-of-focus 'me'. Without this nebulous 'me' even self-evaluation would be impossible, but it is a transformed (provisional) me.

We are mindful of the efficacy of mindfulness—we pay attention to its benefits and watch its obstacles fade away. So our confidence grows and our equanimity grows too. That is, we are careful not to throw ourselves out of balance with likes and dislikes, attractions and rejections. We must continue to make an effort and apply energy. If we do not apply our energy then the adhesive energy of *saṃsāra* (replicating dissatisfaction) will overcome us.

17.4.3 The Five Reflections

The five reflections (so-called Five Aggregates), as we saw in Chapter 13, trap us in cyclical patterns of suffering, patterns which constitute 'me'. This cycle is called *saṃsāra*. Mindfulness of the naturally reflective workings of our own minds reveals the sources of these patterns, thus providing the potential for wisdom, choice and liberation.

Our natural tendency to pleasure, praise, fame and gain and revulsion for pain, blame, ill-repute and loss result in a craving for the former and anxiety about the latter. There is nothing more to 'me' than that, and yet that natural clinging is the base of my reflexive experience of 'me'. It is not 'me' that is *performing* the craving for the attractant; that natural process of clinging and identifying *is* me. No clinging, no me. Mindfulness of mind reveals the clinging of (not dualistic clinging *to*) the Five Aggregates: identifying 'I' and 'me' and 'mine' with (1) body and physical things, (2) pleasures and pains, (3) knowing and perceiving, (4) thinking and willing, and (5) consciousness.

17.4.4 The Six Sense-bases

The six sense-bases referred to many times in the Buddha's teachings are: eye (seeing), ear (hearing), nose (smelling), body (touching), tongue (tasting) and 'mind' (recognizing). In the light of what we have learned, even the senses cannot be what they appear to be. The Buddha has not provided us through enormous effort the teaching on nonduality just to let an *objective* 'sense-base' through the back door. His entire viewpoint would collapse if that were the case. Duality supports the illusion that it is the sense-bases which independently provide us with 'information' about 'the outside world'. But now we know better. If there is ultimately no mind/world division then there can be no discrete mechanism that feeds 'mind' with 'knowledge' of 'the world'. The awakened one sees each sense in full context of Right View and all of the Noble Eightfold Path. One should not take a sense-base to be some sort of objective ground for our view of 'the world', but one should see each sense-base as it actually is. The Buddha says:

> Bhikkhus, when one does not know and see the eye as it actually is, when one does not know and see forms [material stuff] as they actually are, when one does not know and see eye-consciousness as it actually is ... then one abides inflamed by lust, fettered, infatuated, contemplating gratification...[1]

It is not the senses that are the channel of 'reality', as we ordinarily think, for there is no such channel; instead there is insight and the 'direct knowledge' that comes with meditational practice.[2]

Here I need to draw the reader's attention to 'mind' as a 'sense-base'. It might seem odd to include 'mind' among the sense-bases, as the Buddha does. In the modern dualist view, 'mind' is the 'subject' side of the subject-object division. However, this shows us that the Buddha's thinking is radically different from ours today. In the Buddha's meiotic nondual view the senses are not conceived as data-gathering tools located in the material, external world, transmitting data to the non-physical sphere, the mind. The mind, in this context, is not to be contrasted with the non-physical, inner world of thinking, imagining, remembering, and so on. Instead, the Buddha conceived the matter in terms of functions. Each of the six has a formative function, and as the co-condition of mind-objects (e.g., memories treated as objects like trees or rocks) the mind is in the same category as, say, hearing, which is conceived as the function or co-condition of hearing-objects, i.e. sounds. But, importantly, for the Buddha the whole dualist way of looking at our experience is ultimately delusory, and plays a fundamental role in creating the 'me'. Just to stretch our understanding of a nondual reality, I here play with a couple of simple models, which are not to be taken literally.

17.4.4.1 Newton's Cradle

Newton's Cradle (the swinging balls ornament; see below) is fascinating because it does not behave according to expectations. The first ball moves and so does the last one, but all the others remain perfectly still. That seems strange. So what has passed from the first ball to the last? In fact, no substantive entity has travelled. (In this case it is, in scientific terms, the arising of 'kinetic energy'.)

Figure 8: Newton's Cradle

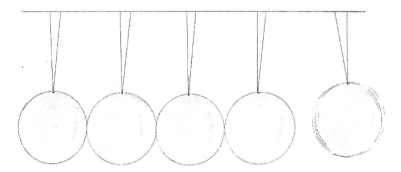

An even simpler analogy is the falling of a line of dominoes. It might appear that some discrete entity has travelled from one end of the line to other, but we know that is not how it is. A wave of kinetic energy has arisen. Such energy is not a separable, graspable 'thing'.

Of course, the Buddha did not live at a time when modern scientific models or analogies could have occurred to him. It was his mindful penetration into the actual ongoing nature of his own experience that showed him the true nature of things. Considered from the highest viewpoint, we may now see that there is neither independent 'world' nor independent 'me'. There is a natural loop-happening, which we call 'human experience'. (This touches on Vipassī's Loop which we mentioned above.) We cannot directly describe the inner characteristics of that loop-happening because all description depends on an already given boundary that one cannot go beyond. But one can try to generate insight by creating metaphors, models and metaphysics as in this book. Unlike some philosophers, I do not think metaphysics is necessarily misleading, as long as one *knows* that it is metaphysics and how that works.

17.4.4.2 Sensory attractants and aversions

The doctrine of the six sense-bases figures in the fourth Foundation of Mindfulness as a reminder to evaluate one's processes of de-clinging in regard to sensory attractants and aversions (and the sensory neutral). I see a colourful bird and there is delight. I see a dead bird and there is aversion. I glance at an unobtrusive dull brown bird and there is neutrality of feeling. I hear the sound of a song thrush singing and there is delight. I hear the squawking of a carrion crow and there is aversion. I barely hear the 'sip-sip' of that dull brown little bird and there is neutrality of feeling. Here there is duality throughout: 'I like this', 'I don't like that'... There is the 'I' (in here) and, independently it appears, there is the 'that' (out there). I am reminded to be mindful of all these contending *dhammas*, mini-laws of nature, tending to 'me-ness', and on better days tending to drop 'me-ness'. I am moving from the like/don't-like of the agitated 'me' to the equanimity of 'not-me'.

Mindful of our senses, we see how a chain reaction leading to craving and dissatisfaction arises at the very touch of experience, so we are able to nip it in the bud or turn away if we so choose. We saw how this works in the case of the 'supra-advert' exercise earlier (Exercise 5). Mindfulness of the senses enables restraint.

17.5 Four Noble Truths

And so we return once more to the Four Noble Truths, but no longer as a doctrine or teaching but as the lived mindfulness of one's own (provisional) mind. There are no such 'Truths' except in the actual experience of a human being watching the workings and potentials of his or her own mind. Where, after all, is the suffering, where the origin of that suffering, where the attenuation of the suffering and where the steps necessary to realize that attenuation? That's right: 'in your mind'. And where is that? Where is the horizon?

With great lucidity the Buddha reminds us of what kind of work or exertion is necessary in applying the Four Noble Truths. He says:

> *Of these Four Noble Truths, bhikkhus, there is a noble truth that is to be fully under-*
> *stood; there is a noble truth that is to be abandoned; there is a noble truth that is to*
> *be realized; there is a noble truth that is to be developed.*[3]

That is, suffering is to be understood as it really is; craving (and rejecting) is to be abandoned; attenuation and cessation of suffering are to be realized in this life; and the Noble Eightfold Path is to be developed by practically following it in all walks of life.

Here there is also a recognition of how these underlying laws of human nature are themselves transient: they arise (with the meditational training) and at last fade away to a vanishing point of realization and liberation. This arising and falling away is itself subject to mindful examination.

17.6 *The Ultimate Paradox*

We can watch our own growth and wonder at the harmfulness of our previous ways of thought, speech and action. Still, it may be asked: Who or what is watching? That core vantage point has not yet been abandoned. The constructed self is put to use as reflector, and therefore is tainted, hence the 'fallacy' of using mundane language to express the inexpressible. However, the reflector reflects even that difficulty. Ultimately, the reflector drops away and the 'me' ceases to be. Peace and silence reign, for some eternal moment.

So mindfulness must be applied even to the Noble Eightfold Path, which provides the standard aspects of the Buddha's teaching itself, aspects that we may eventually be able to let go of as we begin to see them as mere crutches in the development of insight.

You might think that this awakening is a very strange 'state' to be in. But far from being strange, it is in fact the most ordinary and fundamental source of things. Just watch a blackbird looking for worms, or a seagull floating on the wind. They *know* of no division or divisiveness. It is the human conceptualizing, elaborating, remembering and projecting of craving for and rejecting that is a strange dividing of the world into two—'me' in here and 'it' out there. The blackbird and the seagull suffer no such delusion. For you and me it took a lifetime to construct that suffering state. The reorientation is attained by letting go of that fundamental division and returning to the resting state of all things, returning to the source.

When a close follower of the Buddha called *Mahākaccāna* was asked to clarify the 'extinction of craving', he replied:

> *Through the destruction ... of desire ... craving ... clinging ... mental standpoints, adherences, and underlying tendencies towards the feeling element [etc.] ... the mind is said to be well-liberated.*[4]

17.7 *The Path of No Path*

Right Understanding is a unity, a connected whole. For the one with Right Understanding the various parts of the Noble Eightfold Path are not examined as an end in itself, but placed in the context of 'the Unconditioned'; that is, every part gradually reveals itself as a reflected aspect of the whole understanding (wisdom, Right Understanding). Thus there is not a path folded into eight parts, but a unity of understanding of the ultimate truth of things. The 'follower of the path', from the non-vantage point of 'the Unconditioned', has in truth no path and is therefore not a follower of anything, although 'the path' remains a convenient way of speaking, especially for someone who has up to this point been ignorant, who has been an 'uninstructed worldling'.

Chapter 18

Right Resolve: A Change of Heart

Right Resolve
Sammā saṅkappa

Often translated as Right Intention or Right Thought. More accurately, *saṅkappa* means resolving to do x, making up one's mind to do x, making a commitment to do x, garnering the will to do x, or firmly deciding to do x. In this context it means resolving, on the basis of one's Right Understanding of the Four Noble Truths, to work towards the end of craving and aversion, renouncing worldly attachments, and living in harmlessness and love (good-will).

18.1 Crossing the Flood

When the follower of the Noble Eightfold Path has this comprehensive understanding, this new view of the human reality, this truth and peace that come with nonduality, they also acquire an unshakeable but open-minded faith in its rightness, awe in its power to unify all things and resilience to accept that as human reality. There has been a change of heart. The follower has a firm resolve not to revert to earlier ignorance. Actually, once awakened, such a reversion is surely impossible.

The fact is that ultimately there is only a Path for one who clings to a discrete self. The Path, after all, is entirely about the release of the self. In completely releasing the self the Path finally has no further meaning. To use one of the Buddha's own similes: one only uses the raft to cross the flood, and when crossed one lets go of the raft.[1] There will be doubts and obstacles on the way. But once crossed there is no longer a flood ahead, and no need to carry the raft, for in that case the raft would be an encumbrance.

However, there appears to be circularity here. It seems that one can only really be resolved if one has understood, but if one has understood then one is not in need of making the resolution. This is rather a pedantic position to take. Let us compare it to learning the skills of playing the violin like a true maestro or maestra. As one begins to see the great improvement in one's skill, that very knowledge will strengthen the resolve to reach the peak of accomplishment. At that peak there is no further resolve, the energy of which has been absorbed into the masterly skill itself. The maestro does not require instruction but now has the role of encouraging others to be resolved and skilful.

This resonates with what we learned about the Emergence Model. The ability to swim begins co-dependently with the notion of swimming, and through a series of levels one proceeds to higher ones, and each level reinforces the level that went before it as it prepares the one emerging after it. Eventually one sees that there are no further levels and nothing to resolve to do.

Now it should be plain why earlier I presented both the mundane (lower level) and supramundane (higher level) account of the Four Noble Truths. But, of course, it is not a discrete dividing line.

18.2 Why Start on the Path?

Now I shall answer more deeply the question why anyone should resolve to follow the Noble Eightfold Path. That is, what is there about the Buddha's account of our commonplace reality and his alternative vision of reality which would provoke and support, even demand, such a commitment? The basic answer is that once clearly understood, the Path immediately resonates with the experience of life and its disappointments. So many of the suttas in the *Tipiṭaka* end with a declaration of joy from the grateful first-time listener to a talk by the Buddha:

> *Magnificent, Master Gotama* [Buddha]! *Master Gotama has made the Dhamma clear in many ways, as though he were turning upright what had been overthrown, revealing what was hidden, showing the way to one who was lost, or holding up a lamp in the dark for those with eyesight to see forms.*[2]

A powerful metaphorical answer is also deeply embedded in the Buddha Dhamma tradition. If you experience serious sickness, and you are offered a medicine for it, wouldn't you be prepared to try the medicine, or at least consider it? Of course, you would want to some extent to acknowledge and understand the sickness itself before taking the medicine.

It is not unlike having high blood pressure. You might feel fine so you do not acknowledge it. You might resist well-meaning suggestions that a medical check-up might be in order. Then one day you have unexpected dizziness, a nose-bleed or blurred vision, and decide to call on one's doctor. The doctor provides a diagnosis. You are lucky that the high blood pressure, of which you were oblivious, did not kill you without warning. The doctor explains the diagnosis, the treatment, and the consequences of ignoring the advice. Now you are motivated. From Right Understanding has emerged Right Resolve. You resolve to take the medication, even if it is for the rest of your life. Little by little you feel better. In fact, you *are* better. There is no 'why' about Resolve; it happens when Understanding is ripe.

The Buddha is the doctor, and dissatisfaction or anxiety is the sickness. Craving-clinging-rejecting is the diagnosis. The Noble Eightfold Path is the prescription. Dhamma exercise in letting-go of 'I-me-mine' is the taking of the medication.

18.3 Three Aspects of Resolve

In Buddhist doctrine, Right Resolve is usually analysed in terms of three dimensions. I present these three and their opposites in Table 4 below.

Table 4: Right Resolve

'HEALTH'	'ILL-HEALTH'
Renunciation	Sensuality, desire, lust
Non-harm	Harmfulness, exploitation
Love, good-will, compassion	Hatred, ill-will, callousness

'Resolve' is a case of emergent transformation, as discussed earlier. It flows in spurts from Right Understanding itself, and unexpectedly at points of cumulative practice. In a sense, Right Resolve is already contained, as a 'seed' if you like, within Right Understanding. Every growth in understanding cultivates a background aspiration to change; the possibility of change becomes gradually clearer, the potential to change grows stronger, and then the realization of change occurs. What is more, as we saw in the last chapter, resolve doubles back and empowers understanding.

We should remember that Right Understanding is the view in which craving for control and enjoyment of the 'world out there' is revealed as a source of insatiability, anxiety, suffering and conflict, and that *awareness* of the process of mental formation of this Wrong Understanding also shows us the way out. The way out must lie in our taking on a kind of mental *de-construction* and *re-construction* of reality. An ontological shift is seen to be necessary; and a shift of historical proportions necessary in the present age if humans are to save themselves from self-destruction. This shift engenders the *resolve* or commitment to begin and sustain the transition in oneself. The resolve is generated through the insight into a powerfully sense-making supersession of our current historical outlook.

18.4 Clinging and Not Clinging

By now we should have understood enough to see, not just that the 'world is not worth clinging to', but that ultimately there is no *separate* world to cling to. Neither is there an ontologically independent clinger; there is the acknowledgement that there is no substantive 'me' to cling to anything. If no discrete clinger, then no objects of clinging. If no objects of clinging then no discrete clinger.[3] This might shock one, until one sees into the great importance of the qualifying adjectives: 'independent', 'substantive' and 'discrete'. (I have been using the word 'discrete' a lot. Collins Dictionary provides us with a simple definition: 'Discrete ideas or things that are separate and distinct from each other'.)

To make the same point differently: at the same moment, that which is taken to be 'me' is revealed in truth to be embedded in that which is misleadingly called 'the external world', but which I cannot know *in itself* but only as represented in the reflection conceived as 'me'. The 'world' regarded as something external to 'me' is generated within that which we *see as* (is constructed as) 'the world' and of which 'I-me-mine' is a minuscule reflection. The mirror cannot know itself, since that would require it to be another, even greater, mirror. Neither can it know the world *in itself* but only as reflected in itself (the mirror of the mind). Radical ignorance is the foundation of all possible mundane and scientific knowledge. Suffering is the consequence of the futile attempt to go beyond the bounds of knowledge and control 'the world around me'. One form of this we mentioned earlier: scientism (section 14.8).

18.5 Acceptance of a Limit

Another question may arise for the seeker: should we (indeed, *can* we) renounce the world—give up on it entirely? Some religions, or some aspects of some religions (e.g., the Desert Fathers of early Christianity), have tried to do so.[4] The Buddha tried it when, as we mentioned earlier, he practised severe austerities for some years, almost starving himself to death. No, the point is to change the perceived world by radically understanding the conditions of its appearance—not through science (an enterprise fundamentally distorted by its dualism but through meditational insights as they emerge from the instructions laid out in the Noble Eightfold Path.

What then should be our most fundamental intention or attitude to the world as it appears? Since 'world' and 'I-me-mine' arise together ('co-dependence'), this is the same question as what should be our most fundamental attitude to this sense of 'me-ness' (I-me-mine) that I suffer from? That is, our attitude to 'me' as it appears and as we *know* it cannot be what it appears to be? The answer is that this kind of knowing, this acceptance of the limits on human understanding, is itself the attitude that liberates us. Right Understanding gives rise to Right Resolve, and Right Resolve swallows up the rest of the Noble Eightfold Path. With Right Resolve there is right speech, action, livelihood, right meditation and contemplation, and support for the deepening of Right Understanding. The Path is self-sustaining.

18.6 Renunciation is Not Rejection

Renunciation of the division of separate 'world' and separate 'me' (self) is not a passive understanding but a *living out* of what one now understands in the light of what is beyond understanding. Then clinging to 'the material world' and to 'I-me-mine' ceases, or approaches cessation (the 'vanishing point' mentioned earlier). It means neither wallowing blindly in the world nor trying to control it to one's own ends. It also means not casting it off or rejecting it. It means neither possessive infatuation with the world nor hatred of it.

We have to be careful not to understand 'renunciation' in a dualistic sense. We have to go beyond dualism in order properly to understand it. Dualistic renunciation would take the form of the rejection of the apparently material or physical word in favour of the apparently spiritual world, giving up earth for heaven. The very idea of world-rejection terrifies most people, and understandably so. The Mirror Model (Chapter 13) should have helped us to see that it is not a case of a reality divided into subject/object or mind/matter. It is a matter of *reflection* presenting us with the appearance of duality.

But what puts an indelible stamp on the Buddha's meaning of renunciation, of letting go, of living in the light of the Dhamma, is the concept of the 'Middle Way' expressed as neither existence nor non-existence.

The Buddha Dhamma is not a denial of life; it is a denial of a suffering life. It is the will to live truly, not the will to die miserably.

18.7 *Wrong Resolve, Right Resolve*

Our wrong understanding of reality is manifested in our resolve to make gains and avoid losses. As already explained, we see the world as the Universal Container, which contains people, and 'me', among other things. In this container view we (wrongly) make a lifetime resolution to get what we want and avoid what we do not want. This vision is not entirely false, but a limited perspective, and limited in such a way as to generate the very suffering it was meant to evade.

The fact of death can sometimes, not always, shake us out of this wrong understanding. We are often speechless in the face of our own death or the death of someone we love or know well. The thing we seek to understand recedes before us. With our Universal Container delusion we have then to make do with the idea that, as isolated entities, we pop into existence and meaninglessly pop out. There is a clear-cut beginning and a clear-cut end. There is then the constant threat of futility, mean-inglessness, of 'waiting for Godot'. Indeed, I might try to account for my mysterious appearance 'in the world' in one of two basic ways. Firstly, by seeing myself purely as an *object* in the world, for which there is a scien-tific account—and the inadequacy of that was explored earlier in terms of the Mirror. Secondly, by seeing myself as something that was myste-riously *created* out of nothing, or perhaps out of and by some supreme being. And, of course, on this view the only way I can escape from anni-hilation is by insisting that 'I' continue as 'me' separated from the object that is my body, that is, escape as a 'soul' to unite with God. Both views are not to be scorned, for in one form or another they are the greatest creations of the human mind, in its bewildered plight.

The Buddha's view presents an alternative: It is that of our embed-ment in a re-becoming, a continuous resurgence, a self-transforming continuity.

18.8 *Non-Harm, Good-Will*

We now consider the other two closely related dimensions of Right Resolve. Namely, non-harm (compassion, generosity, nurturing) and let-ting go of ill-will (sustaining good-will, forgiveness, love, helpfulness). We also place these two acts of resolution within the context of the Middle

Way (*Majjhimāpaṭipadā*, Mirror Model, subject/object nonduality) and the Waveform Way (*Suññatā*, emptiness, not-self). The two are closely related and are expressed in these terms: at the very least avoid causing deliberate harm to yourself, other people and all life by your thoughts, actions and deeds; and at the very least avoid an attitude of hostility, vengefulness, disliking self and others, jealousy, holding grudges and so on. Yes, this may not be easy in our world, but is the alternative better? It is also worthwhile keeping in mind that those who are harmful and harbouring ill-will are usually expressing their own suffering of the past, present or imagined future.

18.9 Mirror Model of Non-Harm and Ill-Will

The Mirror Model (nondual understanding) teaches us that there is no 'other', that is, no other in the same sense in which there is no 'self'. That is, no discrete/non-connected other.

Put simply, seeing myself as a 'pop-up, pop-out object' in a Universal Container provides a fairly firm basis for the delusion and the belief that I must always put 'myself' first and consolidate and strengthen myself above all else. All other beings and indeed the 'world' itself, it seems, are my potential obstacles and enemies and I have to be wily and persistent to defend myself, to manipulate and exploit where I can. With this dualistic delusion my stance in life is naturally one of harm, be harmed and self-harm.

If, however, I come to see this pop-up self as a delusion, where the reality is actually the boundaryless embedment of myself in the Dhamma, then this of course undermines the very vision that grounds harmfulness. Then I cannot but see our living and transient kinship with all beings and all things. The image in the mirror is of one separated, but the one behind the eyes of flesh looking in the mirror is the same as everyone else's subjective outlook. When as a community we meditate together and leave all difference behind then we are all in the same peaceful 'non-place', a place of no vantage point.

18.10 Waveform Model of Non-Harm and Ill-Will

If you have really taken to heart as a personal discovery that, while you are not 'nothing at all', you cannot identify yourself as any kind of discrete, separate, abiding thing and that what you find instead is more like a wave in a stream or a knot in a thread in a beginningless tapestry, then your whole attitude to life is open to change. This is truly a momentous meditational discovery, not just an intellectual one; it is an insight or 'direct knowledge', not just a thought or belief or item of knowledge.

One dimension of the difference made is the letting go of ill-will or, expressed positively, expressing and demonstrating compassion for the suffering of others, even when or especially when that suffering is engendered by ignorance or resentment. I now have a general attitude of compassion, for now I am not just that small, grasping, protective self. The unhappy delusion of self-separation I see all around me is sometimes tragic, sometimes comical, sometimes tragi-comical, but always ultimately unnecessary.

It may be said that this is an unconvincing account of ill-will, which may be the result of many kinds of conditions. However, in this Waveform Model ill-will is seen, whatever contingent causes there may be, as a failure at root to perceive continuity or affinity between oneself and apparent 'others'.

The Waveform Model teaches us that all is re-becoming, that there is no Universal Container of separated, independent things. This model prompts us to think and act more in terms of unity, continuity, affinity and family resemblance. Abuse, exploitation and violence then release their grip.

Right Resolve, then, involves a shift from harmfulness to non-harmfulness. It is the undermining of the magnetism of harm to oneself, to others near and far, to other species, harm to oceans, to atmosphere and earth. Ultimately, it is duality that draws us progressively into the destructive mode, now resulting in the global catastrophe of climate change.

With renunciation there grows harmlessness and good-will. You see at once that to harm other beings is to harm yourself, and to harbour ill-will is to harbour it against yourself. Here is the true and only meaning of *kamma*.

18.11 Dissolving I-me-mine

Let us now revisit the I-me-mine delusion. Consider what happens to the 'my' and the 'mine' of 'I, me, my, mine' now that the 'I' and the 'me' are quite differently understood.

If I am now 'non-attached to myself' in attitude, understanding and behaviour then any possessiveness or acquisitiveness—even if at quite a 'normal' and acceptable level by ordinary standards—has been undermined since supra-mundanely there is nothing independently substantial for me to feed, protect and build up. Nutriment remains a necessary condition, but not cuisine.

Furthermore, since I not only see my non-separateness but also (what is the same thing) my interconnectedness, I am more than willing to give away, give up, donate, help out, volunteer and renounce. I neither hanker after more stuff nor hesitate to be generous with the stuff that I already have. In short, I have become tendentially selfless and very much at peace in being that way. The constant search for security and reassurance is not the issue it once was, and may no longer be an issue at all. If my whole understanding of myself has been radically transformed, then my whole attitude will also be redirected. In other words, my intentions, aims and purposes will all be pointing in a selfless direction. If I am no longer attached to the world, as though it were something 'out there' that 'I' can take from apparently without consequence, then actually I have renounced the world to some degree.

The discerning reader will have noticed that in the previous two paragraphs the pronouns 'I' and 'me' were used amply. The question arises whether, despite the Buddha's teaching, 'I-me-mine' cannot be escaped. This question takes us to the last chapter: the silence of no discrete things.

Chapter 19

Right Resolve: Silence

19.1 Faith

Resolve is not 'faith' in the way that term is often used in theistic religions such as Christianity. The terms 'belief' and 'faith' are used in special ways in the religious context. There is a perfectly ordinary use, for example, 'I have faith in my dentist's ability', or 'I believed my dentist was honest, but I was wrong'. In theistic religion people speak, for example, of having faith in or believing in God, Jesus, the prophets, saints, and so on. There are also forms of Buddhism that speak of the Buddha or a particular bodhisattva (e.g., Amida/Amitabha) in this way. I would not wish to reject them.

However, I do not think this religious way of speaking and understanding is to be found in the Buddha's *core* teachings, namely in the Buddha Dhamma itself as found in the *Tipiṭaka*. There, religious devotion is not a fundamental soteriological (salvationist) one in the same way it is in, say, evangelical Christianity. What we do find is better understood initially in terms of the talk of the dentist above. Certainly one needs confidence, and even strong confidence or trust, in the Buddha's teachings and in one's abilities to master the practical teachings. When embarking on the Noble Eightfold Path there is need for faith that it is worthwhile 'having'. But generally there is no 'evangelical' sense of faith.

In *Pali* there is the term *saddhā*, usually translated as 'faith', and that term too should be understood in the ordinary way, while in the context of the Buddha Dhamma. In Theravada Buddhism a lay person who has this faith or confidence in the Buddha, the Dhamma and the community (*sangha*) is usually known as an *upāsaka* (male) or *upāsikā* (female). The Buddha Dhamma does not involve a resolution to 'have faith' in an afterlife or in 'God's goodness'.

Once one has the insight into the necessity of the Buddha's silence on certain religious and metaphysical questions then one is close to liberation, but not before then. We now turn to that silence.

19.2 The Buddha after Death

In a famous scenario the local king questions Khemā, a Dhamma nun, about whether the *Tathāgata* (Buddha) himself exists or does not exist after death.[1] Her reply appears rather mundane in so far as she answers that just as the number of grains of sand in the Ganges or amount of water in the ocean are immeasurable, so is the Buddha. I think this should be taken as a rather poor simile or metaphor. Its weakness is that it could allow the interpretation that it is immeasurable simply because it is too vast to measure. After all, the grains of sand or gallons of water are measurable in *principle* even if it is empirically (practically) impossible to do. But the real problem is a conceptual one, and this tenuously comes across in the nun's further answer, and that answer (despite her specific intentions) could be applied to all individuals, not just the Buddha:

> The Tathāgatha ... is liberated from reckoning in terms of form; he is deep, immeasurable, hard to fathom like the great ocean ... [and those 'Five Aggregates'] have been abandoned by the Tathāgatha, cut off at the root..., [so the question of his existence or non-existence] does not apply.[2]

To repeat: the question of existence or non-existence does not apply. That *is* the answer to the king's question to Khemā.

19.3 The Re-becoming Answer

If the application of mindfulness is completely effective then the five reflections (so-called Five Aggregates) no longer apply, then the discrete self no longer applies, and if that no longer applies then the existential question no longer applies. One who persists doggedly with the question of the Buddha's existence (and the Buddha, let us not forget, was a person like the rest of us, albeit an awakened one) is one who, however slightly, is still clinging to one or more of the five reflections. Finally, then, there is the opportunity to be liberated by Right Understanding and from much of religion and philosophy as sources of suffering (however refined or gross the manifestation).

In the same sutta the Buddha considers, more generally, the question of whether there is a 'self' or not. He says that 'all phenomena are not-self', which could (wrongly) be taken to mean that there is no self in *any* sense. The Buddha's implicit logic dictates, in fact, that it is not the case that there is a self and that *it is not the case that there is not a self*.[3] A transient self, a clinging, always and intrinsically in the process of arising/falling, may be rightly understood as such, but a discrete and independent one cannot. Without insight into the transience of 'I-me-mine' my mind bifurcates into belief in a discrete and independent self (the 'eternalism' of theistic religion) and belief in the extinction of the 'I-me-mine' (the 'annihilationism' of atheistic nihilism).

The Waveform Model may help one to see into the truth of this confusing bifurcation: the wave, being a transient aspect of a process, does not exist as a discrete, independent object, but neither is it nothing at all. One may see and speak of 'a wave' but always with an understanding of its transience, its transformational motion. In this case, if it were not transient it would not be a wave at all. In short, the curious statement 'I am a wave' has a truth in it. The phrase 'all phenomena are not-self' was a way of saying this within the limits of the Buddha's modes of thought in his time.

It seems to me that (let's call it) 'the waveform conception' is deeply liberating and has much less suffering in it than the reification (thingification) of myself. Now I can let go of wandering isolation. It implies 'my' deep connection with 'everything else'. 'I' pop up from the 'ground' of conditions and 'I' pop out into the ground of conditions ... surely, that is awesome.

19.4 *Body and Soul*

Again in the *Abyākata saṃyutta*[4] the question is posed whether the body and soul are different or the same, and the Buddha is reported as not having 'declared' this one way or another. The Buddha is silent. This is because his whole teaching reveals how such questions are futile and lead to suffering. The full answer can be deduced from the Buddha's core cluster of concepts of nonduality and the five reflections (so-called 'Five Aggregates'). Attachment to the conviction that I am my body (an aggregate subject to clinging) is an assumption underlying the question. Since the Buddha instructs us on letting go of that conviction, once that letting go is attained, no such question on body and soul is logically possible, because the concept of my (discrete) body has been dissolved.

In fact, so important is it to see this for yourself that as long as one holds the view that the body and soul are the same or different, 'the holy life cannot be lived'.[5] To put it in another way: it is a characteristic of the one trapped in *saṃsāra* to divide body and soul (dualism), or reduce soul to body (materialism), or reduce body to soul (idealist eternalism, theistic religion) or vacillate between all three.

19.5 Death and Afterlife

Many fear that death is annihilation, a nothingness. But nothingness requires a subject. In this case there is no discrete 'me' to experience nothingness. Reflecting on what happens when I die I may conjure up a frightening image of myself looking into a dark, bottomless abyss. That is Wrong Understanding. There is no independent 'you' to look into an abyss or any other kind of presence or absence.

There is no afterlife that we can *experience* any more than there was a before-life that we experienced. As Mark Twain is reputed to have whimsically said: 'I do not fear death. I had been dead for billions and billions of years before I was born, and had not suffered the slightest inconvenience from it'. Now, taking a step beyond Twain's limited understanding, the de-centred meditator will find it more than sufficient that he or she has insight into a wondrous kinship with the life that emerges everywhere always.

There is nothing to be afraid of, since there is no discrete subject that could be afraid. The fear is one that may arise in the mind of the living: 'What happens to me when I die?' But, recognizing it as a futile and suffering thought, I let it go.

As Shakespeare wrote in *The Tempest*: 'We are such stuff as dreams are made on, and our little life is rounded with a sleep.'

19.6 God

The Buddha is quite clear that a supreme being, 'God', plays no part in his Dhamma.[6] But to understand him, one needs first to understand the religious ethos and controversies of his time. In brahminical (Vedic) religion God is conceived at two levels. There is the personal God, Brahmā, conceived as a being, creator of the universe, and that can be characterized in personal terms. This conception of God corresponds more or less to the Western mainstream conception of God, and the Buddha dismisses it. His reason must be that it commits what I call the Fallacy of Mundanity, that is, wrongly understanding a nondual expression, such as a metaphor, in entirely mundane or literal terms.

Furthermore, he thinks that it entails a diminishment of human ethical responsibility. Another reason, consistent with his dismissal of all attachment to I-me-mine, is that such a conception is modelled on our mistaken conception of the discrete human self. This is a criticism of the 'God' concept that is not unknown in the mystical tradition of Western Christianity.[7]

This may lead us to the idea, proposed by Zen master Thich Nhat Hahn, for example, that the Buddha's conception must be apophatic, as opposed to cataphatic.[8] That is, the Buddha would be in agreement with those theist theologians who maintain that while we cannot say what God is, we can say what he is not. This is a generous proposal in so far as it opens the possibility of concord between the Buddha Dhamma and the Christian mystical tradition and similar. This may or may not be correct, but one difficulty is that the Buddha is clearly determined to wipe out the wispiest vestige of 'self' which leaves us with a hard question. When the apophaticist says 'God is inconceivable' we may still ask '*what* is it that is inconceivable'. That is, there appears to be a trace of inconsistency in the statement 'God is inconceivable' or the like. To eradicate even this wispy trace, one option remains: silence. To coin a term, one may say the Buddha is trans-apophatic! He remains silent.

19.7 Brahman

One has to keep in mind that, as mentioned, there is a 'higher' conception of God in the brahminical (Vedic) religion: Brahman. Perhaps confronted with the aforementioned paradox of conceiving the inconceivable the brahmin theologians took the route of an inconceivable God as well as a conceivable one. That would surely keep everyone happy! However, Brahman is also *conceived* to be consciousness, eternal and infinite, and so on. The Buddha would have been fully aware of this notion. It is significant that the Buddha never mentions Brahman in the *Tipiṭaka*. However, could it be that the Buddha did 'hold' onto some vestige of Brahman but, seeing the difficulty, he outwitted the brahmins by taking the route (non-route) of silence?

By the way, in the light of this background we see that the Buddha cannot be described as an agnostic. It is not that he was uncertain about God's existence. He was in a position that had nothing to do with certainty or uncertainty about God's existence. He was beyond that dualizing question. Buddha was not a theist, not an atheist and not an agnostic; he has been described as 'non-theist'.

The foregoing questions are important because they strike at the heart of what the Buddha was aiming at in his quest to end suffering. His strategy, as we have seen in some detail, was to train his followers to let go of any reifying ideas of 'what I am', such as 'body' or 'consciousness'. The question is whether, having attained that dismissal of any clinging to a thing-self, he was easing us towards an alternative, for example some

Brahman-like notion, or a trans-Brahman which was un-nameable and inconceivable? Perhaps '*nibbāna*'? Did he mean to leave us in aporia, that is, a state of bamboozled suspension? Maybe that suspension itself is the ultimate insight into 'the way things really are'? In some way does this correspond to the Vedic 'union with Brahman', but cleansed of all reifying traces?

19.8 Udāna 8

Still, is the Buddha *absolutely* silent? There are some passages in the Pali Canon (passages generally assumed to be authentic) in which it appears that the Buddha himself makes exclamations (asseverations) about *nibbāna* which have the familiar ring of a belief in Brahman. He exclaims: 'Monks, there is a not-born, a not-become, a not-made, a not-compounded'. Then he immediately adds that if that were not the case then there could be no 'stepping-out' from what is born, become, made, and compounded, that is, there could be no 'escape' from the suffering in *saṃsāra*.

I agree with Ven. Bhikkhu K. Ñānananda when he said of this passage that 'the significance of these [negative terms] is purely psychological'.[9] That is, the Buddha is not speaking of a Brahman-like figure, which would contradict everything he teaches with the method of nonduality, but about the *awakening* of the meditator or, if you like, the dissolution of mind-world.

19.9 *Disentangling*

The best way out of this tangle is to go back to the basics of the Buddha's method of ending suffering: particularly *anattā* and the five reflections subject to clinging (*pañc'upadanakkhandha*). So we now return to the 'body and soul' discussion just above and how it might throw light on the God concept. Just as we analysed the body/soul duality we now analyse the material world/God duality in similar fashion. The first point to note is that for centuries there has been Western debate about whether 'God' is the same as, or different from, the 'material world' (external world, physical world). This has resulted in all sorts of theological theories including pantheism, panentheism, materialist atheism, agnosticism, immanentism, theism and objective idealism (Hegel's philosophy). The Buddha does not fall into any of these and his view has been labelled 'non-theism'. He is not a theist or an atheist because he works with the different fundamental assumptions of nondualism.

We could put it this way: once we assume a discrete (independent) 'me', all sorts of philosophical difficulties arise, and those are swept away by denying a discrete I/me, while admitting a conditioned I/me, as has been illuminated throughout this book. Now, although the cases are not parallel in every respect we see that, similarly, once we assume a discrete, supreme or ultimate being (whether Western or Eastern) a wide range of difficulties arise, ranging from 'the Ontological Argument' to the 'the Problem of Evil'. Those too are swept away by denying a discrete, independent and personal super-being, while admitting the *appearance* of a personal God similarly '*constructed*' from human experience. One should perhaps add that just as 'self' or 'soul' has its reality in ordinary language, so does 'God'. The Buddha does not say 'self' does 'not exist', and neither does he say anywhere that God does not exist. One has to quickly add: neither does he say either of them 'exist' in the ordinary sense of 'exist'.

Many Western theologians have admitted that there is a conceptual problem here: a 'constructed' or 'conditioned' God is not fit for purpose. To be fit for purpose it would have to be free of all humanly conceived characteristics. Therefore, it seems that it has to be more like the impersonal and abstract Indian Brahman. That throws us back onto the other horn of the dilemma: a characterless, impersonal God (besides being not fit to offer human comfort and solace) cannot be conceived at all. Strictly, 'it' cannot even be conceived as 'inconceivable'). So, the Buddha was, quite rightly, silent. You have to find the answer *for yourself* in the deeper region of your experience.

We began this book with an awareness of speaking and we end it with an awareness of how much more can be *shown* by silence.

19.10 *The Nub: Exist/Not-exist*

The Buddha's silence when asked to answer ten to fourteen metaphysical questions is due to his dismissal of a pervasive ontological assumption underlying those questions as well as much of mundane ways of thinking.[10] The misleading assumption underlies our common-sense understanding of reality: that things either exist or they do not exist, that things pop into existence and pop out of existence. That generally things are separate and independent, not inter-related and akin. This includes the conviction that 'I' pop into existence (birth) and 'I' pop out again

(death); that even the universe pops into existence (nowadays conceived scientifically as 'the Big Bang') and pops out again ('Heat Death').

Put as simply as possible: the Buddha's implicit view is of re-becoming (*punabbhava*), a kind of process that has a transformational continuity; but is a process which by means of 'clinging' generates the divisive delusion of either absolute existence (born) or absolute non-existence (not-born, dead) (see Chapter 15: 'Self and the Waveform Model'). So the mundane dualized 'me/universe' experience is not really a matter of existence/ non-existence (birth/death) as it appears, but of the emergence of transformations. On this new understanding, questions such as 'Do I cease to exist at death?' or 'Is the universe finite or infinite?' are unanswerable (hence the Buddha's silence) because their very framing assumes an absolute division (exist/not-exist) where there cannot be one.

19.11 Universal Peace

Some readers may conclude that I have really been saying all along that there is no such thing as awakening (enlightenment), no attainment of *nibbāna*, and no liberation.

What I am showing is that it is all a matter of an extraordinary change of *understanding*, a profound Gestalt shift, and *that* change is an awakening, a superseding of vantage points, a change of reality and a universal peace.

Conclusion: A Global Awakening?

Not Worth It?

The question may arise: If the world is 'not worth clinging to' then why save it from climate change or any other global catastrophe? Mundane positive answers would refer to the worthiness of diverse beautiful creatures, to the millions of years of evolution and struggle, to the uniqueness (or specialness) of planet Earth, to the great achievements of human beings, to the love for our grandchildren, and to our responsibility to future generations. The Buddha would not reject such answers but would encourage a Gestalt shift, to see the issue more deeply, in ultimate (supramundane) terms.

Homo avidus

Climate change is now said to be the greatest problem facing humankind. However, it is not the climate that is ultimately the problem, nor even carbon dioxide and methane. It is *Homo avidus* that is the problem. And who is *H. avidus* or Craving Man? *We* are, of course. To move beyond this evolutionary impasse we must first of all recognize the self-destructive mutation we have become. We are no longer *Homo sapiens* or Wise Man, son of *Homo erectus*; we are now *Homo avidus*, the Craving Man, whose little wisdom has degenerated into the mere cleverness to acquire, possess and cling by any means.

We are the first species in the history of planet Earth to be defined not by genetic variation but by our deluded fantasies. Our insatiable craving, a limitless desire for *more*, now uniquely rests on our false assumption that reality is dual: a controlling 'we' in here overcoming a submissive '*it*' out there—so-called 'Nature'. If insanity is a detachment from reality, a delusion about the fundamental nature of things, then *H. avidus* may also be defined as an insane being. Never before has the earth witnessed an evolutionarily insane creature gradually and meticulously setting up the conditions for its own destruction, not only by its physical configuration but by its mental one.

Eight Worldly Intentions

Right Resolve is the antidote to Wrong Resolve. The Buddha's teaching wraps up a bundle of delusory human intentions quite neatly and comprehensively in what is sometimes called 'The Eight Worldly Intentions (Conditions)'. We might also call it the *Ignoble* Eightfold Path. As we have seen in this book, special understanding and firm resolution are necessary to move from the Ignoble Path to the Noble Path. Table 5 summarizes the Ignoble Path.[1]

Table 5: Eight Worldly Intentions

CRAVING AND CLINGING TO	REJECTING
Pleasure	Pain, discomfort
Praise	Blame
Fame, recognition	Bad reputation (or obscurity?)
Gain	Loss, want

We only have to look around us, at the activities of corporations, marketers, advertisers, salespeople, shopping, the media, the entertainments industry, tourism and politicians—and look into ourselves, of course—to see these eight intentions energetically at work. This is not to moralize from on high. It is, as a matter of fact, what we find within and without.

We tend to hold before us the image of the perfectly happy and free human being as one who has 'got it all': who indulges pleasure regularly (tasty food, fun, sex, luxuries, etc.), who is praised by everyone for their success and achievements, who is a celebrity, world-renowned, receiving accolades from every quarter, and who gains wealth, possessions and physical attractiveness.

The miserable wretch, who apparently suffers a fate worse than death, is the one who is in discomfort and pain, blamed by everyone for their failures, who is either humiliated or living in complete obscurity, and who is poor, hungry and deemed to be physically ugly.

This is the world wholly created by our human intentions and Wrong Resolve, a resolve to gobble up as much of 'the world' as possible. It is our chosen hell. We intend to escape from pain and discomfort by seeking pleasure, escape from blame by seeking praise, escape from obscurity by seeking fame, and escape from want and loss by seeking wealth. When we have gratified our intentions we come up against the truth: we may not be any happier, we may feel the insecurity of losing what we have, and we may also become aware that nothing is permanent in any case.

So, in this frame of mind, we may be quite mystified by the fact that poor people often seem happy and rich ones often unhappy, and that if the rich are sometimes happy it is not because of their wealth but despite it. We may wonder at how much the rich and comfortable have to spend on security systems, bodyguards and insurance policies. We may scratch our heads trying to remember the name of someone once famous, and shake our heads at how those who were once praised for their success are blamed for the failure that suddenly pulls them down.

But perhaps we should really wonder why it is that we wonder, when *we* set it up in our minds in the first place.

Apocalypse in the Mind

Dualism, and the fantasy of Heroic Man conquering Nature for 'her' fruits, has perhaps already prepared us for apocalypse. For the apocalypse we should be concerned about is not the one spoken of as though it is something that will come to us from outside like an alien monster. We are the alien monster.

One characteristic of *Homo avidus* is the now dominant belief that 'the universe' beyond the thin shell of Earth is most likely just rock, gas, electrons, photons and plasma for billions upon billions of miles in every direction, and for ever. Actually, even our home Earth is seen as fundamentally the same insensate meaningless stuff. The universe, we are led to believe, is just the storm wreckage of exploding stars, cosmic waves and galactic collisions. In this debris-field, human life is of miniscule significance. But this apocalypse is in truth an ongoing invention of the human mind and it leaves us with no comfort, no meaning and no sense. In the logic of mental apocalypse many believe that even without the human mind the Universal Container will continue interminably, cold, dark and empty. In this bleak view, when we humans cease to exist, it will not matter; there will for ever be no one and nothing to notice we have departed or that we ever existed. This is a picture of the nihilism that the Buddha roundly rejected.

Re-becoming Homo sapiens

So what is the nondual alternative? Kamma, we recall, is instant. It is nondual action/reaction; there is no apocalypse coming *around later*. The apocalypse is built into the contemporary lived-out *conception* of human life, namely, *saṃsāra*. This unenlightened life is the 'apocalypse', inner and outer at once. 'If the world is not worth clinging to then why save it from climate change?' is the wrong question. There is no Heroic Man that will save Mother Nature, for there is no such division in the first place. It is a fantasy. We just need to stop abusing ourselves with that fantasy.

We have a chance to wake up. The Buddha's path of peace is a way to make that awakening our reality. The question is now posed for all of us: Is a re-become and revivified *Homo sapiens* possible? This is not an objective question. It is a question of *your* next action.

Appendix 1: Posture

Many lay people will have seen monks or nuns of various traditions in a sitting posture. You might imagine that they are very peaceful. You may wonder whether you can or want to adopt such a posture, and what it has to do with meditation anyway. Well, it is your state of mind that is important, not concern about posture. The Buddha's path of peace is not to be confused with yoga, beneficial as yoga may be. Posture does have something to do with meditation, but probably not as directly as you think. Let us now consider what specific postures there are and what the benefits might be.

Why Posture?

First, adopting an 'Eastern' posture such as sitting cross-legged on a cushion is not essential to, nor does it guarantee, meditational benefits. Indeed, it is positively a hindrance to believe that meditation is something bodily. Unhelpful attachment to the body, which sometimes takes the form of clinging to physical appearance and abilities, is a major obstacle to practising the Dhamma. A healthy body is certainly not an obstacle and it generally helps to be healthy; but it is the *attitude* to the body that is all-important. An attitude in which success in contorted postures is considered the key to existential insight is about as helpful as believing manicured fingernails are the key to writing good poems.

So are there meditational benefits in certain postures? Yes, but it is not the posture *per se* that is beneficial but how the particular posture encourages you in developing mindfulness, concentration and insight. Any posture at all, including standing on your head, would be recommended if it harmlessly facilitated meditation.

How can posture facilitate in this way? The Buddha suggests that there is some parallel between the ease of one's posture or gait and that of one's mind. He said:

Just as a man walking fast might consider: 'Why am I walking fast? What if I walk slowly?' and he would walk slowly; then he might consider: 'Why am I walking slowly? What if I stand?' and he would stand; then he might consider: 'Why am I sitting? What if I lie down?' and he would lie down. By doing so he would substitute for each grosser posture one that was subtler. So too ... when a bhikkhu gives attention to stilling the thought-formation of those thoughts ... his mind becomes steadied internally, quieted, brought to singleness, and concentrated.[1]

The Buddha was not recommending lying down to meditate, of course. He was saying that calming the mind is like calming the body. These days, we believe the reverse to be true: we consider that stabilizing and calming the body is like stabilizing and calming the mind.

There are some specific ways in which posture facilitates meditation:

- Optimal breathing
- Sustainability
- Discipline
- Humility.

Thus a sick or dying person confined to a bed or wheelchair may not only meditate well but may meditate far better than a body enthusiast in the Lotus position with little or no awareness of their true bodily *status*. Before we look at specific postures, let us consider these facilitating factors.

Optimal Breathing

Any posture should, for a particular person in his or her own circumstances, facilitate breathing. In other words, a posture that inhibits or distorts regular breathing will generally be a hindrance to meditation. This is because, as we shall see below, a certain kind of breathing is critical to developing meditation. However, there is no gold standard of breathing that is the same for everyone. It is a matter of breathing optimally for your personal circumstances, whether you are young, old, healthy or sick.

Sustainability

Any posture should be sustainable—that is, it should not eventually undermine itself because it is straining against gravity and/or the body's anatomy and physiology. It should be a posture that can continue long enough for meditation to do its work. A posture is unsustainable if, for example, it induces pain in the lower back, neck or knees. You might have to overcome short-term discomforts in learning to adopt a good posture, but this is a different matter. In any case, these short-term 'sacrifices' will not usually be in the back or neck but perhaps somewhere in the legs.

A real hindrance to meditation is slouching in any position, as encouraged by Western-style armchairs. To begin with, such a posture may induce sleepiness ... just before the back pain induces its opposite!

Discipline

Meditation requires self-discipline. The work involved in adopting a good posture and staying with it in stillness and alertness facilitates the mental discipline required for growing attention, mindfulness and concentration, with their attendant merits.

Humility

Conceit and pride reveal themselves in posture—granted the context and culture. Consider the slouch, elbows on the table, the feet on the chair or table, looking down the nose, the gunslinger ambling gait, or hands in pockets even when meeting someone for the first time.

Adopting a posture appropriate for meditation, which is ultimately an exercise in radically dissolving self-centredness, means developing something that blends in gently with the ground of one's being. Such a posture speaks of respect, gratitude, acceptance, stability and alertness. You may not notice the grey heron in its total stillness among the reeds, until it catches the fish in one single-pointed thrust. A slouching heron never caught anything but a cold.

Chair Posture

You can meditate perfectly well on a chair. A soft armchair or divan of any sort is unsuitable. The chair should preferably be quite hard, something like a plain dining-room chair.

Figure 9: Chair Posture

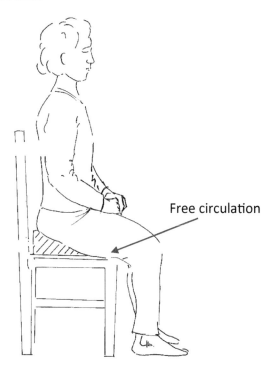

Free circulation

As shown in Figure 9, the front edge of the chair should not interfere with the circulation in your thighs, so a cushion under the feet may help to raise the thighs sufficiently.

There are also firm wedge cushions available to place on the chair, and these tilt the body forward slightly in a way that assists both the spine and the thigh circulation. Your legs should not be crossed, and the soles of your feet should be squarely on the ground, about a shoulder's width apart.

In most ordinary circumstances it is not advisable to lean back in the chair, but to sit in self-supporting fashion with an upright posture. Slouching is definitely unhelpful. Your head should be ever so slightly tilted forward and your shoulders gently held back.

Enclose your left thumb in your right hand and rest both hands together in your lap. There should be no unnecessary tension anywhere in the body, such as neck, shoulders, arms or knees. Do not allow the weight of your arms and hands to pull your shoulders and back forward.

You may prefer simply to place your palms on your knees. Your hands should rest palms down on the knees, not face up.

Symbolic gesturing positions with the hands (called *mudrā*) are unnecessary and in any case are just inappropriate out of their religious context.

Should your eyes be open or closed? It is best to begin with eyes closed, which will help to calm the mind. After a while you may choose to open them and rest your eyes on the ground at about 45 degrees. Do not stare at or examine anything. If you are sleepy then keep the eyes open from the start.

All I have said here (and about the postures that follow) would have to be qualified in cases of sickness, physical challenges and infirmity. Since I cannot run through all of these possibilities here, and in any case I am not competent do so, supplementary advice may be needed from a doctor or therapist.

Whatever your condition, you *can* meditate if you remember to optimize your posture within your abilities and in terms of the mental and ethical context already described.

Stool Posture

Figure 10: Stool Posture

You might like to try using a stool. Simple, three-part, folding stools for meditation are widely available on the Internet. Be sure to find, or make, a stool of the right size for your body proportions. You should sit on it with your legs under the stool in a kneeling position, as in Figure 10.

The stress point in this posture will be the front of the ankles, as the feet are pushed backwards. One could encourage flexibility by sometimes carefully trying to kneel without a stool, so as to stretch the ankle musculature, although you may find that this is not easy to do for any period of time. With some gentle coaching, the ankles may get used to this. The rest of the instructions for stool-sitting are largely the same as for the chair, but you will need a meditation mat.

Cushion Posture

Figure 11: Cushion Posture

Knees down

You could also try using a meditation cushion, and again it is important to choose one that is supportive for your body proportions. Depth, width and firmness are all important. Household cushions are generally not suitable as they are too soft to support the body's weight. Taller or less flexible people usually find they need a deeper cushion. It is best to try out several shapes and sizes before purchasing one. If you wish to try this, then the position I recommend is the ankles-down one (Figure 11). There is a technique for moving into this position.

Sit on the front half to one-third of the cushion, which is placed a little towards the rear of the meditation mat. Lean forward. Put the outside of the left ankle on the ground, with the side of the knee on the ground too. Put the outside of the right ankle on the ground, with the side of that knee on the ground too. The right foot will now be in front of the left foot. You have to lean forward to be able to get the legs into this position. As you lean forward, pull the cushion under you, so that it is comfortably positioned to hold you in an erect posture. You will be sitting on the front half to one-third of the cushion and you may need to wriggle a little to establish a firm, comfortable and erect posture.

The knees *must* be on the ground, because sitting with knees raised will eventually cause backache and is not suitable for meditation. After some time in this position, you could change the legs around, so that the left foot will be in front. The instructions for body position, hands and eyes are as for the chair posture.

Other postures that involve sitting on a cushion are taught in some kinds of Yoga. These include putting one foot onto the opposite calf or thigh, or both feet onto opposite thighs. The ability to do these difficult positions does not automatically confer the ability to meditate. For those not brought up sitting on the floor as in many Eastern countries, it is far more fruitful to adopt a posture that is accessible to you and put the real effort into the mental and attitudinal exercises.

Standing Posture

Standing may be a good posture for meditation in two circumstances: to take a break from sitting meditation, and for those who have back problems. Generally speaking, one can maintain a sitting posture for a much longer period than standing, so some form of sitting is more common in meditation practices.

For standing, the posture should be erect, the feet placed firmly and equally weighted on the ground with about 25cm (ten inches) separating the big toes. The back should be straightened and the head tilted ever so slightly forward, with the eyes resting on the ground at about 45 degrees.

The arms should either be hanging at the sides or you can place the right hand over the left hand in the dip of the chest.

The all-important meditational aspects that the postures facilitate will be discussed further in the chapters that follow. Walking meditation is discussed separately further on.

Lying Posture

Lying down may also be a good posture for meditation in two circumstances: just before sleeping for the night or when sick in bed. If you have been practising meditation during the day, it is helpful to continue with a posture that does not stress the neck, back and limbs during the night and to focus on the breathing for a while, as described below.

Doing the same, as far as possible, when sick in bed is also calming. An alternative to focusing on the breathing is to focus on an inner image of something restful such as the sea, clouds or a flower. If agitated or distressed before sleeping, then replaying in your mind a happy scene or episode is sometimes calming and helps over a period of time to generate a generally calm attitude that is conducive to meditation.

The last point to be made about posture, as ergonomics experts tell us, is that optimal posture throughout the day and night helps maintain health, whatever one's health status happens to be, which is always helpful for good meditation. This book is probably not the right place to dwell on the patent benefits of good diet and exercise. One sentence of advice may be allowable: decrease the 'Four White Stuffs' (sugar, salt, processed flour and animal fat) and increase the 'Four Sunny Stuffs' (vegetables, fruit, walking in the greenery, and laughing at ourselves).

Challenges

Many of us have or will have serious health challenges in life. Meditation is not designed just for the hale and hearty. Indeed, it was when the Buddha saw for the first time illness, old age and death that compassion arose in him with a wish to understand the human condition at its roots.

If one is physically challenged in some way then hopefully it is possible to draw some points from the above descriptions that you can bring together for a posture helpful to Dhamma meditation.

Pain, of course, is always a challenge and following the Path may help, combined with the advice and/or prescription of a sensible doctor. If one is mentally challenged then, again, Dhamma meditation may help.

Those caring for the sick, whether at home or in a hospice or hospital, are thereby giving a great gift, and may also learn a great deal that will guide them in the ethical, meditational and compassion-arousing practices of the Buddha.

This discussion of posture will have got you paying attention to what your body is doing at certain points. Now we should take advantage of this attention to develop meditation.

Appendix 2: Glossary of Neologisms

A neologism is a new or invented word. The author has invented a number of terms in this book, usually in connection with the models deployed to clarify the nondual (supramundane) viewpoint.

Aporia—a conceptual blockage; when trying to solve an apparent problem the mind reaches a point at the boundary of sense at which it sees no possible way forward

Buddha's path of peace—traditionally known as 'The Noble Eightfold Path'.

DNA of Ignorance—*Saṃsāra*, or the deepening of human ignorance as one condition of life leads to another, that is, co-dependent origination (emergence).

Embedment—the relation of an entity A and a general form B, in which the entity appears separate but is only a manifestation of the 'same' general form B; like a lump of ice in water. See 'Knot' below.

Emergence Model—a non-reductionist representation of the relations between the key mental arisings that give rise to ignorance and suffering. Reductionist: the wrong idea that a whole can be understood as nothing more than the sum of its parts.

Ethico-cosmos—a view of reality in which value (moral, ethical, aesthetic) is embedded in the cosmos (the whole). (See 'Embedment'.)

Horizons Model—a representation of how, in pursuing the Noble Eightfold Path, the 'goal' appears to recede, for it is not a place.

Hovering—the outlook of someone who is poised between mundane duality and supramundane nonduality.

Knot (slipping)—a representation of embedment (see above).

Leap-frog—using reified (object or 'thing') language to leapfrog over itself into a non-reified (nondual) insight. The method of this book.

Meiosis—borrowed from cell biology, a representation of how the unity of experience gradually splits (over centuries) into subject-object duality; and a name for the early stage of such splitting (e.g., the Buddha's time).

Mirror Model—a representation of the dual appearance of mind and body (subject and object; 'me in here' and 'it out there').

Mundanity, fallacy of—wrongly understanding a nondual expression, such as a metaphor, in entirely mundane or literal terms.

Ontology—a theory of ultimate reality. (Not a neologism; but not generally used outside philosophy.)

Rebecoming, resurgence—the concept that all things emerge from what has gone before (a network of conditions), as in organic growth. There is no discoverable beginning to such rebecoming.

Reflections, the five—a concept substituting for the doctrine of 'The Five Aggregates', having the advantage of a nondual perspective on the clinging from which suffering emerges.

Reification—the process of treating a non-physical concept, for example, 'mind' as though it were an 'object' or 'thing' or physical entity.

Supra-advert—a consumer advertisement as it appears when interpreted with mindful investigation, namely, as a manipulation of human greed, hatred and delusion.

Think-ism—an attitude of the Western mind based on the assumption that every life-problem can be resolved by merely reasoning or thinking about it.

Universal Container—the delusion in which the 'world' is treated as a vast container (empty space) containing discrete objects such as planets, rocks, trees, people and 'me'.

Vipassī's Loop—a 10-linked (rather than 12-linked) version of co-dependent origination (see 'Emergence Model' above) presented by buddha Vipassī as spiritual development over a single human life rather than over a past, present and future life or lives by means of repeated rebirth.

Waveform Model—a representation of the nondual relation of apparently discrete objects; a representation in the form of the (no-essence) continuity/discontinuity of waves.

References and Notes

Abbreviations

AN

Aṅguttara Nikāya: Numerical Discourses of the Buddha, translated by Bhikkhu Bodhi, Wisdom Publications, Somerville, MA, USA, 2012.

DN

Dīgha Nikāya: The Long Discourses of the Buddha, translated by Maurice Walshe, in 'Teachings of the Buddha' series, Wisdom Publications, Somerville, MA, USA, 1995.

MN

Majjhima Nikāya: The Middle Length Discourses of the Buddha, translated by Bhikkhu Ñāṇamoli and Bhikkhu Bodhi, in 'Teachings of the Buddha' series, Wisdom Publications, Somerville, MA, USA, 1995.

SN

Samyutta Nikāya: The Connected Discourses of the Buddha, translated by Bhikkhu Bodhi, 2 volumes, 'Teachings of the Buddha' series, Wisdom Publications, Somerville, MA, USA, 2000.

Preface

1. 'Models in Science', *Stanford Encyclopedia of Philosophy*, https://plato.stanford.edu/entries/models-science/ (accessed 26 February 2019).

Introduction

1. SN vol. 2, 56.11, Wisdom Publications [hereafter, Wisdom], pp. 1843–47.
2. SN vol. 2, 56.11, Wisdom, p. 1844. All Buddha's quotations in this book have been italicized by this author for emphasis.
3. AN 3.65, Wisdom, p. 281.

Chapter 1

1. See, for example, MN 21, Wisdom, pp. 217–23.

Chapter 2

1. AN 6.63(5), Wisdom, pp. 963–64.
2. Lyndal Roper, *Martin Luther: Renegade and Prophet* (London: Vintage, 2016), esp. pp. 3–6.
3. DN 16 (2.25), Wisdom, p. 245.
4. Bhadantācariya Buddhaghosa, *The Path of Purification* (*Visuddhimagga*), trans. Bhikkhu Ñāṇamoli (Kandy, Sri Lanka: Buddhist Publication Society, 1991), chap. IX, sec. 23, p. 294. Also on letting go of anger and resentment see AN 5(161–62), Wisdom, pp. 773–74.
5. Lots of food for thought in Timothy D. Wilson, *Strangers to Ourselves: Discovering the Adaptive Unconscious* (Cambridge, MA: Belknap Press, 2002), and Bessel van der Kolk, *The Body Keeps the Score: Mind, Brain and Body in the Transformation of Trauma* (London: Penguin, 2014).
6. Information accessed on 26 February 2019 at: https://www.oxfam.org/en/even-it/5-shocking-facts-about-extreme-global-inequality-and-how-even-it-davos.
7. SN vol. 1, 1.7, Wisdom, pp. 255–56.

Chapter 3

1. AN 5.177(7), Wisdom, p. 790. Also, for monastic people see DN 2; and on not 'pursuing gain with gain', MN 117(29), Wisdom, p. 938.
2. SN vol. 1, 7.11(1), Wisdom, pp. 267–68, and notes 459–63.

Chapter 4

1. For example, AN 10.176, Wisdom, pp. 1518–23.
2. See, for example, AN 4.12(2) and 13(3), Wisdom, pp. 400–401.
3. MN 141.29, Wisdom, p. 1100.
4. AN 5.51(1) and 52(2), Wisdom pp. 679–81.
5. Vance Packard's 1957 book *The Hidden Persuaders* was the first radical critique of the psychological power of advertising, and still has validity today.
6. MN 20, Wisdom, pp. 211–14.
7. For monastic practitioners trying to remedy lust there are a number of extreme practices involving the 'foulness' of the body. See MN 10, Wisdom, pp. 147–49.
8. MN 141.29, Wisdom, p. 1100.
9. For the monastic view and practice of loving kindness see Buddhaghosa, *The Path of Purification* (*Visuddhimagga*), trans. Ñāṇamoli, chap. IX, secs. 1–76, pp. 288–306.
10. MN 7(2), Wisdom, p. 118.

Chapter 5

1. The classic source on mindfulness of breathing is the *Ānāpānasati Sutta*; MN 118, Wisdom, pp. 941–58.

Chapter 6

1. AN 1.19(9), Wisdom, p. 92.

Chapter 7

1. AN 10.55(5), Wisdom, p. 1408.

Chapter 8

1. The Buddha is not a 'sense-data theorist' (or any kind of analytic philosopher); on which subject see 'Sense-Data' in *Stanford Encyclopedia of Philosophy*, https://plato.stanford.edu/entries/sense-data/ (accessed 4 March 2019).
2. AN 6.47(5), Wisdom, pp. 919–20.
3. 'Dhamma' is the overall law of reality, whereas '*dhamma*' is a specific or particular phenomenon, e.g. a tactile sensation. Broadly speaking, it is the examination of '*dhammas*' that can lead us to an understanding of the Dhamma. 'The Dhamma' is always singular, whereas '*dhamma*' can be plural ('*dhammas*').
4. DN 22.1, Wisdom, p. 335.

Chapter 9

1. SN vol. 1, 12.20, Wisdom, p. 552; MN 72.1.14, Wisdom, p. 591.
2. DN 22.4 (*Mahāsatipaṭṭhāna sutta*), p. 336.
3. DN 22.4 (*Mahāsatipaṭṭhāna sutta*), p. 337.
4. MN 10.6-9, Wisdom, pp. 146–47.
5. MN 10: *Satipaṭṭhāna Sutta* (The Foundations of Mindfulness), Wisdom, pp. 145–55.
6. MN 10, Wisdom, p. 1189 note 138.
7. *Pali Text Society Dictionary*: http://dsal.uchicago.edu/dictionaries/pali/ (accessed 4 March 2019).
8. See Commentary on the *Satipaṭṭhāna Sutta*, translated in Soma Thera, *The Way of Mindfulness* (Kandy, Sri Lanka: Buddhist Publication Society, 2003 [1st edn, 1941]).
9. MN 123.22, Wisdom, p. 983.

Chapter 10

1. MN 10.32, Wisdom, p. 149; DN 22.11, Wisdom, p. 339.
2. MN 10.34, Wisdom, p. 150.
3. MN 10.37, Wisdom, pp. 150–51; and see Wisdom, p. 1192 note 155.

Chapter 11

1. Consider AN 8.6(6), Wisdom, pp. 1116–18.

2. I am told by a monastic friend that, here, account should be taken of the distinction between *pakatti sīla* (natural morality) and *panatti sīla* (formulated or prescribed morality).

3. On the difference in attitude to misfortune between the uninstructed and the instructed, see SN vol. 2, 36.6(6), Wisdom, pp. 1263–65.

4. SN vol. 2, 43.14 et seq., Wisdom, p. 1378.

5. SN vol. 2, 56.11(1), Wisdom, p. 1844.

Chapter 12

1. SN vol. 2, 56.11(1), Wisdom, p. 1844.

2. MN 102.24; Wisdom, p. 846.

3. I thank Ajahn Amaro of Amaravati Monastery, UK, for our exchange of ideas in December 2018 on *nibbāna*, horizons and the event horizon of black holes. Also see Ajahn Pasanno and Ajahn Amaro, *The Island: An Anthology of the Buddha's Teachings on Nibbāna* (Redwood Valley, CA: Abhayagiri Monastic Foundation, 2009), p. 181.

4. This is the most probable cause of death as described by Bhikkhu Mettanando MD, in his article, 'The Cause of the Buddha's Death', *Journal of the Pali Text Society* XXVI (2000): 105–17.

5. AN 3.65, Wisdom, p. 281.

6. Lewis Carroll, *Alice's Adventures in Wonderland* (London: Penguin, 2003).

Chapter 13

1. SN vol. 1, 12.15, Wisdom, p. 544.

2. SN vol. 2, 56.11, Wisdom, pp. 1843–47.

3. SN vol. 2, 56.11(1), Wisdom, p. 1844.

4. DN 1.2.23, Wisdom, p. 80.

5. SN vol. 2, 51.15(5), Wisdom, pp. 1732–34. Ajahn Amaro kindly drew my attention to this sutta.

6. See 'René Descartes', in *Stanford Encyclopedia of Philosophy*, https://plato.stanford.edu/entries/descartes/#MinRel (accessed 5 March 2019).

Chapter 14

1. MN 122.16-17, Wisdom, p. 975.

2. See Geoffrey Hunt, 'The Lambda Limit: The Incompletability of Science', *Journal of Biological Physics & Chemistry* 12.3 (2012): 121–28; online at: http://amsi.ge/jbpc/31212/12-3-abs6.htm (accessed 13 August 2018).

3. *The Dhammapada*, trans. V. J. Roebuck (London: Penguin Classics, 2010), chapter 1, p. 3. There are many other translations.

4. By comparison see the Hindu classic *Brihadāraṇyaka Upanishad*, in *The Upanishads*, trans. V. J. Roebuck (London: Penguin Classics, 2003), chapter 4(2), p. 46: 'You cannot see the seer of seeing...' etc.

Chapter 15

1. SN vol. 1, 1(1), Wisdom, p. 89.
2. SN vol. 1, 22.95(3), Wisdom, p. 951.
3. SN 35.85, Wisdom, pp. 1163–64.
4. SN vol. 1, 12.35(5), Wisdom, pp. 573–74.

Chapter 16

1. For example, Empedocles of Sicily (c. 490–c.430 BC); see 'Empedocles', in *Stanford Encyclopedia of Philosophy*, https://leibniz.stanford.edu/friends/members/preview/empedocles/ (accessed 6 March 2019).
2. A good entry-level book on the subject is Roger Lewin, *Complexity: Life at the Edge of Chaos* (Chicago: University of Chicago Press, 2000).
3. The concept of *paṭisandhi-viññāṇa* does not appear in the Buddha's teachings. It probably makes its first appearance in Ps (*Majjhima Nikāya* commentary), I.52, followed by VbhA (*Vibhanga* commentary), 192. See the entry 'rebirth-linking (*paṭisandhi*)' in the Index of Buddhaghosa, *The Path of Purification* (*Visuddhimagga*), trans. Ñāṇamoli. For more information on this entangled metaphysical notion see: https://www.wisdomlib.org/definition/vinnana (accessed 3 January 2019).
4. DN 14.2(18-22), Wisdom, pp. 210–13.
5. DN 14.2(19), Wisdom, p. 211.
6. It may be said that the *Abhidhamma*, the third *piṭaka* of the *Tipiṭaka*, does precisely set out to achieve such an analysis.
7. SN vol. 1, 15.1(1), Wisdom, p. 651.

Chapter 17

1. MN 149, Wisdom, p. 1137.
2. MN 149, Wisdom, pp. 1137–39.
3. SN vol. 2, 56.29(9), Wisdom, p. 1856.
4. SN vol. 1, 22.4(4)2, p. 863.

Chapter 18

1. MN 22(13), Wisdom, pp. 228–29.
2. MN 72.22, p. 594.
3. MN 37.3, p. 344.
4. Benedicta Ward, *The Desert Fathers: Sayings of the Early Christian Monks* (London: Penguin, 2003).

Chapter 19

1. SN vol. 2, 44.1, Wisdom, pp. 1380–83.
2. SN vol. 2, 44.1, Wisdom, p. 1382.
3. SN vol. 2, 44.10, Wisdom, pp. 1393–94.
4. SN vol. 2, 44.7, Wisdom, pp. 1388–89.
5. MN 63.6, Wisdom, p. 535.
6. Relevant sections of the *Sutta Piṭaka* on devas (gods), Brahmā, Brahman, and 'God' include the following: AN 61(2), Wisdom, p. 267; DN 1 (2.1 et seq.), Wisdom, pp. 75–76; DN 11.80-85, Wisdom, pp. 178–80; DN 13, Wisdom, pp. 187–95.
7. For example, the Christian theologian Pseudo-Dionysius the Areopagite (fifth/ sixth CE) emphasized in *De divinus nominibus* (V:4) that God is not a 'being among beings'.
8. Thich Nhat Hahn, *Living Buddha, Living Christ* (London: Rider, 1995).
9. *Udāna*, 8.3 in *A Pali-English Bilingual Study Edition* (Theravada Tipitaka Press, 2010), pp. 227–28 and n. 169; see also *Itivuttaka*, sec. 43.
10. MN 63, Wisdom, pp. 533–36; MN 72, Wisdom, pp. 590–94; MN 2, Wisdom, pp. 91–93.

Conclusion

1. AN 8.5(5) et seq., Wisdom, pp. 1116–18.

Appendix 1

1. MN 20, Wisdom, p. 212.

Bibliography

Bodhi, Bhikkhu (trans). *Samyutta Nikāya: The Connected Discourses of the Buddha*. In 'Teachings of the Buddha' series. Somerville, MA: Wisdom Publications, 2000.

Bodhi, Bhikkhu (trans). *Aṅguttara Nikāya: Numerical Discourses of the Buddha*. Somerville, MA: Wisdom Publications, 2012.

Brihadāraṇyaka Upanishad, in *The Upanishads*. Trans V. J. Roebuck. London: Penguin Classics, 2003.

Buddhaghosa, Bhadantācariya. *The Path of Purification (Visuddhimagga)*. Trans. Bhikkhu Ñāṇamoli. Kandy, Sri Lanka: Buddhist Publication Society, 1991.

Carroll, Lewis. *Alice's Adventures in Wonderland*. London: Penguin, 2003.

The Dhammapada. Trans. V. J. Roebuck. London: Penguin Classics, 2010.

'Empedocles'. In *Stanford Encyclopedia of Philosophy*. Centre for the Study of Language and Information, Stanford University, 2014. https://leibniz.stanford.edu/friends/members/preview/empedocles/ (accessed 6 March 2019).

Hunt, Geoffrey. 'The Lambda Limit: The Incompletability of Science'. *Journal of Biological Physics & Chemistry* 12.3 (2012): 121–22; online at: http://amsi.ge/jbpc/31212/12-3-abs6.htm (accessed 13 August 2018).

Itivuttaka, sec. 43. Trans. Thanissaro Bhikkhu. 2001. https://www.accesstoinsight.org/tipitaka/kn/iti/iti.2.028-049.than.html (accessed 10 December 2019).

Lewin, Roger. *Complexity: Life at the Edge of Chaos*. Chicago: University of Chicago Press, 2000.

Mettanando, Bhikkhu. 'The Cause of the Buddha's Death'. *Journal of the Pali Text Society* XXVI (2000): 105–17.

Ñāṇamoli, Bhikkhu and Bhikkhu Bodhi (trans). *Majjhima Nikāya: The Middle Length Discourses of the Buddha*. 'Teachings of the Buddha' series. Somerville, MA: Wisdom Publications, 1995.

Nhat Hahn, Thich. *Living Buddha, Living Christ*. London: Rider, 1995.

Packard, Vance. *The Hidden Persuaders*. New York: Ig Publishing, 2007 (1st edn, 1957).

Pasanno, Ajahn and Ajahn Amaro. *The Island: An Anthology of the Buddha's Teachings on Nibbāna*. Redwood Valley, CA: Abhayagiri Monastic Foundation, 2009.

Pseudo-Dionysius the Areopagite. *De divinus nominibus (The Divine Names)*, V:4 in *Pseudo-Dionysius: The Complete Works*. New York: Paulist Press, 1987.

Roper, Lyndal. *Martin Luther: Renegade and Prophet*. London: Vintage, 2016.

Stanford Encyclopedia of Philosophy. Centre for the Study of Language and Information. Stanford University, 2014. https://plato.stanford.edu/ (accessed 1 November 2018).

Thera, Soma. *The Way of Mindfulness*. Kandy, Sri Lanka: Buddhist Publication Society, 2003 (1st edn, 1941).

Udāna, 8.3 in *A Pali-English Bilingual Study Edition*. Intro by Lennart Lopin. Theravada Tipitaka Press, 2010, pp. 227–28.

Van der Kolk, Bessel. *The Body Keeps the Score: Mind, Brain and Body in the Transformation of Trauma*. London: Penguin, 2014.

Walshe, Maurice (trans). *Dīgha Nikāya: The Long Discourses of the Buddha*. 'Teachings of the Buddha' series. Somerville, MA: Wisdom Publications, 1995.

Ward, Benedicta. *The Desert Fathers: Sayings of the Early Christian Monks*. London: Penguin, 2003.

Wilson, Timothy D. *Strangers to Ourselves: Discovering the Adaptive Unconscious*. Cambridge, MA: Belknap Press, 2002.

Index

abdomen 4, 64–66, 71–72, 96–97
acceptance 9, 32, 208
acting 25–27
addiction 10
advertising 47, 52–53
after-life 216
age of blindness 69, 152
Aggregates, the Five *see* reflections, five
agitation 62–63, 66
agnostic 152, 160, 217–19
Alice in Wonderland 143
anchor and buoy 93–97, 119
anger 16, 18, 27, 30–32, 167, 183
annihilation 136, 177–78, 209, 215
anonymized shared reflection 117
anxiety 3, 6–7, 206
apocalypse 223–24
apophatic theology 142, 217
aporia 124, 149, 159
arahant 138–39
assumptions 192–93
asymptote 135–36
attachment 29, 78–79
attention 55–56, 62, 75–77, 82–83, 86–88
attitude 18–19
authenticity 124–25
awakening 141, 221
awareness (*sampajañña*) 100–1

balance (loss of) 34
beauty products 104
beginning 195
bell 73, 109
bewilderment 129–30
body scan 93
Brahman 217
brahminical view (Hinduism) 25–26

brain 158, 160–61, 163
breathing 63–68, 102
broccoli 5–6

catching oneself 30–31
cessation (*nirodha*) 133–35
cherry tree 58
choice 27–28, 84
civilization 3–4, 34, 37, 153, 158, 166
clinging *see* craving
clock 92
cloth (stained) 60
co-dependent origination (arising)
    180–81
cognition 106, 155, 166
collectivizing ethics 30
compassion (*karuṇā*) 142–43, 206, 211
complexity 181–83
concentration 61–67, 195
conditionality 188–89
consciousness 157–60, 166–67
consumers 38, 166
cosmos 127–28, 162, 171
craving (clinging) 10, 130–31, 207,
    221–22
crossing the flood 170, 204
cultivation of loving-kindness (*mettā
    bhavana*) 58–59
cynicism 18, 35–36

darkness (and light) 76–77, 80–81
death 8, 209, 214
depression 38
Descartes 153
Desert Fathers 207
detox (ethical) 47–48
devas (gods) xv *see also* Chap. 19 n.6

Dhamma (*Dharma*) directly visible 2, 90
dhammas 98–99, 147, 157, 197 *see also*
    Chap. 8 n.3
diaphragm 64
diary 116–17 *see also* states of mind
distraction 63, 82–83, 95
DNA of ignorance 192
downward counter-flow 189–90
dualism (duality) 147, 151–53, 156–57,
    208
dukkha see suffering

eel-wriggling 150
effort 43–46
Eight Worldly Intentions 222–23
elaboration 99, 192
elimination of life 140
embedment 209
emergence model 139, 179–84
Empedocles 179
emptiness (*suññatā*) 101, 172
energy, habitual 48
enlightenment 141
equanimity 109, 126
eternalism 215
ethico-cosmos (ethico-natural) 127–28
evil 35, 88–89
existence 117–18, 145, 219–20
experience (bare) 89–90

faith (*saddhā*) 213
floating man 46
flood *see* crossing the flood
flypaper mind 63, 79
foam 170
four foundations 98–99
Four Noble Truths 6, 201–2

Ganges 170
Gestalt shift 140, 220
God 216–18

happiness 68, 236
hatred 113, 163, 208
Hindrances, the Five 49–50, 72, 198
holism 184–85
Homo avidus (Craving Man) 221
horizons model 137–44

hovering 150, 153–54

ice in water 154, 174
ignorance 195
ill-will 198, 209–11
I-me-mine 211
immunity 163, 168
impermanence (*anicca*) 11, 118, 191, 194
inconceivable 150, 160, 217–19
insight 69, 95–98
insubstantiality 106, 118, 170, 194
intention (in speaking) 19
Iron Age xiv, 30, 179

John the Buddhist 89

kamma (*karma*) xvi–xvii, 25–27
Khemā 214
killing 29
kindly family 31–32
knot, slipping 154, 174–75
know for yourself 11
Kofi Annan 22
Koṇḍañña 2

ladder 143
lay people (laity) 138
leaf 70
leap-frog 154, 162, 165–66, 197
lethargy *see* Hindrances, the Five
letting go 29, 82, 85, 96, 114, 217, 162
light switch 103
limit 207–8, 194
livelihood *see* work
loving-kindness (*mettā*) 58–59

Mahāyāna 138, 167
Mandela, Nelson 22
mantra 44
Māra (the devil) xv
me 7, 9, 92, 105–6, 141–42, 152, 158–59,
    162, 196
meditation xvi–xvii, 15, 43–44
meiosis 157–58
memory 51, 75
mesenteric infarction 139 *see also* Chap.
    12 n.4
meta-horizon 143–44

mettā bhavana see cultivation of loving-kindness
middle way 146–47, 177, 208–9
mind and matter 132
mindful action 32
mindfulness (as consumer commodity) 38–39
Möbius Strip 148
models xiv–xv, 149
monastic life 138–39
mundane level (worldly) 7
mundanity, fallacy of 150–51

name and form (*nāmarūpa*) 180
natural law 98, 128, 180, 197
Newton's Cradle 200
nibbāna (*nirvana*) 105, 136–37
nirodha (ending suffering) 7, 134–35
Noble Eightfold Path xv, 2, 7–8
nonduality 67
non-harm (*ahimsa*) 209
non-reducibility 185
nostril sensations 71
not-me *see* me
not-self (*anattā*) 171, 196, 214
non-theism 218–19

object of meditation 61, 63, 70, 86–87
obstacle course 56
ocean 177–78
Oxfam 30

pain 98–99, 112, 165
Pali Canon 75, 105, 218
paradox 154, 202
philosophy 109
physical things 108
ploughs 37–38
precepts 28–29
progress 33, 36
psychosomatic experience 165
punabbhava see rebecoming
purification 104

rebecoming (*punabbhava*) 183, 214, 220
rebirth 135, 177–78
reductionism 181–82, 185

reflections, five (Five Aggregates) 151, 156–59, 198–99
Reformation (the Christian) 26
reification 172, 215
reincarnation *see* rebirth
rejection *see* craving
renunciation 208–9
resolve (resolution) 209
right 127–28, 132
root 39, 130, 132, 146, 149, 214
rules, attachment to 28–29

Śākya (*Shakya*) 157
sampajañña (awareness) 102–3
saṃsāra 67
samudaya (origin of suffering) 6
sangha (monastic community) 7, 28, 213
satellite dish 82
scanning body 77, 93
scientism 163–64
self and not-self (*anattā*) 153
self-evaluation 196–97
self-mortification 2, 146
self-organization 163, 184, 186
sense-bases 186, 199–200
sensory attraction 201
Seven Factors of Enlightenment 197–98
sign 52–53
silence 217
sleepless woman 51
slipping knot 174
soul 176–78, 215
sounds 82–83
speech, right 15
standing meditation 111–12
states of mind (fruitful or not) 49, 114–16
still point 73
stool posture 229–30
stopping (random) 32
strange shopping 193–94
subtleties of speech 17–18
suffering (*dukkha*) 9–10
supra-advert 52–54
supramundane level (transcendent) 133
swimming 91

Tathāgata 214
teaching, Buddha's way of 11
technology 4, 37
television 164
Theravāda xiii, 138, 188, 213
think-ism 90–91
tick, the 'clocking' 92
timeliness in speaking 22–23, 180
Tipiṭaka 98, 190
torch beam 77, 80–81
toxic environment 40–41
tradition 11
transcendence 196
transformation 182–83
tribal languages 163

Udāna 218
unanswerable questions 9, 150, 194–95, 220
Unconditioned, the 150, 203
uninstructed worldlings 125, 138

universal container 153, 171, 209–11, 223

vanishing point *see* horizons model
vantage point 137–38
Vedas (Vedic religion) 25–26, 218
views 84
viharati ātāpi (dwelling ardently) 105
Vipassī (Vipassī's Loop) 188

walking meditation 110–11
Wall Street 34
watchful walking 85–86
wave 154, 171–73
Wheel (of *Dhamma* in motion) 2, 146
(the) wonderful and marvellous 106
work 33–37
worry 72

yakkhas (spirits) xv
yoga 44

CPSIA information can be obtained
at www.ICGtesting.com
Printed in the USA
LVHW081818080920
665354LV00004B/157